CASS LIBRARY OF VICTORIAN TIMES

No. 5

General Editor : Anne Humpherys
Herbert H. Lehman College, New York

THE ROOKERIES OF LONDON

THE
ROOKERIES OF LONDON

BY

THOMAS BEAMES

NEW IMPRESSION OF
SECOND EDITION

FRANK CASS & CO. LTD.
1970

Published by
FRANK CASS AND COMPANY LIMITED
67 Great Russell Street, London WC1B 3BT

First edition   1850
Second edition   1852
New impression of Second edition   1970

ISBN 0 7146 2415 2

·664492

Printed in Great Britain by Clarke, Doble & Brendon Ltd.
Plymouth and London

The Rookeries of London.

The Rookeries of London:

Past, Present, and Prospective.

By Thomas Beames, M.A.
Preacher and Assistant of St. James, Westminster.

Second Edition.

London:
THOMAS BOSWORTH, 215, REGENT STREET.

m.dccc.lii.

To the Honoured Memory

OF

THE WISE AND GOOD DR. ARNOLD,

HISTORIAN, SCHOLAR, AND DIVINE,

THE SOCIAL REFORMER OF HIS AGE,

THIS PLEA FOR THE WORKING CLASSES,

IN WHOSE CAUSE HE GAVE OF THE LABOURS OF HIS PEN

AND THE EARNINGS OF HIS PROFESSION,

Is Dedicated

WITH PROFOUND RESPECT.

Contents.

viii   Contents.

Preface
to
The Second Edition.

———◆———

When I was called upon by my Publishers to prepare a Second Edition, I determined, as far as possible, to amend the many defects of the first. I had reason to be grateful for the very favourable criticisms delivered upon it, with one exception; and the animadversions of the dissentient were too just to be passed over without an attempt to reverse the sentence. A great part, therefore, of the work has been re-written; large additions have been made, some of the antiquarian portions of it omitted or abridged, whilst the lighter and more satirical parts have also been left out. Herein I have been swayed by the opinion of a near relative, whose wishes I am bound to obey, and whose judgment is well known, his own professional works having not

only an English but American circulation. Other kind
and candid friends recommended me to apply the knife;
which, I hope, has been done unsparingly.

To my dear old friend, the Rev. T. T. HAVERFIELD, of
St. James' Chapel, I owe more than I can express, for
his corrections whilst the work was passing through the
press—corrections the more valuable, because proceeding
from a man of the most varied accomplishments and
refined taste. To MONTAGUE GORE, Esq., late M.P.
for Barnstaple, I am indebted for an opportunity of
visiting, in his company and under his guidance, one of
the worst districts in London. To my colleague and
brother Wykehamist, the Rev. MACKENZIE WALCOTT,
the author of " The English Ordinal," I thankfully acknowledge obligations which the reader will appreciate
when he peruses the account of Pye Street, Westminster.

To many kind friends among the Working Classes I
tender my sincere thanks;—among them have I laboured
as a London Clergyman for twelve chequered years,
having previously held a curacy in the country. Amidst
many severe trials they have cheered me. I felt I owed
them a debt of gratitude; it was not sufficient to tend
them in their sickness, and to plead for them in my
public ministry; but, if any would listen, to tell the

naked tale, as many among them had told it me, or as the record of what I had so often witnessed.

Thankful am I, that the seed which the master hand of Arnold planted has taken root—that the dwellings of the Working Classes are thought worthy the attention of earnest and wealthy men; and I deem it a fair auspice of the success of this little volume, that it should issue from the press at this time, when our own parish is striving to erect a Model Lodging House, of ample size, upon a spot of ground hitherto occupied by one of the lowest Rookeries of London; when the untiring exertions of LORD INGESTRE have already obtained large subscriptions; and when he may hope that some of the evils which he has so often witnessed with me, in the homes of our poorer brethren, are about to be removed.

London,
March 1852.

The Rookeries of London.

Chapter I.

There is much in a name, one significant phrase which spares circumlocution, and the reader, without wading through two or three pages, sees what you mean. We had not otherwise been bold enough to call our book

" The Rookeries of London."

There is a period in all languages, when words pass from the mint in which they are coined, their questionable origin is forgotten, and they are used among the current money of the realm of thought. We believe that such is the case with the word **Rookery**. The uninitiated may ask its meaning, and the philologist wish to know the stages by which it arrived at its present acceptation. It would be wrong to call the dwellings of the working classes generally **Rookeries**: in country villages they hardly lie close enough for that; they are not high enough—sufficiently crowded; there is not the same economy of space which **The legitimate Rookery** demands.

Doubtless there is some analogy between these pauper colonies and the nests of the birds from whom they take their name; the houses for the most part high and narrow, the largest possible number crowded together in a given space,—common necessity their bond of union: though the occupation of the different tenants varies, yet they belong to the same section of the social body, having all descended to the lowest scale which is compatible with human life. Other birds are broken up into separate families—occupy separate nests ; rooks seem to know no such distinction. So it is with the class whose dwellings we are to describe. We must speak of the dwellings of the poor in crowded cities, where large masses of men are brought together; where, by the unwritten laws of competition, rents rise and room is economised in proportion; where, because there is no restraint to check the progress of avarice, no statute to make men do their duty, they turn to profit the necessities of their fellow-creatures, and riot on the unhallowed gains which injustice has amassed at the expense of the poor.

We must speak of human masses pent up, crowded, crammed into courts and allies; here, as by a fatal attraction, opposite houses grow together at the top, seem to nod one against one another, conspiring to shut out the little air which would pierce through for the relief of those beneath. We must speak of men and women sleeping in the same apartment, whom, in some cases, not even the tie of relationship unites ; of a married couple with their offspring, who have already come to the age of maturity, with a common dormitory; and we ask, if a malignant spirit wished to demoralise the working classes of the country, could he find a plan more congenial to his wishes? We must speak of stories piled on stories in the older part of our towns; not each floor, but each room tenanted by a family; in some cases the dormitory of several occupants, thrown together without distinction of sex or age in the chance scramble for the night's lodging, each swelling the gains of some middleman, whose heart is seared by the recollection of his own poverty, and who learns to grind as he was once ground by others. We trust to the hands of the most ignorant and most injured, an instrument which even the best and the wisest can scarce wield as they should. We put an engine, fitted with momentous powers, into the hands of one trained to abuse it by a long course of oppression—of oppression which, under the name of custom and the sanction of law, eats into men's hearts; their natures are insensibly changed by it; against which they first rebel, then bear with, then submit to, then acquiesce in, then adopt, then exercise, then defend, to the injury of their brethren. But of this we will speak anon: the middle-man and the broker are persons whom we must sketch at length, when we have proceeded further. Are not these colonies Rookeries, if the description given by the natu-ralist be correct? "A Rookery, a village in the air peopled " with numerous inhabitants: it is the nature of birds to " associate together, and they build in numbers in the " same or adjoining trees." Rookeries they are, if rooks

build high and lie thick together, young and old in one
nest.   Colonies are wedged up, not so much because of
connection between families as by common wants and a
common nature, and with the fierce discord and occa-
sional combats of the inhabitants.   The tenants of these
Rookeries, like the birds from whom they take their
names, have much in common—want, with its offspring,
recklessness; they the pariahs, so to speak, of the body
social, a distinct caste, yet not bound together otherwise
than by common wants—with their jealousies, discords,
and antipathies; as if it were not too true of them, as of
others, that a man's foes may be they of his own household.

Whence came these Rookeries ?   Were they prison
colonies, safety valves, so many Alsatias needed for the
wants, tolerated as the least of two evils by the authorities
of all towns of above a certain population—allowed to
fester, so they did not infect—upon sufferance, because
they had their use—poisoned wells, yet girdled round by
certain barriers which confined the pestilence within a given
circle ?   Were they formed by some greedy speculator or
needy adventurer ?   Modelled after a common type, or,
indeed, modelled at all ?   Have they grown out of the
wants, or were they shaped by the policy, of the age ?
Are they peculiar to London, to England, to Europe ?
Are they sinks into which, as Tacitus says of Rome,
everything bad and vicious flows ?   Is vice alone the
bond of union among the inmates ?   Or, as the proverb
says, Is it necessity which makes men acquainted with

strange bedfellows in haunts like these? Do these
Rookeries obey some general law, which assigns to a given
number of people a certain pariah class, which, in its proportion to the other divisions, shall not vary; so that you
cannot diminish them, or give them better dwellings, or
fix the cubic feet of air each man shall inhale, the area
he shall occupy, the amount of light which may be justly
placed at his disposal, with something like a reference to
what God intended for all his creatures, and of which
they who would rob their fellows must do so at their peril?
Are these Rookeries entailed on us by a law of our being,
so that you allow men to build huts without the com
monest comforts, without drains, without supply of water,
where they live shut out almost from the air which feeds
existence, and the light which comes down from heaven?
Will you rest contented because you know these hovels
will not want tenants, and that there must be human
beings whose necessities these dens will supply? Are
men created for this state of social isolation? Do they
come into the world, like the hero of Greek drama, to
fulfil a hereditary curse, destined before they are born to
a condition from which no human institution can shield
them? Do men cling to these colonies through perverse
adherence to the errors or traditions of their fathers;
because fancied immunities and privileges are connected
with them; or because none better adapted to their comforts are ready to receive them? Do these strongholds
of corrupt antiquity yield advantages which decent habitations could not supply? When you plead for these

anomalies, do you plead for some mysterious benefit
which they alone appreciate who enjoy it; must efforts
called forth and energies taxed on their behalf be abortive?

It might have been well to give some statistics on
these points, were not the most perfect collection of
reports ever placed within the reach of the Political
Economist, the Poor Law Annual Reports, now sold for
waste paper; still we may ask how these Rookeries grew
to their present size, or degenerated, if you will, to their
present abuse?

The subject is not without its interest; it falls within
the compass of our plan, if we would consider Rookeries
in the past as well as present tense. This vast Babel or
Babylon,—as Cobbett called it, The Great Wen—whence
came it? what changes has it seen? rather, more strictly,
from what beginnings did these Rookeries grow to their
present size? Do you mean to tell us, the reader asks,
that the poor are worse lodged now than they have ever
been, or only comparatively worse? because it occurs at
once to us that there were plagues, periodical pestilences,
making vast inroads, carrying off perhaps 10,000 men at
a time, so that the great plague of 1665, which was
supposed to have killed 80,000 people, was only the last
of a series; so that the disorder, the sweating sickness,
was fatal to thousands, and returned, as West Indians
tell us the yellow fever does, at intervals, not fixed
indeed, yet not varying much in their length! From
this, it is argued, that London must be more healthy than
it was, for such things are almost unknown among us.

The cholera, in 1832, only swept away 6000, out of a population of nearly 2,000,000. The last ravaging disorder of which we know, the gaol fever, has long left us. Small pox, that scourge of our countrymen a hundred years ago, is much mitigated, seldom fatal, promptly dealt with, easily warded off, and yielding readily to the remedies applied. Men gladly infer, it is a sort of opiate to our consciences, that there is less physical suffering among the poor than formerly—less absolutely and relatively. We think this an error. Let us look back then and see how men were lodged of old, and glean at the same time what information we can respecting those plague spots which still remain, and, under the name of Rookeries, are so unenviably notorious.

A great city then may present many objects of interest and be even architecturally grand, yet its grandeur be the screen of its deformity. Witness Paris, for instance, the centre of modern civilisation ; walk through the streets in the very neighbourhood of the Louvre, and the Palais Royal, with their shelving pavements, the gutter in the middle, their narrow streets, no place for foot passengers, the lamps hanging from ropes and making you think you still, as in the Revolution, hear the cry, Away with him to the Lantern ! Survey the whole district between the Port St. Denis and the river, look at the neighbourhood of Père la Chaise, the Panthéon and the Luxembourg. Or again in Brussels, you walk through the beautiful streets in the neighbourhood of the Parc, you are delighted with the space they occupy, the lofty rooms in the houses, the evidences of luxury and wealth ; you marvel at that combination of architectural beauty, the Grande Place, with its Hôtel de Ville, the mansion which commemorates the cessation of the plague and others. You have scarcely turned from a spot that interests by its historical, equally as its picturesque associations, scarcely ceased to revel in the glories which Spain and Austria have bequeathed, when narrow streets, and fetid gutters, poison at once the air you breathe, and the thoughts you have evoked. Thus too in London, during the Plantagenet dynasty, we are feasted with accounts of shows and processions, the houses decorated with banners, the conduits running with wine, the gorgeous masques, the figures of angelic beings who greeted the sovereign, and we infer from these stories, not merely the riches of the people, but the splendour of the city in which they dwelt.

Despite of this, till within two hundred and fifty years from the present time, the houses were for the most part built of wood ; the nobility and the sovereign alone seemed to have used a more durable material ; the streets were narrow, the buildings with their pent-houses or projecting first story overhanging the causeway ; each story, in fact, projecting further into the street than that below it ; the roads were neglected, abounding with ruts or holes, and were generally narrow and unsafe.

In the reign of Elizabeth, the houses in the cities and towns were built in the fashion of those still in being at Staple's Inn, the Holborn front of which is a fair specimen of domestic architecture towards the close of the Tudor period; each story projected over that immediately beneath it, so that when the streets were not very wide, the people, at the top of opposite houses, might talk and converse with one another. Stowe even tells us, though one would think this is exaggerated, that they could shake hands together. To prevent decay of wood, it was enjoined, about the year 1606, that all persons should build the front of their houses with stone or brick.

We can scarce bring ourselves to believe that, three hundred years since, houses were generally built of wood, because so few specimens still exist; and yet, in foreign cities, many of the buildings are four and even five hundred years old. We have few specimens extant of very old houses, for the great fire of 1666 commenced in the neighbourhood of the Monument, and extended nearly to Temple Bar ; and the streets which were not burnt down, were affected by the change which took place. Wooden houses are still to be found in the neighbourhood of the Minories, and in some old towns : in Bristol, Winchester, and other cities, they are frequently to be met with.

Building with brick only came into general use, in the early part of the reign of Charles I. ; it was introduced by the Earl of Arundel, who imported the custom from Italy, where it generally prevailed. Carpets are luxuries comparatively of modern date; the palace of Henry VIII. was strewed with rushes, the floors were generally thus covered :—in many cases, the straw was suffered to remain a long time; bones and refuse meat were plentifully scattered about and became imbedded in the straw; the general want of cleanliness which prevailed, and the insufficient supply of water, coupled with the narrow and badly ventilated streets, produced the various plagues of which we hear so much. In few houses were chimneys found; the fires were kindled by the side of the wall, and the smoke was permitted to escape through the windows; the pallets on which men slept, were of straw, and round logs for pillows were in general use. It is not asserted, that there were no Rookeries then, but rather that they were common, and the distinction between the dwellings of the rich and poor not so obvious.

Many edicts were passed from the time of Henry VIII. to the Commonwealth, which forbade the erection of more houses in the suburbs of London, or, at least, encumbered the permission to build with so many conditions, that it became inoperative; London increased in spite of the resistance of the authorities. Such a prohibition multiplied buildings within narrow spaces, and whilst it made ground dear, confined a dense population within narrow limits; public fountains were the only cisterns which supplied the people with water; just as in foreign cities, especially in the German towns, the inhabitants derive their supply from conduits, which are constantly kept running for the use of the citizens; few, if any, of the continental cities being supplied with water as we are, by pipes communicating with the houses.

Few have not heard of the New River, and those who know the neighbourhood of Sadler's Wells, may recollect the public-house, with a picture of Sir Hugh Myddleton for its sign, a grave and reverend Signior, in the rich dress of the age of James I., bearded and bedizened as became a citizen of the ancient times, chain of office and laced ruff bespeaking civic dignity when it was wont to be valued by the best the city bred. London is more indebted to this good man than to any of its benefactors. In 1608 he began the good work; in five years that immense canal, called the New River, was completed, and London ever since supplied with water.

Has the improvement in the condition of the poor kept pace with that of the higher and middle classes? There are no houses, even in Rookeries, without chimneys, though 300 years ago they were comparatively scarce; but then, firewood was cheap, and so were cattle, and the diet of the labouring man, consequently, better than at present. It was the boast of Sir John Fortescue, speaking of those times, that the English lived far more upon animal diet than their rivals the French, and to this cause he ascribes their strength and courage. The people generally suffered through bad drainage, wretched roads, unhealthy houses, and want of water: the rich were victims as well as the poor. The accession of James I. was quickly followed by a destructive plague, the spreading of which was doubtless accelerated by the narrowness of the streets, and the crowded state of the houses, whilst every extension of the suburbs seems to have been resisted by successive administrations.

These anomalies have been, in a degree, removed; improvement has swept on with mighty strides; pity that there should still remain the monuments of this olden time in the Rookeries of London,—that the close alley, the undrained court, the narrow window, the unpaved footpath, the distant pump, the typhus or Irish fever, should still remind us of what London once was to all, what it still is to the poor! The wealthy, we are told, hastened from the town when the plague was announced, satisfied that its ravages would soon be felt amongst them. The poor, with an accuracy which startles, can now tell the spot which fever, when it comes, will occupy; a fetid odour has long warned them that a nucleus is not wanting,—that neglect has spared materials for disease; and if we wonder that of old, enactments enclosed, as within a prison wall, the space already occupied by buildings in these days, the poor man dare not remove the dust-heap, which offends the nose and digusts the eye, lest he should be punished for breaking the parish contract with him who is pledged, but is slow, to remove it; he must wait till the heap is large enough to justify the dustman's interference, to make it worth the functionary's while to send a horse and cart for its removal.

We reckon our coal beds a great source of national wealth: the iron and coal of England are more available advantages, than the gold of Peru to the Spaniards who first discovered it; yet, in former times, coal was used sparingly, large forests, as in France, supplied fuel for the wants alike of rich and poor. We are thankful for the treasure which we not only possess, and so amply enjoy; its use is not without some drawbacks, not merely that our public buildings are spoiled by it, but that it clogs and darkens the atmosphere,—it creates an incessant demand on the cleanliness of the poor,—it adds much to the unhealthiness of their dwellings, so that even Rookeries are blacker still, and another coating of coal smoke is added to the dingy hue, which is their congenial colour. This evil, were we in earnest, we might remove, and effect a positive saving in the consumption of coal.

It is often asserted, that London is better lighted, paved, drained, and supplied with water, than any city in the world; this improvement has only been arrived at by gradual stages in a long course of years. When Charles II. was restored, the early attention of the Legislature was directed to the lighting and cleansing of the streets, and the repairing of highways; the salutary effects of which were gradually communicated to St. Giles's, and the novel exhibition was seen of candles, or lights in lanterns; these were directed by the Act to be hung out by every householder, from the time of its becoming dark till nine every evening, from Michaelmas to Lady-day. In the neighbourhood of St. Giles, 150 years since, there was a Rookery, for Strype describes Whetstone Park, at the back of Holborn, as being noted for its once infamous and vicious inhabitants, who, some years since, he says, were forced away. On this ground, which, from lying waste, was frequently the scene of low dissipation, houses were first erected by Mr. Whetstone, a vestryman of St. Giles, and from him it obtained the name of Whetstone Park. Strange comment this of the quaint historian, that this benevolent or speculating vestryman should have destroyed a haunt of vice, and erected houses which, we may suppose, were intended as an antidote to the evils described, and that about five or six years since, a fatal epidemic broke out in this very place which puzzled all the doctors.

This place is now inhabited by some of the lowest characters in London; and we may almost believe old Stowe, when he tells us that so narrow were some of the streets in ancient London, that people could shake hands across them; for this, if anywhere, might be done in the street called Little Turnstile, which is just at the back of Whetstone Park.

A change has come over us. The rich have room, have air, have houses endeared to them, by every comfort civilisation can minister ; the poor still remain sad heralds of the past, alone bearing the iniquities, and inheriting the curse of their fathers. Worse paid, do they breathe a purer air ? Worse fed, are they better housed than their ancestors ? Regent Street attracts the eye ! Rookeries still remain ! Westminster, at once the seat of a palace and a plague spot ; senators declaim, where sewers poison ; theology holds her councils, where thieves learn their trade ; and Europe's grandest hall is flanked by England's foulest grave-yard.

Chapter II.

Whence sprang The Rookeries of London?

Various causes combined to produce them. Many, from the first, were intended for the occupation of the poor. In the parish of St. Pancras, you have streets of the class Rookery, which cannot be fifty years old ; small houses are now building which will soon become Rookeries. Agar Town, in that immense parish, contains a squalid population, originally a band of settlers, who seem, as they would say in America, to have squatted there, and now it is almost impossible to remove them. In other districts, rows of small houses are constantly erected ; the ground around them is not drained, and they are as so many depôts for the investment of money by rapacious speculators. These houses are badly built, mere lath and plaster ; built, we should think, by contract, solely as a profitable investment, with an evident desire to evade the provisions which the Legislature, at last, has been forced, from a sense of decency, to enjoin. In this attempt to neutralise Acts of Parliament, contractors have been eminently successful, owing to the want of a public prosecutor, whose business it is, as in France and other countries, to uphold the law. The recklessness of

poverty, the greediness of avarice combined,—what
pledge have you that such dwellings shall serve more
than the temporary purposes for which they were erected ?
No real reform will take place till the size, materials
employed, drainage, &c. are fixed by Act of Parliament;
dilapidated houses, insecure dwellings, all, in a word,
which do not answer the purpose proposed, and will not
bear the strictest examination, should be condemned by
a committee appointed for the purpose. A wholesome
check would soon be imposed upon the heartlessness of
capitalists, and poverty protected in spite of self. A
large class of the genus Rookery, are very ancient houses,
deserted by those to whose ancestors they once belonged.
The tide of fashion—the rage for novelty—the changes
of the times, have also changed the character of the
population who now tenant these buildings. In the
dingiest streets of the Metropolis are found houses, the
rooms of which are lofty, the walls panelled, the ceilings
beautifully ornamented, (although the gilding which
encrusted the ornaments is worn off,) the chimney-
pieces models for the sculptor. In many rooms there
still remain the grotesque carvings for which a former
age was so celebrated. You have the heavy balustrades,
the wide staircase, with its massive rails, or, as we now
call them, bannisters ; you have the strong doorway,
with its carvings, the large unwieldy door, and those
well-known features of the olden time, in keeping with the
quaint and dust-stained engravings which seem to have
descended as heirlooms from one poor family to another.

The names of the courts remind you of decayed glory,—
Villiers, Dorset, Buckingham, Norfolk, telling of the
stately edifices which once stood where you now breathe
the impure atmosphere of a thickly-peopled court. A
street, now remarkable only for its narrowness and dirt,
is called Garden, because once there was a garden there ;
some term of chivalry distinguishes another ; some
article of dress, now in disuse, a third; some alley,
without a pump, bears the pompous name of Fountain
Court. The houses themselves are in keeping externally,
with what we have described of the interior; the dark
redbrick, the pillars, with their capitals and quaint
figures, speaking of art called forth by wealth, and taxed
to produce novelty, to stamp on the buildings in which
he lived, the rank of the owner.

In other parts of London, groups of small houses,
with their background of courts and alleys, have been
erected upon the site of large gardens, which formerly
were the pleasure grounds of stately mansions. Two
hundred years since, one side of the Strand consisted
of the houses of the nobility ; of these mansions, Nor-
thumberland House is the only remnant, the grounds
belonging to which extended to the river. The famous
Villiers, Duke of Buckingham, the courtier in the times
of Charles II., pulled down the magnificent house in
which he lived; the site of it, together with the gardens,
is occupied by streets which bear his name and title :
some of these are rapidly degenerating, and will become
Rookeries, if no change take place in the social con-

dition of the poor; the beautiful water gate seen from the river, was the entrance to the grounds.

Such are the general features of 𝕷𝖔𝖓𝖉𝖔𝖓 𝕽𝖔𝖔𝖐𝖊𝖗𝖎𝖊𝖘. We may be interested in inquiring how any particular nest of these buildings grew to its present size, or became appropriated to its present use. Men generally connect St. Giles's and Seven Dials with squalid misery and a degraded population; most people suppose that extreme poverty and abject distress are confined to this spot, and that pauperism in other parishes is merely comparative.

To omit mention of the Minories, Saffron Hill, and other notorious plague spots,—we may safely assert, that very few parishes in London are without these haunts of destitution. The most aristocratic parishes, as they are termed, have a background of wretchedness, and are too often so many screens for misery which would shock the mind and make men avert their gaze, could they indeed see them as they really are.

Chapter III.

In an inquiry like this, it is good to have something definite to fix on. We will, therefore, begin with the Parish of St. Giles. In common parlance, St. Giles's and Billingsgate are types—the one, of the lowest conditions under which human life is possible,—the other, of the lowest point to which the English language can descend : and yet, when we look back, there is nothing peculiar about the situation of the former parish ; it is not on the banks of a river, connected with shipping, and therefore affording a harvest for crimps, thieves, and abandoned women ; it never had the privilege of sanctuary, as far as we can learn, and thus degenerated from a refuge of the unfortunate, to become a rendezvous of the scum of society. About the time of the Northern Conquest, it was not built on, was scarcely even a suburb, and but thinly dotted with habitations*. The parish derived its name from the hospital dedicated to the saint, built on the site of the present church, by Matilda, Queen of Henry I., before which time there had only been a small church or oratory on the spot.

* *Vide* Aggas, Stowe, and Dobie's History of St. Giles's, published in 1834.

It is described in old records as abounding in gardens
and dwellings in the flourishing times of the hospital;
it declined in population after the suppression of that
establishment, and remained an inconsiderable village
till the end of the reign of Elizabeth, after which it was
rapidly built on, and became distinguished for the
number and rank of its inhabitants. In the reign of
Henry I., the hospital mentioned was founded for the
reception of lepers,—and in that of Henry V., the famous
Lord Cobham, the founder or patron of the Lollards,
was executed here, after much barbarous treatment.
After the suppression of the hospital, the parish, called
of old "the verie pleasaunt village of St. Giles's," was
built over, and a cluster of houses erected there ; and, in
the reign of Elizabeth, the Lord Mayor visiting the
conduits at Tyburn, hunted the hare in the great black
forest of Marylebone, and, after dining, killed a fox at
the end of St. Giles's. Towards the end of this reign,
Holborn had extended so far westward as nearly to join
St. Giles's, which was increasing rapidly. In the reign
of James I., Drury Lane was built on, and, in 1628, the
whole number of houses rated, amounted to 897, and
more than twenty courts and alleys are mentioned by
name. Soon after this, mention is made of the erection
of fifty-six houses which, it is supposed, were inhabited
by people of rank and wealth. Thus, more than two
hundred years since, a nucleus for Rookeries was formed
in these very courts and alleys; they must have been
built as the dwellings of the poor, and we are not

surprised to find that the larger houses in the vicinity
were gradually deserted by their inhabitants, as the tide
swept westward. But we cease to wonder at the size,
internal decorations, and external ornaments of many of
the houses tenanted by the very refuse of the population. There is yet standing in Great Queen Street, a
very fine old dark red brick house, the front well ornamented with carving; and, though it has been somewhat
defaced, still giving us a fair sample of the residence of
an opulent man two hundred years since, which is
believed to have been the residence of the eccentric
Lord Herbert of Cherbury, and afterwards of Sir Godfrey
Kneller;—the back of this mansion is surrounded by
some of the lowest houses in the parish of St. Giles's.
Great Queen Street seems to preserve some share of its
ancient importance, whilst the surrounding neighbourhood has gone fast to decay. In the reign of Charles II.
the place, afterwards called Seven Dials, was erected, in
expectation that it would soon become the abode of
the gay and wealthy. Soho Square, and Covent or
Convent Garden, were the residence of the aristocracy,—
the *Spectator* telling us that " Sir Roger de Coverley,
" a baronet of good fortune and ancient family, lived
" in Soho Square," which is in the immediate neighbourhood of Seven Dials. In the reign of Queen
Anne, the whole parish of St. Giles, except the neighbourhood of Bedford Square and what is now called
Bloomsbury, was covered with houses. In the days of
the Commonwealth, an attempt was made to promote

the better observance of Sunday, and victuallers were
forbidden to open their houses on that day. Seven
Dials, even then the resort of questionable characters,
became the rendezvous of what the writer calls " op-
" pressed tipplers." A Doric pillar was set up by a
person whose name was Neale, who introduced lotteries
into this country; this was afterwards surmounted by a
clock having seven dials, and hence the name by which
this neighbourhood is known. Many hundreds of French
refugees, driven to this country by the revocation of the
edict of Nantes, fixed their abode in the neighbourhood
of Long Acre, the Seven Dials, and Soho. On the site
of Wylde Street, or, as it used to be spelt, Welde Street,
resided the family of the Welds of Lulworth Castle.
Bainbridge and Buckeridge Street were built prior to
1672, and derive their names from their owners, who
were men of wealth in the time of Charles II.; as Dyott
Street does its title from Mr. Dyott, a man of consideration in the same reign. On the spot occupied by these
very streets, in fact formed out of these streets, was the
famous Rookery, pulled down to form a continuation of
Oxford Street: from a comparatively early period, this
was the resort of the Irish, and the place they first
colonised. It has long been remarkable for poverty and
vice; for, in Smollett's novels, we read of one of his
heroes, whose rescue from the hands of the soldiers was
attempted by " two tatterdermalions from the purlieus
" of St. Giles's, and between them both was but one
" shirt and a pair of breeches." Allowing for exaggera-

PIERCON.

A Scene in St. Giles's.

tion in this sketch of 1740, we have the place and the class which we are at present describing.

These Rookeries then were haunts of crime in days of old,—are they more select now ? Or, do you suppose that they only conceal the accomplished felon,—that the labourers amongst whom he takes shelter for a while connive at his hiding place merely from mistaken compassion ? Do you suppose that such a man can live among them, without a fellow feeling between him who hides and him who is hidden ? that the plague spot does not spread, and that the very sight of the excesses in which one so abandoned revels when his trade is flourishing, has no temptations for him who, by hard labour, can barely earn a precarious subsistence ? Suppose that felon colonies were tolerated among us ; not penal places of banishment, but licensed Alsatias, and that thus the dwellings of the industrious poor were separated by a marked line from these gulfs of infamy ;—would not crime be fostered of itself by the very recklessness which Rookeries produce ? If they who make a gain of the necessities of the poor break one of God's commandments, will the victims be more fastidious ? You reduce men well nigh to the level of the beasts of the field,—can you expect them to be careful of nice distinctions, or not to glide by the slippery gradation of habit from less to greater delinquencies ?

In the time of the Commonwealth, then, St. Giles was the sanctuary for the vagabondism which seems the necessary curse of great cities ; there were even then

dense and skulking places where evil doers could lie hid
till the hue and cry was over. The scene of some of
Hogarth's most celebrated prints lies in this parish :—thus
his picture of Gin Lane has for its back-ground the
Church of St. George, Bloomsbury, the date is 1751.
" When," says Hogarth, " these two prints were designed
" and engraved, the dreadful consequences of gin
" drinking appeared in every street in Gin Lane, every
" circumstance of its horrid effect is brought to view *in*
" *terrorem,* not a house in tolerable condition, but the
" pawnbrokers, the gin shop, and the coffin makers in
" the distance." St. Giles's, then, was not in any degree
behind what it is at the present day, if we may take this
and other prints as fair types of its appearance ; for the
present Church often forms the background, or is introduced in the distance into his paintings; the houses seem
as mouldy and dilapidated, more so, even, than they do
now. A hundred years since, there was a large pauper
colony in St. Giles's; this increased year by year, till, in
the beginning of this century, it swelled to most alarming
proportions.

In a work, by the celebrated Fielding, called " Crimes
" and Offences," written in 1749, occurs the following
notice of St. Giles's in his time :—

" Thus in the parish of St. Giles's there are a great
" number of houses set apart for the reception of idle
" rogues and vagabonds who have their lodging there
" for two-pence a night; and in the above parish, and
" St. George's, Bloomsbury, one woman alone occupies

" seven of these houses, all properly accommodated with
" miserable beds, from the cellar to the garret, for such
" twopenny lodgers ; in these beds, several of which are
" in the same room, men and women, ôften strangers to
" each other, lie promiscuously, the price of a double
" bed being no more than three-pence as an encourage-
" ment to them to lie together: gin is sold to them a
" penny a quartern : in the execution of search warrants,
" Mr. Welch rarely finds less than twenty of them open
" at a time. In one of these houses, and that not a
" large one, he hath numbered fifty-eight persons of
" both sexes, the stench of whom was so intolerable,
" that it compelled him, in a short time, to quit the
" place; nay, I can add what I myself saw in the parish
" of Shoreditch, where two little houses were emptied of
" near seventy men and women."

In 1807, this colony is mentioned, in one of the
periodicals of the day; the difficulty of collecting rents,
and the drunken habits of the renters being pathetically
described. But, as even pauper colonies have their
degrees of wretchedness, so the worst sink of iniquity
was 𝕿𝖍𝖊 𝕽𝖔𝖔𝖐𝖊𝖗𝖞,—a place or rather district, so named,
whose shape was triangular, bounded by Bainbridge
street, George street, and High street, St. Giles's.
While the New Oxford Street was building, the recesses
of this Alsatia were laid open partially to the public, the
débris were exposed to view; the colony, called 𝕿𝖍𝖊
𝕽𝖔𝖔𝖐𝖊𝖗𝖞, was like an honeycomb, perforated by a number
of courts and blind alleys, *culs de sac,* without any outlet

other than the entrance. Here were the lowest lodging
houses in London, inhabited by the various classes of
thieves common to large cities,—the housebreaker, who
did not profess to have any other means of livelihood ;
the tramp and vagrant, whose assumed occupation was
a cloak for roguery ; the labourer who came to London
to look for work; the hordes of Irish who annually seem to
come in and go out with the flies and the fruit,—were here
banded together : driven by their various necessities to
these dens, they were content to take shelter there, till
the thief had opportunity to repair his fortune, and the
labourer means to provide better lodging. The streets
were narrow ; the windows stuffed up with rags, or
patched with paper; strings hung across from house to
house, on which clothes were put out to dry ; the
gutters stagnant, choked up with filth ; the pavement
strewed with decayed cabbage stalks and other vegetables ; the walls of the houses mouldy, discoloured, the
whitewash peeling off from damp ; the walls in parts
bulging, in parts receding,—the floor covered with a
coating of dirt. In the centre of this hive was the
famous thieves' public house, called Rat's Castle ; this
den of iniquity was the common rendezvous of outcasts.
In the ground floor was a large room, appropriated to
the general entertainment of all comers ;—in the first
floor, a free and easy, where dancing and singing went on
during the greater part of the night, suppers were laid,
and the luxuries which tempt intoxication freely displayed. The frequenters of this place were bound together

by a common tie, and they spoke openly of incidents which they had long ceased to blush at, but which hardened habits of crime alone could teach them to avow. Even by day it was scarcely safe to pass through this district! Did not the loathsome sights appal you, it was crowded with loiterers, whose broken hats and ragged shooting jackets were in keeping with their dwellings ; round them, lounged boys with dogs, birds, and other appurtenances ; these being their only visible means of support, it was possible, though very improbable, that they lived solely by the sale of them : by day, then, you might inspect the dingy alley with its thievish population; women with short pipes in their mouths and bloated faces and men who filled every immediate occupation between greengrocer and bird-catcher. Thieves lurk here now, their very semblances worn to conceal a less reputable calling; dog-breakers, dealers in birds, marine store-keepers, water-cress sellers, costermongers (*i.e.* small greengrocers), sellers of sprats and herrings, hawkers of prints and toys, street sweepers, dealers in coffee, lozenges, and other kinds of confectionery ; men, whom indolence and dissipation unfit for more regular employment, throng these haunts even by day ; there the bill-stickers retire, there go the bands of placard carriers who have obstructed the causeway, marching in column shouldering their weapons of offence; there beggars throng to count, divide, and spend their gains,—but night alone witnesses the real condition of our Rookeries. Then the stream of vagrants who have

driven their profitable trade return to their lair—trampers
come in for their night's lodging ; the beggar's operas,
as they were wont to be called, then open their doors to
those whom necessity or crime has made skulkers or
outcasts ; no questions are asked, it is sufficient that the
money is forthcoming,—and they, who are driven to such
dens, are seldom in a condition to ask questions. Not
in St. Giles's alone, but in most London parishes, are
rooms where chance lodgers are gathered at nightfall ;
these are crammed by those whom poverty assembles,
and the landlord derives a large revenue from the necessities of his customers ; so that you cannot judge by the
daylight aspect of the Rookery, what face it wears by
night. In St. Giles's, especially, rooms are opened as
night lodgings, where, as a general rule, several men
sleep who have never met before ; in many cases, there
are double beds, where married couples sleep, five
or six pairs, in the same room : you would be startled
to witness the crowding of inmates even in favoured
localities ; to see the industrious mechanic, his wife,
and his children huddled into a single apartment,—by
day, the common sitting room, by night, the common
dormitory ; you would be startled to find that such is
the rule among the working classes, the meed of honesty
and diligence, so that it has few exceptions. In the
genuine Rookery, even this remnant of decency, this
slender rag, which betokens a lingering regard to the
proprieties of social life is removed ; men and women
are brought together in the same apartment whom no

marriage tie unites, and who have no other bond than that of common want; children of all ages sleep with their parents; and even the miserable boon of laying the head in such places as these, though paid for, is often made of none effect, through the cries of infants, which break the silence of the night. In some of these places, bedsteads are supplied,—in some only straw,—and the charge, of course, varies with the accommodation. In these houses there is generally, on the ground floor, a common room, answering to the coffee room of an inn, or rather combining coffee room and kitchen; this is sometimes hung round with beds at the side, but not always; here is a good fire; spirits and beer are brought in, bacon fried, meals prepared; boys and girls are lying on the floor gambling or playing with marbles, sometimes exercising their ingenuity in tricks with dirty cards. Because all are taken in who can pay their footing, the thief and the prostitute are harboured among those whose only crime is poverty, and there is thus always a comparatively secure retreat for him who has outraged his country's laws. Sums are here paid, a tithe of which, if well laid out, would provide at once a decent and an ample lodging for the deserving poor; and that surplus, which might add to the comfort and better the condition of the industrious, finds its way into the pocket of the middleman.

We have lately had an opportunity of visiting the worst district of St. Giles's—George street and Church lane; through this part of the parish runs the New Oxford street, and they are thus the remains of the famous

Rookery—the still standing plague-spots of that colony. You cannot gain an idea of what 𝕿𝖍𝖊 𝕽𝖔𝖔𝖐𝖊𝖗𝖞 was without visiting these streets. Rows of crumbling houses, flanked by courts and alleys, *culs de sac,* &c. in the very densest part of which the wretchedness of London takes shelter. You seem for a time to leave the day, and life, and habits of your fellow-creatures behind you—just to step out of the din and bustle of a crowded thoroughfare—to turn aside from streets whose shops teem with every luxury—where Art has brought together its most beautiful varieties,—and you have scarce gone a hundred yards when you are in 𝕿𝖍𝖊 𝕽𝖔𝖔𝖐𝖊𝖗𝖞. The change is marvellous : squalid children, haggard men, with long uncombed hair, in rags, most of them smoking, many speaking Irish ; women without shoes or stockings —a babe perhaps at the breast, with a single garment, confined to the waist by a bit of string ; wolfish looking dogs ; decayed vegetables strewing the pavement ; low public houses ; linen hanging across the street to dry ; the population stagnant in the midst of activity ; lounging about in remnants of shooting jackets, leaning on the window frames, blocking up the courts and alleys ; with young boys gathered round them, looking exhausted as though they had not been to bed. Never was there so little connection between masses of living beings and their means of livelihood. And then these dens, the fronts of a small court—square you can scarce call it— more wretched, more utterly destitute of all that is needed for the purposes of life, than the lanes of which they are the background. These alleys were thickly populated, as though a close atmosphere had more attractions, and drew by a sympathetic cord more lodgers than the open thoroughfares ; you could scarcely have an idea of the number of persons crowded together in a single room. At first, when the average proportion of sleepers is stated to you, you feel inclined to calculate the number of square feet contained in the area of the room, to see whether it is possible that so many human beings can lie down there. You begin to fancy that the process so familiar to the prisons of the middle ages must take place here ; that persons do not sleep in a recumbent posture, but by leaning against the walls ; or perhaps, at night, some purgatory like a steamer's cabin is erected, and men sleep in tiers, as in one of those marine Pande-moniums. Thus in one room, measuring six feet by five broad, we were assured that eight people, some of them, of course, children, slept. You will tell us this must be exaggeration ; however, the tendency amongst the inhabitants, was to conceal, or qualify ; for the landlords had made wholesale clearances in many houses, where they had reason to believe that information on the subject of lodgings had been given by the tenants. The landlords were alarmed at the inquiries made of late, and determined to elude them. In one house 100 persons have been known to sleep on a given night. In a particular instance, we ascertained that three rooms were thus occupied—first room, by eight persons, second by fifteen, third by twenty-four. We ourselves saw as many as twenty-four persons in the same room ; they were assembled there even in the day-

time, and yet you are assured that night alone affords a
fair criterion.   In these rooms are piled the wares by
which *some* of the inhabitants gain their precarious
living,—oranges, herrings, water-cresses, onions, seemed
to be the most marketable articles; and there were
sweepers, cadgers or beggars, stray luggage porters, &c.
lounging about.   In another house, the average number
of persons who slept in a room was twelve; in others, of
course larger, forty persons are known to have slept in a
single night.

In a back alley, opening into Church street, was a
den which looked more like a cow-house than a room
for human beings—little, if any light, through the small
diamond panes of the windows; and that, obstructed by
the rags which replaced the broken glass—a door whose
hinges were rotting, in which time had made many
crevices, and yet seventeen human beings eat, drank, and
slept there; the floor was damp and below the level of the
court; the gutters overflowed; when it rained, the rain
gushed in at the apertures.   On a wretched mattress lay
a poor young man, with a fearful racking consumptive
cough; he was quite naked, had not a rag to his back,
but over him was thrown a thin blanket, and a blue rug
like a horse cloth,—these he removed to let us see there
was no deception.   This room was so low, that a tall
man could not stand upright in it—the rest of the inhabitants slept on shavings; the ceiling was broken,
several of the inhabitants were ill, and had all suffered
more or less.   In Church lane, it has been computed
that from 1000 to 1100 persons live; our informant

thinks, even at present, there are more than 800; and he has long known it, and indeed, from what we saw, this is likely to be accurate; in another room, about 8 feet by 12, twelve people slept.

We asked several questions respecting the inhabitants, and in one house some information was given us, which, in many points, was corroborated by our companion— that in an upper room as many as seventeen juvenile thieves had been collected, and used to live together; that one of these had been transported, and their ages ranged from six to twelve. It seems unlikely that sentence of transportation should have been carried out in the case of one so young; perhaps sentence was passed, and he was sent to a model prison in virtue of that sentence: but, substantially, the account was no doubt true; the extreme youth of the criminals, their habits, their plan of clubbing together, we fear, cannot be mis-stated. Many of the houses are so far below the level of the street, that, in wet weather, they are flooded; perhaps this is the only washing the wretched floorings get; the boards seem matted together by filth.

The aspect of these rooms is singular; in some, heaps of bedding—that is to say, blanket and mattress are tied up in a bundle, and placed against the wall so as to leave the middle of the room clear for meals; little bags, containing the whole of their small stock, are hung on a nail; shavings carefully gathered into a heap, occupy one corner; old hats, reaping hooks, bonnets, another—some sick child moaning in another part of

the room. These peculiums are arranged with some
neatness; there is an individuality about them, the idea
of a *meum* and *tuum,* the little stake in the country's
welfare, which is not altogether lost; there seemed
something like attachment to these shadows, which we
wished we could see exercised on more substantial
comforts; some clinging still as to a home, miserable as
it was, enough to show that reformation was not quite
hopeless. Many, perhaps most of the inhabitants, were
Irish; how strong their attachment to their native
country! One old man, breaking fast, was about to
return, to lay his bones in the " ould country." Those
about him spoke with warm enthusiasm of his return;
their eyes glistened, and some of them, we ascertained,
had wrung a little horde even from the wretchedness
around them, as a fund on which to subsist in their
native land. Seldom have we seen the love of country so
strong; and strong it must be to survive long separation,
the wrongs they had suffered before they had left their
native shore, the demoralising air of Rookeries, and the
ties they had formed in England. In several of the
rooms four and five distinct families lodged together; in
the time of the cholera, this induced fearful suffering.
It was warm weather; those who were well, were engaged
either in their daily business, or in their out-door lounge.
In one room a benevolent man told us he saw three
persons dying at the same time of the epidemic; there
were several cases where, because the disorder was
sudden, or they had no connections, or perhaps from

fear, those stricken were left to die alone, untended, unheeded, " they died and made no sign," without mentioning their relatives, without a word which betokened religious feeling on their lips, without God in the world, poor hapless outcasts, acclimatised long to the atmosphere they breathed, reckless from want of knowing better !

In these lodging-houses many of the families are stationary, that is, comparatively so, remaining for the week, the month, or the quarter; but we have said trampers come in, and the poverty of the inhabitants makes them glad to receive these chance customers. We were curious to know the charge for the night's lodging, and found it to be 1*d*. per night upon the bare boards, 3*d*. per night on a mattrass. The habits of the dwellers in these Rookeries are of course strange. Women will be seen crawling out to beg, who have been only two days confined. Marriage is too often dispensed with ; men leave their wives, and wives their husbands, in Ireland, and come over here with other partners, or else pick them up in England. Thus, some years since, in our noviciate, we paid the passage of a poor woman, who was very ill, to Ireland. She left her husband, he intending to join her; she soon returned, and found him provided with a partner ; and it is difficult to convince them this is wrong ; indeed, when anything happens, which, in higher circles, would lead to a divorce, the working classes generally take the law into their own hands, separate from their erring wives, and live with

some other woman; and they justify themselves on
religious grounds,—defend, as they think, this breach of
morality. Among these people, superstition abounds.
We saw a sick child, whose sufferings were severe; we
asked why it was not in the infirmary? The answer was,
it had been there, but the mother took her babe away,
conveyed it to Mile End, that it might be *charmed*, and
thus restored to health. In another house was a young
man who said he had been "in trouble;" in other words,
he had just returned from the House of Correction. He
said he had stolen a desk purposely, that he might be
committed, for he was starving; that he would now
willingly work, but that he had pawned his shoes, and
therefore must resort to the old trade for a livelihood.
He could read and write; we asked why he did not
enlist before he took to thieving? and he answered, that
his arm had been broken. Prostitution prevailed here to a
fearful extent. In one large house it is said that £.10, in
a smaller that £.5 per week, are cleared by this traffic ;
the most open and shameless immorality is carried on ;
the middle classes contribute to the evil. Six or seven
houses in one street are applied to this nefarious trade,
and there are from 200 to 300 fallen females here, for
mothers send out their own daughters on these errands,
and live on the proceeds.

Juvenile theft is also recruited by the same means,
and there are parents in this neighbourhood, training
their children to this iniquity, punishing them severely
when they return home empty-handed, and living on the

fruits of their success. Yet Ragged Schools are not wanting in the neighbourhood, nor do they labour in vain, although scarcely a tenth part of the juvenile population is educated.

We have said that a large majority of the inhabitants are Irish; they fly from starvation, and thus colonies are formed, not merely Hibernian in all their attributes, but separate colonies from different parts of the country, or plough lands, as they call them: thus, when an emigration takes place, the emigrants on arriving in London drop into the places prepared for them, as much as if they were billeted on the different wards of a hospital or a barrack. In one wretched room where eleven beds were ranged against the wall, two of them double beds, the landlady of the house was confined, and the occupants witnessed the pains of labour. When asked if she was not ashamed, her answer was, she had no other room in which to live.

This description will startle you, gentle reader: you thought, perhaps, as we did, that New Oxford Street had superseded 𝕿𝖍𝖊 𝕽𝖔𝖔𝖐𝖊𝖗𝖞. Was any colony of old worse than this—more thoroughly wretched and demoralising? Will any one now say we don't want an Act of Parliament to regulate the number of families per house, of inmates per room, and public prosecutors to see that the law is enforced? A religious society employ an Irish missionary in this district. When he first sent in his journal, the committee complained that he had only selected cases of open vice and extraordinary ignorance: his answer was, that he had passed over the worst cases; yet, that if his journal was to be a fair criterion of his labours, it could contain nothing but details of ignorance and vice—that in such a district anything else was impossible. But nine-tenths of the inhabitants are Irish; do we, then, set down to Irish nurture this amount of wretchedness and immorality? God forbid! We believe that examples of female profligacy are more rare in Ireland than England, though poverty is more excessive, and accompanied with more utter prostration of the individual than among us; yet the Irish coming to London seem to regard it as a heathen city, and to give themselves up at once to a course of recklessness and crime. Some regulations then should be framed to meet this great and pressing evil. Rookeries, at least such as Church Lane, should at once be proscribed; it would be difficult, with our free institutions, to stop these descents of Irish upon our great towns; but the names of those who land here should be entered in a book, their progress observed, and, if they did not get work within a certain time, they should be sent back to their own Unions; or, at any rate, not be allowed to congregate in such masses in the worst parts of our towns: they bring their bad habits with them, and leave their virtues behind. The misery, filth, and crowded condition of an Irish cabin, is realised in St. Giles's. The purity of the female character, which is the boast of Irish historians, here, at least, is a fable. Rookeries are bad, but what are they to Irish Rookeries? Within the ordinary boundaries of a district, we are assured, on the authority last mentioned, there is scarcely a family which is not Irish.

We do not aim in this sketch at describing minutely

the condition of those who inhabit Rookeries, and have therefore contented ourselves with few details. We must otherwise, in the cause of truth, enter upon inquiries, whose results are too disgusting for our pages. Such descriptions very properly fill the reports of Sanatory Commissioners, for, if they were left out, many an evil would be unchecked. *The Times, The Morning Chronicle*, and, above all, Mr. Mayhew, have told the naked tale. Thus, in the following pages, though much to the uninitiated may seem exaggeration, not one tithe of the nuisances which disgrace Rookeries, has been enumerated. Yet still a few facts, and they not the most startling, may prepare us for further investigation ; and, as we have derived them from official sources, we are less likely to be misled.

In the report of the Statistical Society, we have the following remarks, respecting the district visited by its members, which was one of the most densely populated in St. Giles's :—

" The inhabitants may be classed as follows :—

" 1*st*. Shopkeepers, lodging-house keepers, publicans, " and some of the under-landlords of the houses, who " make a considerable profit by letting the rooms, " furnished and unfurnished.

" 2*nd*. Street dealers in fruit, vegetables, damaged " provisions, and sundries ; sweeps, knife-grinders, and " door-mat makers.

" 3*rd*. Mendicants, crossing sweepers, street singers, " persons who obtain a precarious subsistence, and " country tramps.

" 4th. Persons calling themselves dealers, who are
" probably thieves, and the occupants of houses of ill-
" fame.

" 5th. Young men and lads, of ages varying from
" ten to thirty, known as pickpockets, and thieves of
" various degrees.

" About one half of the inhabitants are Irish, chiefly
" natives of Cork, who for the most part have been long
" resident in London. About one eighth are of Irish
" descent, born in England; the remainder consist of
" English, some of whom have been in better circum-
" stances." This last remark must be taken with some
allowance, because of the obvious difficulty attending
such classifications.

You are much struck in visiting the rooms and houses
where the working classes live, by the absence, not
merely of the comforts, but almost the necessaries of life.
Take, for instance, a family consisting of man and wife,
and five children; they are lucky if they have one bed-
stead and three beds; in many instances, there are no
bedsteads; in some cases, in the worst districts, as we
have seen, straw furnishes the bed, and the day clothes
the covering by night. The houses of the poor are, for
years together, guiltless of paint; and even whitewash,
cheap as it is, is sparingly laid on. The inmates suffer
much, too, from the want of water, with which these courts
are very inadequately supplied, even where it is turned
on; and this takes place, in many instances, only twice
a-week, though the companies have a plentiful supply at

command ; and few investments have turned out so profitable as those made in the shares of these different societies.

We need not wonder that such dens exist, that several persons unconnected by birth or even similar occupation are massed together in the same room, when the in-dependent labourer, the artisan, the mechanic, seldom rent more than a single apartment severally for themselves and their families. Below them in the scale of society are several degrees ;—the man of uncertain occupation, the beggar, the thief, the felon, each a grade in itself, and that grade distinguished, not only by more reckless habits than the one above it, but also worse clothed and lodged.

𝕿𝖍𝖊 𝕽𝖔𝖔𝖐𝖊𝖗𝖞 is no more ! a spacious street is in its stead ; but will you tell us that any poor man has gained by the change—that any section of the working classes has reaped an advantage—that any band of ruffians is dispersed—that middlemen have felt a mortal blow—that vagabondism, pauperism, alms-asking, or any other un-licensed trade has been broken up ? Certainly not ; there must be poor, and they lodged and fed ; how or where the Legislature must provide. The effects of the late removal are thus shown in the Report of a Committee of the Council of the Statistical Society :—

" The Council consider that a main cause of this evil
" is what are falsely called the improvements, which
" have recently taken place in this part in the formation
" of New Oxford Street. It would seem to raise a
" suspicion of the sanatory value of that kind of im-

" provement which consists in occupying, with first or
" second-rate houses, ground previously covered by the
" tenements of the poorer classes. The expelled in-
" habitants cannot, of course, derive any advantage
" from new erections, and are forced to invade the yet
" remaining hovels suited to their means ; the circle of
" their habitations is contracted while their numbers
" are increased, and thus a large population is crowded
" into less space. Church Lane consists of twenty-
" seven houses. The Council proceeded in their ex-
" amination from No. 1 to No. 18, passing over No. 1
" as a corner house and shop, and 11, 12, 13, 15, and
" 16, as lodging-houses, and therefore no fair specimens
" of the ordinary population. The number of houses
" examined were thus reduced to twelve, and the popula-
" tion of each was compared with that of the census
" of 1841—the great increase of overcrowding since
" is exhibited in the following most remarkable table :—

	Population in 1841.	1847.
No. 2 . .	33	61
„ 3 . .	14	49
„ 4 . .	27	61
„ 5 . .	35	47
„ 6 . .	29	32
„ 7 . .	29	62
„ 8 . .	13	48
„ 9 . .	25	26
„ 10 . .	17	13
„ 14 . .	17	19
„ 17 . .	12	26
„ 18 . .	26	17

' The increase of population in twelve houses being
' thus 186. Dividing the number of cubic feet of air
" in these twelve houses by the number of individuals
" found in them, the average supply for each individual
" was only 175 feet—while 1000 is the number deemed
" necessary for a single prisoner in England. The
" largest supply of air in these twelve houses was 605
" cubic feet, and the smallest was as low as fifty-two."

The conclusion is obvious: if Rookeries are pulled down, you must build habitable dwellings for the population you have displaced, otherwise, you will not merely have typhus, but plague; some fearful pestilence worse than cholera or Irish fever, which will rage, as the periodical miasmata of other times were wont to do, numbering its victims by tens of thousands!

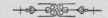

Chapter IV.

We would next inquire into the origin and present condition of the district called Saffron Hill. It is very interesting to trace the steps by which any particular district degenerated into a pauper colony, because it shows the gradations by which the hotel of the peer may become the hovel of the pauper; and we may, perhaps, learn at what point to interpose, and when it becomes necessary to declare a house unfit for human habitation.

Saffron Hill is now divided and subdivided into innumerable courts and alleys. It is difficult to ascertain the precise period when it became a Rookery, since many of the houses now used as lodging-houses bear the marks of wealth, and were evidently erected with some regard to the comfort of the owners. The streets are narrow, but not more so than many of the lanes and thoroughfares belonging to the Inns of Court, and the alleys in which a large business is carried on in the City; and could you suppose the business of the Courts transferred to Westminster, in thirty years' time many buildings now leased at an extravagant rent might degenerate to the condition of Saffron Hill. The ground on which this Rookery stands, formerly belonged to the Bishops of

Ely,—the names of some of the streets, Vine Street, and others, seem to indicate this. The gardens attached to this mansion, as appears from the curious map published by Ralph Aggas, occupied the present site of this district; they formed an irregular parallelogram, extending northward from Holborn Hill to the present Hatton Wall, and Vine Street, and east and west from Saffron Hill to the present Leather Lane ; but except a line or cluster of houses on Holborn Hill (some of which belonged to the See of Ely, and were called Ely Rents), the surrounding grounds were entirely open and unbuilt upon. Ely House, we are informed by Brayley, or Ely Inn, as it was anciently called, stood on the north side of Holborn Hill, and was the town mansion of the Bishops of Ely. Its first occupier was Bishop John de Kirkeby*, who, dying in 1290, bequeathed a messuage and nine cottages on this spot to his successors in the diocese. William de Luda, the next Bishop, annexed some lands and other dwellings to this residence ; and in 1298 devised them to his See, on condition that 1000 marks should be paid by his immediate successor towards the maintenance of three chaplains, for the service of the chapel here. On the west side of Ely Place, are the remains of this very chapel; the present edifice, though well nigh rebuilt, retains still some traces of its ancient glories, the tracery of the east window especially denoting the times of Richard II. Bishop John de Hotham, who died in

* The modern Kirby Street, near Saffron Hill, is evidently called after him, the " k " being omitted, a frequent Atticism.

1336, enlarged the property by annexing to it a vineyard, kitchen garden, and orchard. The good Bishop little thought that the memory of his terrestrial paradise would live in the crumbling streets of a Rookery, where it is unsafe to enter by night, and where day lends its light, only to shock you by its revelations. Shakspeare refers to this mansion, with its pleasure grounds, in his Richard III., in which drama the Duke of Gloucester, at the council in the Tower, thus addresses the Bishop of Ely :—

"My Lord of Ely, when I was last in Holborn,
I saw good strawberries in your garden there ;
I do beseech you, send for some of them."

This is but the paraphrase of a passage in Hall, one of the old chroniclers. A great feast was given at Ely House, by the Sergeants-at-Law, in November 1531, when eleven new members were added to their body ; they kept open house for five successive days; and on Monday, November 13th, which was the fourth and principal day, King Henry himself, with his Queen, Katharine of Arragon, and the foreign ambassadors, were feasted in different chambers.

In the eighteenth year of Queen Elizabeth, an important change took place at her mandatory request. She required the Bishop, who then inhabited Ely House, to resign it to her favourite Hatton : the prelate objected that, as tenant for life, he could not alienate the rights of his successor. On this occasion she is reported to have written the memorable letter :—" Proud Prelate, " I understand you are backward in complying with your

" agreement; but I would have you know that I, who
" made you what you are, can unmake you; and if you
" do not forthwith fulfil your engagement, by God I will
" unfrock you." Bishop Cox granted to Richard Hatton,
after whose family Hatton Garden was called, the gate-
house of the palace, (except two rooms, used as prisons
for those that were arrested, or delivered in execution to
the Bishop's bailiff, and the lower rooms, used for the
Porters' Lodge,) the first court-yard within the gate-
house to the long gallery dividing it from the second, the
stables there, the long gallery with the rooms above and
below it, and some other fourteen acres of land, and the
keeping of the garden and orchard, for twenty-one years,
Hatton paying at Midsummer day a red rose for the gate-
house and garden, and for the ground ten loads of hay,
and £.10 per annum; the Bishop reserving to himself
and his successors free access through the gate-house,
walking in the gardens, and *gathering twenty bushels
of roses* yearly. Mr. Hatton undertaking to repair, and
make the gate-house a convenient dwelling.

Successive Bishops endeavoured to regain the property thus alienated, and suits were entered into by them
with this view. During the Protectorate of Cromwell,
Ely House, and its attached offices, were appropriated
by the ruling powers to the uses both of a prison and a
hospital; and the crypt under the chapel became a
kind of military canteen. Thus occupied, and during
the protracted suit for the redemption of the Hatton
estate, which followed, the buildings were greatly dilapi-

dated, and at length being deemed incapable of repair, the entire premises were purchased by the Crown, under the authority of an Act of Parliament, which received the royal assent, in June 1772. The situation had been considered suitable for the erection of public offices; that design was eventually relinquished, and this estate was in consequence sold to a Mr. Cole, an eminent surveyor and builder. By him all the old edifices, except the chapel, were taken down, and the present Ely Place was built upon the vacant ground, about the year 1775. A few years before this, part of the house was still standing, almost opposite to St. Andrew's Church, its entrance being through a large gateway, or porters' lodge, into a small paved court. To the north-west of the Hall, was then attached a quadrangular cloister; in a field containing about an acre of ground stood the chapel; the field was planted with trees, and surrounded by a wall;—a print of the building as it stood before 1772, may be found in the edition of Grose, at the British Museum. It would seem that the money obtained by the sale of the ground still attached to the Hall was applied, with other sums, to the purchase of a house in Dover Street, Piccadilly, which is now attached to the See of Ely, and on which is carved a mitre.

Ely Place, then, would seem to have been a comparatively modern erection, yet we may not suppose that any part of the genuine Rookery is of an origin so recent; for, in Aggas's map, made in the reign of Elizabeth, there was a row of houses from Cow Lane to about Ely Place,

whose backs were opened to the fields. Clerkenwell,
which joins this district, had been, long before this,
famous for its St. John's Hospital ; Smithfield, previously
to this, had a melancholy notoriety ; the fires of persecu-
tion kindled, and the faithful martyrs perishing in the
flames, connect its memory with some of the most touching
records of our annals. Clerkenwell is not only referred
to as a spot generally inhabited at this time, for part of
it was, before this, the resort of thieves, loose characters,
and desperados. Shakspeare mentions Pickt Hatch
in his play of the Merry Wives of Windsor; and anti-
quarians tell us it was near Clerkenwell Green, the
refuge of the destitute, the sanctuary of the disorderly.
The great Dramatist puts these words into the mouth of
Falstaff* :—

"At a word, hang no more about me, I am no gibbet
"for you, go, a short knife and a thong to your manor
"of Pickt Hatch; go, you'll not bear a letter for me, you
"rogue, you stand upon your honour; why, thou unconfi-
"nable baseness, it is as much as I can do to keep the
"term of mine honour precise." This Pickt Hatch is
thus characterised in the celebrated memoirs of Colonel
Hutchinson :—"Robinson fell a railing at the Colonel,
"giving him the base term of rebel and murderer, and
"such language as none could have learned, but such as
"had been conversant with the evil society of Picked
"Hatch, Turbull Street, and Billingsgate, near which
"last place the hero got his education."

* Act II., Scene 2.

Hatton, the antiquarian, writing in 1708, speaks of Saffron Hill, between Field Lane and Holborne Bridge, and of St. Andrew's, Holborn, as comprising Cross Street, Kirkby Street, Field Lane, part of Chick Lane, all Saffron Hill, Vine Street, Hatton Wall; and of the number of houses in the Liberty of Saffron Hill as 819.

The famous Gordon riots broke out in 1780, in June,— and Newgate was burnt down. The people made a stand at the bottom of Holborn Hill, although they were soon dispersed, but not before they had done much damage ; for a large distillery stood on the brow of the hill near Fetter Lane, which was sacked by the mob, the vats were broken up, and their contents ran down the gutters at the side, and many of the mob lay down in the kennel, and drank the raw spirits to such an extent, that some were taken up dead. This scene must have taken place in the neighbourhood of the Rookery, and we cannot but suppose, that the rioters were recruited by the denizens of these haunts. The distiller had incurred the displeasure of the mob because he was a Papist, and they were hounded on to deeds of atrocious violence, by the cry of " No Popery." Within the memory of many now living, the object of this attack was residing at Mitcham, Surrey, where he is said to have reached a good old age; a heavy fine, we believe, was levied on the City of London, from the proceeds of which they, who suffered from the riot, were indemnified.

This district has seen strange scenes then ; the imagination paints its infancy in glowing colours,—the lordly

Bishop,—some mitred abbot with his stately palace, his garden, through which the impetuous river rushed in its course to the Thames, a pleasant place for eye to look on, with its tiers of terraces and goodly trees,— its aviaries,—its fountains,—its sculptures of fantastic and grotesque forms,—its oratories shaded from observation by hanging groves; and then the long retinue, —the train of attendants,—the pomp,—the state,—the portly form, which seemed to mock the accents of humility which the lips repeated. Yet, with all this, there were the large charities which graced the old faith, the crowds of poor whose wants and sickness alike were tended, and the learned clerks whom the prelate sustained around him, the goodly company, who under his guidance and beneath his roof, went forth on errands of health to the body, and of comfort to the soul. The scene changes, and there is the Lord Hatton, Elizabeth's Chancellor, with his train of menials, and the ensigns of a judge's state, in days when the younger sons of decayed families were glad to discharge a menial office about the person of one whom the Queen honoured;—the open fields, ringing to the cry of hounds, or the shouts of the gay train pursuing the sport of hawking in the very neighbourhood of Ely House; and the pleasant village of Islington in the distance, where men went to breathe the pure air of the country. Now squalid misery and crowded courts, the black ditch, and the mouldering Rookery, supply the place once tenanted by forms the painter would love to depict, and by scenes which call up the merry days of good Queen Bess.

The modern condition of Saffron Hill entitles it to high rank among 𝕿𝖍𝖊 𝕽𝖔𝖔𝖐𝖊𝖗𝖎𝖊𝖘 𝖔𝖋 𝕷𝖔𝖓𝖉𝖔𝖓; such colonies there are, we need not repeat, in most parishes; St. Giles's does not stand alone, and Saffron Hill has strong claims to the second place. Perhaps for this, it is indebted to Mr. Dickens, whose researches have dragged it into light: some of the scenes of his Oliver Twist are laid there ; there, if we remember, the poor friendless boy is enticed into a den of thieves. The place is connected in the minds of many with the disappearance of pocket handkerchiefs, and these thefts are with them types of greater iniquities. The far-famed Jack Sheppard had his lair there, and some few years since, a thieves' house in West Street was the popular exhibition of the day. The veritable Saffron Hill is bounded by Ely Place on the west; Clerkenwell and St. Saviour's parishes on the east ; on the south by Holborn Hill ; on the north by Brook Street, generally called Mutton Hill. On the east runs a large sewer, commonly termed the Fleet Ditch, once so wide a creek of the Thames, that at high water vessels of small size came up it to a considerable distance, though more than two hundred years since a protest was entered against its filthy condition, or rather its abuse.

From the back of a cottage the writer was enabled to see the Fleet Ditch, a window opening on it. It is a most unsavoury black stream of some width, it does not so much flow as rush impetuously between the walls of the houses on each side. The stream is only visible from the back of these tenements, it carries along with its current all sorts of refuse, corks, &c. floating on the surface. Its waters are dark and fetid, and it is difficult, even in cold weather, to stand a few minutes in the room when the windows looking down upon it are opened. In summer, the inhabitants tell you, the stench is intolerable. This may be supposed, when a wide deep open sewer momentarily recharged with putrid matter is running just under the kitchens of the houses.

Clerkenwell, in the neighbourhood, is famed for its Printing Houses; this district for several trades peculiar, we believe, to its precincts. In one street was an establishment where the skins of horses' legs were boiled, and then hung up to dry; and other branches of commerce, not less redolent, were carried on not far off.

The Rookeries of this district consist, for the most part, of lodging houses, where trampers and others of uncertain occupation are received; several thieves live in the neighbourhood: in some of these receiving houses families are taken in, others seem only intended for single men; the rooms are small and the beds closely packed. Two bills were given as setting forth the charges and advantages of their several receptacles. The first is as follows :—

" CLEANLINESS *v.* FILTH !"

" Do you want a comfortable lodging ? Then go to
" 8, Upper Union Court, opposite St. Andrew's Church,
" Holborn Hill, where you can be accommodated with
" a single bed at the low charge of 3*d*. per night, or
" 1*s*. 9*d*. per week, a good fire and every accommodation.

" Please to notice, the first lodging house on the left
" from Holborn Hill.

" Gas lamp over the door,
" Opposite the Public House ! ! ! "
Another runs thus :—
" THE PHILANTHROPIC LODGING HOUSE,
" 11, *Union Court, Holborn Hill.*
" The above house is open for the reception of single
" men, at the charge of 2*d.* and 3*d.* a night, fire for
" cooking and other necessaries provided. This house
" is opened for the purpose of providing a home (during
" the coming inclement season) for those who may be
" peculiarly situated."

Here, as in most Rookeries, are colonies of Irish, who
seem particularly given to courts in which the only
egress is a narrow alley. Many a *cul-de-sac* is there in
this district, which the sons of Erin have chosen as their
own.

The arrangement of these lodgings is for the most
part as follows :—

At the bottom of the house is a low narrow cellar,
the receptacle of all sorts of refuse; over this, separated
only by thin boards, is the common sitting room allotted
to the lodgers, the flooring in many cases much decayed,
and not thick enough to prevent the evaporation from
below ascending to this apartment : in this room, especially after night-fall, are gathered the motley groups
whose necessities, or whose evil deeds force them to take
refuge here. Persons of uncertain occupation, trampers,
beggars, thieves, are for the most part housed here; even in
the better part of the district, the population is of a fluctuating character, street singers, dogs' meat men, crossing

sweepers (in some cases a lucrative trade), pie-men, muffin-sellers, dealers in lucifer matches, watercresses, fruit, and sweet-meats, cabmen, dustmen, and a host of others, who prefer a desultory to a regular employment, settle in this quarter. They who ply a regular trade, choose out a home where they soon become known, where they frequently live for many years; so that where the inhabitants of a district are migratory, there poverty and recklessness put on their worst garb.

The bed chambers in which these lodgers for the night sleep, are over the common room, and the tenants ascend by a ladder, to a few small rooms where the beds are packed so close, that there is only space to walk between them. We were informed that water is let on three times a week in these courts, and then only in limited quantities, so that there is much quarrelling, and even fighting for the supply. Many ash heaps were found in different streets; and a bystander to whom we spoke on the subject, told us that the dustman always left a portion behind him when he came on his rounds—though he removed the rest; as though the size of his cart, not the amount of deposit, was the question he was most concerned in. Some of the inhabitants ran across the court without shoes or stockings; the windows in many places were stuffed up with rags in lieu of the glass which had been broken. Field Lane, in this district, is a place of such bad repute, that policemen are constantly employed in it.

In one house are four rooms, with shop and parlour,

the latter is used as a kitchen, where the lodgers sit in the day time, and cook what they require ; two of the rooms have two beds in each, in these rooms they take men and their wives,—two families in each room ; the double beds, 6d. each. In two rooms, they have four single beds in each, at 4d. each per night. This is a moral house.

In another house there are six rooms ; in the two front there are six double beds,—three in each, paying 2d. each person. In the other four rooms are ten single beds ; two have three single beds, and two have two single beds in each : charge, 3d. per night. They receive none but males. This is a moral house.

Two houses are used by known thieves, and the police are very often there in search of bad characters, both male and female, also *boys and girls.*

In another house they have ninety beds (single) for males only.

Two houses are occupied by thieves, both men and women, two beds in each room. A woman was confined in one of these houses, with another family in the same room, which is not ten feet square. On the same side, next door, are two houses, in which they have twenty-four single beds at 3d. per night each, this house is used by known thieves. In one of them are three beds in a very small room, so close that there was not space to pass up the side to make them. They were occupied by six females, paying 1s. 6d. each per week ;—the persons in charge of the houses are not the owners, and are not

willing to give any information, fearing it might be made
public. The parlours, or kitchens of these houses, re-
semble the tap-room of a low public house. Some of the
worst characters in London—men, and in others men and
women sitting, conversing, and smoking—using the most
disgusting conversation.

We have spoken of the celebrated Thieves' houses* in
this district; these were destroyed six or seven years
since, when the line of the New Street was opened between
Farringdon Street and Clerkenwell. The houses were
situated in West Street, formerly called Chick Lane;
it is supposed that they were built in the year 1683, by
a man named McWaullen, or McWelland, chief of a tribe
of Gypsies; these buildings went under the name of the
Red Lion, but this was only a *nom de guerre*, to conceal
the real character of the place, its true purpose was to be
a rendezvous for thieves, and a depôt for stolen property :
the buildings behind were used as stables, where the
horses were kept in constant readiness ; these horses were
always selected for their speed and breeding ;—and among
the inhabitants have been at different times, Jonathan

* We are indebted to the kindness of the Reverend J. Garwood, one of
the Secretaries to the City Mission, for much information on this head,
especially for access to the interesting paper published in that Society's
journal for October 1844, where is an account given by Mr. Andrew
Provan, of this locality. We acknowledge our deep debt of obligation
to that excellent Society. Those only who, like the writer, have long
known Mr. Garwood, and been conversant with the workings of this the
Parent Society, can appreciate the inestimable amount of good which
has been done.

Wild, Jack Sheppard, Jerry Abershaw, and Richard Turpin.

Many circumstances contributed to render this district the resort of thieves and low characters; the Fleet Ditch flowed through the middle of it; though its dark and rapid stream was concealed by the houses built on each side, its current swept away at once into the Thames whatever was thrown into it. In the Thieves' house were dark closets, trap-doors, sliding panels, and other means of escape. In shop No. 3, were two trap-doors in the floor, one for the concealment of property, the other to provide means of escape to those who were hard run; a wooden door was cleverly let into the floor, of which, to all appearance, it formed part; through this, the thief, who was in danger of being captured, escaped; as immediately beneath was a cellar, about three feet square; from this there was an outlet to the Fleet Ditch, a plank was thrown across this, and the thief was soon in Black Boy Alley, —out of reach of his pursuers. The cellar is described as a most dismal filthy place, the light was let in through a small window, or hole, immediately above the Fleet Ditch. In one corner was a den or cellar concealed by a wall besmeared with soot and dirt, to prevent detection : this measured about 4 feet by 8; here, it is asserted, that a chimney sweep, who escaped from the prison of Newgate, a few years since, was concealed for a long time, and kept alive by food which was let down through an opening, made by removing a brick near the rafters. In a corner on the opposite side, was a small blast furnace, which a gang of coiners had used some years since ; and a private still had long been at work in the same locality.

Our informant, who saw the place in its original state, before it was pulled down states, " The most extraordinary " and ingenious part of the premises, I consider to be " the means of escape. If a prisoner once got within " their walls, it was almost impossible to capture him, " there were so many outlets and communications. The " most active officer had scarcely a chance of taking the " thief, if the latter only got a few minutes start of him. " There were four means of escape. The staircase was " very peculiar, scarcely to be described ; for though the " pursuer and pursued might only be a few feet distant, " the one would escape to the roof of the house, while " the other would be descending steps, and, in a moment " or two, would find himself in the room he had first left " by another door. This was managed by a pivoted " panel being turned between the two. A large room on " the first floor back, is said to be the place where the " abandoned inmates held their nightly orgies, and " planned their future robberies. From the upper room, " there were means of escape, by an aperture made in the " wall, leading to the house No. 2, containing no less " than twenty-four rooms, with four distinct staircases. " Here, also, level with the floor, was a shoot or spout, " which remained covered, except when required, about " two feet in breadth and three feet in length, by which " goods could be conveyed to the cellar in an instant.

" Immediately behind the premises just described, stood
" a dilapidated building, lately used as penny lodgings,
" where men and women slept promiscuously. Scenes
" commonly occurred here in the middle of the day in
" the public street, before this house, too gross and
" revolting to be described."

In the visit we paid, we had an opportunity of seeing
much, which the public has already known by hearsay.
Several of the courts were entered by a low arch or passage, which was formed of boards and planks ; they were
uneven squares, or parallelograms, some of them steep,
sloping down the hill on which they were built ;—they
were very narrow,—enclosed on three sides,—open only
at the entrance we have described ; some were entered
by a long alley, or through a stable yard, or by some
twisting passage, refuse and dirt-heaps being placed
against the walls. You entered the house, and much the
same sort of scene met your eyes, which we have before
pictured in Church Lane. We will just state what we saw
in one of these wretched abodes, which may be taken as a
type of the whole ; it is not needful to go over the same
ground we have once trodden before, or to present again
the same results. The house we select contained five
rooms, one of which was inhabited only by a man and his
wife ; whether the landlord was the occupant here, we know
not, but in the four remaining rooms, 86 human beings
were massed together ; in room we will call No. 1, 28,—
No. 2, 27,—No. 3, 14,—No. 4, 17,—No. 3 was the front
attic at the top of the house, it was a low square room,

inhabited chiefly by Irish. Although our visit took place in the day time, there were three or four families there,— women suckling their children, men lounging about the floor or cooking potatoes, a little heap of sacking for bed-clothes; sundry lines running across the room, on which were hung divers articles of clothing; the walls were discoloured, blackened by soot, or the plaster was peeling off; shelves were extemporized with marvellous dexterity. One of the women had been in Ireland during the fatal Skibbereen fever in 1847; she spoke in warm, and even eloquent terms of the kindness of a Protestant clergyman, whose name was Tyrrell, a man of property, who, having given his substance, at last gave his life, dying by fever, caught in visiting those who were stricken; the poor creatures round her, although Catholics, joined heartily in the benediction she poured out upon his head, saying, " Aye, Sir, he is rewarded for it now!" There was all the courtesy and warmth of heart about these poverty stricken tenants, which we find generally in the Irish; the language, although betraying the brogue, good and appropriate, reminding us strongly of Miss Edge-worth's description of them, where she says, " That in " stead of the Englishman's benediction, long life to " your honour, the Irishman prays that you may live as " long as water runs, or the sun shines." They were playing with, or nursing the children, and when asked whether their rest was not disturbed by the crying of infants, where so many were brought together, the answer was, "the children are very good." In the room we have

called No. 4, seventeen men, women, and children, lived
and slept; the size of the room was as follows,—length,
10 feet, or thereabouts, width in one part, 8 feet; in the
other, where the fireplace was, 5 feet. We doubted whether
it were possible that on such an area seventeen people
could be placed? The answer was, " We make shift."
This room was half filled with onions, the children must
have slept on them; there were a few pieces of the coarsest
brownest crockery, old hats and bonnets, no chairs, or
tables—two men, and several women and children were
here. One of the men was what is called a mud-larker,
or one who prowls about the banks of the river, and
picks up the coals which are scattered there by the men
who unload colliers; another, nearly blind, was supported
evidently by the earnings of the rest. Their welcome to
us rung cheeringly on our ears, and the salute which they
gave us as we left, was full of warmth, and in a style
which would not have disgraced noble blood. Round the
room were the same number of cords, cupboards, and
shelves, as in the other; a small fire was burning, at which
an old woman was cooking. Children seemed, if we may
judge by the number we saw, to thrive there, and to be
fondled with an affection, the want of which renders many
mansions desolate. You could not but grieve, that so
much kindness and courtesy should be neutralised by
wretchedness,—and that these poor creatures should live
in the neighbourhood of the worst thieves and lowest
prostitutes of London.

In another part of the district, were houses for single

"The last of Field Lane."

men; in those tenanted by married couples, four or five families per room seemed the rule.

In Field Lane, and the courts which run out of it, were several lurking places for thieves, lodging houses and places of resort frequented by them; although others, whose only vice is gross intemperance, are often obliged to live in these dens, so that professional men have been known to inhabit these localities, dragged down to this lowest abyss, by their passion for drinking. Of the thieves, the greater proportion are English; for the most part, the receivers of stolen goods, the negociators in this fearful traffic, are Jews, who, with their families, reside here, and drive their nefarious trade. These thieves are often the children of honest, though drunken and debauched parents, father and mother spending their earnings, and devoting their spare time to the public house; their children have become the easy prey of the villains who lurk in the neighbourhood; soon do they learn, in thieves' training houses, the jugglery of their trade, and apt pupils do they become. Even if they were sober, the inhabitants of Rookeries cannot take care of their children,—they are too much from home; the children are allowed to run about, without any one to take care of them, or, if even sent to school, are not quite out of the reach of temptation; and what influence must the example of a thieves' quarter have upon them all. With such a neighbourhood are connected the lowest prostitutes and the worst public houses—for in these two species of enjoyment, the unhallowed gains of felons are wasted, scattered profusely, rather than spent,—these different species of intoxication, the lures which wed them to their infamous calling.

The City authorities, some years since, proposed to build a long street to connect Farringdon Street with Clerkenwell; after having erected a few handsome houses, obstacles were put in their way—the purchase of the houses in the line of road about to be made was not completed, and therefore the works were suspended. The open space thus formed the nucleus for an assemblage of ragged boys; near it is a Ragged School, where a hundred beds, in a large, lofty, and airy apartment, are provided for those pupils who are houseless; and baths and other comforts are attached to the establishment, and it is said that in summer, the poor often sleep under the arches which have already been erected. The proposed street, if carried out, would be a great blessing to the neighbourhood, the inhabitants would never be at rest till the back ground of wretchedness had been removed.

If this wholesale clearance answered its end, other landlords would be tempted to build better houses in the place of the present dens, courts, and alleys. It would be letting light upon Pluto's gloomy dominions, the astonished ghosts would vanish at the unexpected sight, and the spirits of pestilence, hunger, crime, and despair, betake themselves to Rookeries yet unexplored.

But Plough and Plumtree Courts, in the same parish; Harp Alley, Churchyard and Cockpit Courts, in St.

Bride's; Crown Court, Hanging Sword Alley, and other worse plague spots than these would be crowded with inmates,—room economised, rents raised to the gain of the middleman and the ruin of the poor, unless lodging houses were built to receive those turned out.

Ere we carry on the historical picture, a few remarks cannot be out of place. There were plague spots in former days, and a population dangerous alike to the State and itself. Because, with the exception of the Gordon riots, for forty years later, no popular commotion took place, it is argued that the danger of fostering such a class is exaggerated; that life and property are still secure, though men like these remain; that by speaking of such haunts as these you cannot alarm selfishness, though there is a strong argument addressed to the conscience of the Legislature. We are not quite so certain that even the first assertion is true. St. Antoine, the St. Giles's of Paris, contributed her hordes in the revolution of 1789. The Bastille was reared amidst her precincts, and was the first victim of revolutionary fury. We say not that these divisions of the body social originate popular disturbances, but they are the fuel on which agitation feeds, ready to take fire the moment the flame is kindled by great party feuds. A hundred years ago the distinction between rich and poor was not so visible, the middle class so large and so wealthy. Now a gulf yawns—is daily growing wider, and we may fear that at no distant time the legend of old Rome may be here brought to pass, the chasm opening only to close because filled up by the best and choicest the country breeds. You have put the weapons into these men's hands,—have taught them, educated them, given them a free press, free to licentiousness, the parent of sedition. They meet, discuss, harangue, plot, combine—wait their time. England's domestic difficulties, her foreign embroilments, a crisis in her councils, a split in her parties, will alike evoke ready instruments to do by violence what should have been done by a paternal Government.

The sketch we have thus far given will describe in what way the most celebrated Rookeries have grown to their present size and condition—a condition not likely to be improved, until the subject of dwellings for the poorer classes really engages the attention of our Rulers.

One remark we cannot forbear. The finest squares of the metropolis are comparatively of modern date,—Grosvenor, Hanover, and St. James's, not two hunded years old,—barely, perhaps, one hundred and fifty. The parish church of St. James was built by Sir Christopher Wren, and some of the carving of the interior is by Grinling Gibbons. We know that these renowned individuals, architect and artisan, flourished towards the close of the seventeenth century, the Church itself having been finished about the era of the Revolution. The Square near it dates its origin from the same period; and Hanover Square was coeval with the introduction of the reigning family; yet the haunts of poverty have been in many instances what they are for more than two hundred years. These squares have been supplanted by new colonies of aristocratic buildings whose sites are supposed to be better, more airy, laid out on a more commodious plan than were those which were wont to be in vogue. The citizen spends his first surplus on a country house; though for the greater part of the day he toil in London, his family have the benefit of pure air, country scenery, and a detached abode. Whole streets—once residences—are now warehouses, counting houses, and places solely for business. Why? Because they are supposed to be too close for dwellings: and though the houses are often lofty and spacious, with large courts in front—though they lodged our ancestors--though they are handsomely built, —the very retail tradesman hurries from their neighbourhood to the country house, or the cockney villa. Time is lost in going and returning, though Time, in commercial phrase, be money; the underlings in City establishments are left without the wholesome control of the master during greater part of the twenty-four hours; property is jeopardied; opportunities of correspondence lost, because it is confessedly worth the while of the principal to buy a portion of health at the cost of a portion of emolument, with risk and with certain loss.

Rookeries still survive by their very isolation, by their retention of past anomalies,—possessing still the errors and handing down the discomforts of our ancestors,—sad memorials of the past. Meanwhile, when rebellion recruits her forces she is fed by the denizens of these retreats. It is on record that during the combats in Paris in 1848, and on the famous 10th of April here, multitudes of strange figures issued from these lurking places, distinguished by their appearance from the rest even of the poor population. They bide their time ; the agitator calls, and " they will come when he doth call."

St. Antoine, riddled by bullets as when we last saw it, still remains ; shall we neglect our duty, because St. Giles and Saffron Hill, unscathed by war, crumble peacefully beneath the hand of Time ?

Chapter V.

Up to this point we have had to do with genuine Rookeries; Rookeries, which have become so through the changing circumstances of the age, or through the abuse or former provisions for the decent lodging of the working classes. Men build small houses, which are not drained, supplied with water, ventilated as they ought to be,—these easily degenerate into Rookeries, but they were not originally designed for this; they were, in advertising phrase, *eligible premises, multum in parvo's ;* we now turn to a different part of the town, not strictly within the city boundaries, though not excluded from the bills of mortality, where Rookeries wear a different shape. The houses are not particularly small, ill ventilated, or crammed, yet they are begirt with a set of nuisances sufficient to degrade them to the lowest state of habitable dwellings. So that Rookeries may become fever depôts through the avarice of speculators, who poison the water and pollute the air for the sake of an additional per centage upon the trade in which they are employed, much in the same way that wretches might be found who would retail poison, did not the Legislature curtail *the freedom of the subject,* when he would be rid

of the life which God gave him for a noble purpose.
Tan-pits, glue-yards,—the head quarters of some odorife-
rous traffic,—subtract about seventy per cent. not only
from the comforts but the necessaries of life. If air and
water be essential for beings constituted as we are,
Rookeries in such localities become dens of pestilence,
and the full pressure of poverty is here exposed, by the
loathsome dwellings to which it drives its victims. Men
must be sunk indeed—desperate, reckless, past power of
redemption, we had well nigh said—who could tolerate
such a neighbourhood as the scene where they are to
know the blessed influence of wedded love, and which is
to be pictured in their children's memories as the place
where first they saw the light. Suppose a man to marry,
with some of the usual aspirations of his kind,—with
some love for, and interest in, the being to whom he is
united; allow him only the smallest particle of that
romance which ought to gild unions such as these,
how soon must he lose every finer feeling, how rapidly
become demoralized by the loathsome attributes of a
plague spot! Moralists have ever ranked among the
great panaceas of our kind the hallowed influence of
marriage,—how it destroys selfishness; what a stake it
gives a man in the welfare of his country; how it opens
the heart to the wants and feelings of others; what an
object to live for; what benefit the country reaps from
well-trained families; with what cheerfulness the man
who is happily married goes to his daily work; what an
aid to the sway of pure and sober religion these home

sympathies are ! How does the romance of affection give
a delicacy to the thoughts and refinement to the taste ?
All is checked, or rather distorted in neighbourhoods such
as these ; we blot out from the catalogue of God's gifts
to men the holiest, the most precious of earthly blessings.
The body soon becomes enfeebled by inhaling a fetid
atmosphere, disease is generated, seizes hold upon some
flaw in a weak constitution, makes one for itself in the
stronger frame, and the mind sympathizes, is clouded, is
driven to seek questionable relaxations, to purchase
moments of forgetfulness in intoxication ; the image the
man has drawn of the partner of his life soon recedes
before the figure of her who is a fellow sufferer with himself ; the annoyances with which he is surrounded leave
their traces in his family and his home ; childhood's
innocence seems a fable in such haunts, wedded love a
mockery, when poverty and custom assign for its enjoy-
ments receptacles like these.   Who shall say how much
the crime which pollutes England is owing to our St.
Giles's and Saffron Hills ? how much to this,—the failure
in our education schemes ? how much to this,—the abortive efforts of Churchmen and Dissenters for the religious
improvement of their fellow creatures ?   Can you think
to lift a man's eyes heavenward, when his vision is
distorted by gazing ever on these objects,—to fill his
heart with love who is reaping the fruits of a more than
heathen avarice,—to teach him reverence for human
laws, when the only exercise of law which he knows is the
protection afforded to plague spots and the victimizers

of their fellow creatures ?   When legislation would root
out the disease which decimates the poor, it is feebler
than the child.

𝕿𝖍𝖊 late visitation has brought to light many sores
in the body corporate of London ; and, thanks to the
able articles in the *Morning Chronicle*, Bermondsey, a
Rookery quarter like those we have just described, has
come in for its full share of infamous notoriety.   Our
attention has been directed to that parish by this able
paper ; and we have therefore wished to include it in our
sketch, though we would much rather refer our readers
to the articles themselves (which we trust will be published separately), and more especially to a tract, entitled
" Jacob's Island, and the Tidal ditches of Bermondsey."
Our plan has been hitherto to show how a Rookery
became what it now is ; whether it ever knew palmy
days, and what and when these were ; because it is
interesting to the mass to learn this, even if, in addition,
it did not point out by what steps such changes* were
accomplished.

Bermondsey, then, is supposed to have derived its
name from some Saxon proprietor whose name was
Bermond, the termination *eu*, or *eye*, in that language,
signifying water.   This was added to denote the nature
of the soil, and is frequent in the names of places whose
situation on the banks of rivers renders them insular or
marshy.

* See Wilkinson's Londiniana Illustrata.

King Edward was lord of the manor, as Harold had been before him, in whose time it was rated to the land tax (including the manor, afterwards called Rotherhithe) at thirteen hundred acres. There were eight hundred acres of arable land ; a new and fair church, with twenty acres of meadow ; and as much woodland as yielded to the lord's share in pasnage * time five fat swine. The reputed annual value of the manor, or whole lordship, in the time of Edward the Confessor, was £.900 of our present money, out of which the sheriff was allowed 20s. or £.60 of our present currency, for collecting the rents and paying them into the Exchequer. The manor house, or palace, was given by William II., in 1094, to the monks of Bermondsey. After its surrender to Henry VIII., it was granted by him to Sir Robert Southwell, who in the same year sold it to Sir Thomas Pope; by whom soon afterwards the ancient edifice was taken down, and a capital mansion erected. Having been occupied by the Earl of Sussex and various owners, part of it, in 1792, was the property of William Richardson; and as late as 1821 of James Riley, Esq., in whose garden, at that time, was an ancient wall, with crosses and other devices in glazed bricks.

Whether from its situation by the side of the river, or from what other cause is not mentioned, the ravages of

---

* Pasnage, or pannage, is an ancient law term for the most of the oak and other forest trees used to feed swine. The time for receiving these animals into the woods and keeping them, was from Holyrood Day, or fifteen days before Michaelmas, to St. Martin's day.——WILKINSON.

the plague are stated to have been greater here than at
Lambeth, although the latter was the more populous
parish. In 1625, this distemper was most fatal, the
number of deaths being 1117; twenty bodies were frequently interred in one night. In 1636, 203 persons died
of this disease; in 1665, 263.

The importance of this place in the olden time was
derived from its famous Abbey or Priory, to which
were attached lands, bounded by the Thames, on which
now stands the colony, called Jacob's Island : the
present condition of this place is the subject of the
strictures in the *Morning Chronicle*, for we are told
that the prior and convent of Bermondsey had a park
and other lands adjoining the Banks of the Thames,
called Rotherhithe Wall. This sustained so much damage
in 1309, by a breach in those parts (probably a high
tide), that they were exempted from the purveyance of
hay and corn. " The mill of St. Saviour (still the place
" keeps the name St. Saviour's Dock) was converted
" into a water machine to supply the inhabitants with
" water, and was, on the first of June, 1536, demised by
" the abbot and monks to John Curlew, at the annual
" rent of £.6 (the value of eighteen quarters of good
" wheat), and to grind all the corn for the use of the
" convent, which Curlew was to fetch home. The annual
" charge of the whole was computed at £.2 3s. 8d.,
" which made the annual rate of the said mill amount to
" £.8 3s. 8d."——MANNING'S *Surrey*.

An indenture was executed between Henry VII. the

Mayor and commonalty of London, the Abbot and Convent of St. Peter, Westminster, and the Abbot and Convent of St. Saviour, Bermondsey, for holding an anniversary in the Abbey Church of Bermondsey, on the 6th of February, to pray for the prosperity of the king and his family, and to pray for the souls of the Earl and Countess of Richmond, the King's parents. The deed contains directions as to the manner in which this anniversary is to be solemnized. " The Abbot and Convent " of St. Saviour, Bermondsey, shall provide at every " such anniversary an herse, to be sett in the myddes of " the high chancell of the same monasterie, before the " high Aulter cov'd and appareled w^t the best and most " honorable stuff in the same monasterie convenyent for " the same. And also four tap's of wax, ev'y of them " weighing VIII. lb., to be sett aboute the same herse, " that is to say on either side thereof o'on taper, and at " either end of the same herse another taper. And all " the same four tap's to be light, and burning continually " during all the tyme of ev'y such placebo, dirige, w^t nyne " lessons, laudes, and masse of reg'ni, w^t the prayers and " obs'vances above rehersed. And ymmediately eeny of " the same high masses singin and fynïshed, the abbot " of the said monasterie of Seynt Sau'yor, of Bermondsey, " if he be p'sent, and the Convet of the same," &c. The decree goes on to direct that in the absence of the abbot the prior of the said Convent shall go with his monks to the same hearse, in a most solemn and devout manner, and shall sing *Libera me de morte eternâ*. At the disso-

lution of monasteries, that of Bermondsey was valued at
£.474 14s. 4d.

The water-side division of Bermondsey, or that part
of the parish situate east of St. Saviour's Dock, and
adjoining the parish of Rotherhithe, is intersected by
several streams or water-courses. Upon the south bank
of one of these, between Mill Street and George Row,
stand a number of very ancient houses, called London
Street ; of this locality, as connected with Jacob's Island,
we shall speak hereafter.

In the year 1804 there were still in being many
fragments of the venerable foundation of Bermondsey
Abbey, probably more than of almost any religious
edifice in or near London, owing, it is supposed, to its
remote situation, which did not encourage the improvements generally so fatal to old buildings. The principal
entrance, called the Gate House, was then nearly entire ;
it stood direct north and faced Bermondsey Church. An
old stone wall ran eastward the whole extent of the
churchyard. On the other side of this wall was a row
of very old houses, whose stone-framed windows and
style of building were witnesses to their antiquity. The
great Gate House and nearly all the ancient buildings,
with the exception of two or three dwelling houses, have,
since 1805, been destroyed, and a modern street, called
Abbey Street, has been erected on their site. A small
portion of the Abbey walls yet remains on the south side,
and a fragment of the same wall on the north side of Long
Walk ; the latter being a part of that which surrounded the

conventual churchyard. There is reason to think that the monastic buildings were separated from the Grange, which extended to the water side, by a long brick wall. This Grange, or pasture, is the site of the abominations we have undertaken to describe. The writer in *The Morning Chronicle* states that, in the reign of Henry II., the foul stagnant ditch, which now makes an island of this pestilential spot, was a running stream, supplied with the waters which poured down from the hills about Sydenham and Nunhead, and was used for the working of the mills which then stood on its banks. These had been granted to the monks of St. Mary and St. John to grind their flour, and were dependencies upon the Priory of Bermondsey; and what is now a straw yard skirting the river, was once the city Ranelagh, called Cupid's Gardens; and the trees, now black with mud, were the bowers under which the citizens loved, on the summer evenings, to sit beside the stream drinking their sack and ale. We have no doubt that the statement here made was founded on respectable authority, although we have not been able to find it; the paper to which we allude is so ably written, and with so much feeling for the poor creatures whose cause it pleads, that it should be read by all who feel an interest in the subject, and for this pur- pose has been published in a separate form. We, as in duty bound, visited this district; the stagnant water which insulates this spot has no appearance of ever having been a stream, though doubtless part of it was so; it seems rather to have been an artificial reservoir,

where the water flowed into channels cut to receive it ;
and this idea is strengthened by the circumstances of the
case : there is a paper mill at a little distance from the
spot ; and, on inquiry, we found that the waters of the
Thames were let into these tidal ditches, as they were
called, three times a week ; the form of the ditch is also
quadrangular. To those accustomed to 𝕽𝖔𝖔𝖐𝖊𝖗𝖎𝖊𝖘, the
appearance of the houses is not worse than that which
they generally wear in such localities.   On entering many
of them, as is often the case in old houses, you descend,
and thus are made sensible that the floor is below the
level of the ground ; there is the usual amount of ricketty
furniture, with a ladder on which to mount to the bed-
rooms : but the houses are not inconveniently crowded,
nor could we find that the rooms were tenanted by more
than one family each.   London Street is a curious
assemblage of houses, and retains very much the same
appearance as it did when it furnished a sketch, in 1814,
for Wilkinson's Londiniana Illustrata.   The houses are
evidently old, the first stories slightly overhanging the
ground floor, yet not no much as in many of our old
towns where these projections form penthouses : there is
nothing particularly quaint and interesting about them ;
hovels they were, and hovels will they remain as long as
they exist.   Still, the whole locality is curious because
surrounded on four sides by stagnant water : part of this
channel must be artificial, and it is not easy to learn
when the district became thus insulated ; this quadrangular ditch is crossed by means of bridges made of wood,

and the whole is separated from the Thames by a long row of large warehouses, which are the glory of that land. Paper mills, sufferance wharves, and other commercial enterprises, have their emporiums there; so that you might pass along the district again and again without stumbling on this isolated Rookery.

We do not say there is nothing to startle a stranger in the buildings of this place—there is much; but, unhappily, twelve years of experience in crowded districts of London have shown us many such sights,—Chelsea, Whitechapel, St. Andrew's Holborn, have many such Rookeries. The floors of the houses being below the level of the foot-path must be flooded in wet weather; the rooms are mouldy and ill savoured; dark, small, and confined, they could not be peopled as the alleys of St. Giles's, because their size would not admit of it. There is the usual amount of decaying vegetable matter, the uneven foot-path, the rotten doors, the broken windows patched with rags, ash heaps in front of the houses, dogs, &c. housed there, ragged children, and other features well known to those conversant with such neighbourhoods. But here the parallel ends:—there are peculiar nuisances in this spot which go far to justify the language used by the writer of the articles in *The Morning Chronicle*, and which he describes technically as perhaps a surgeon alone could do. These abominations we proceed to notice; not, of course, that we can go into many details; —the gentleman we have alluded to has done it much better than we could pretend to do,—done it too with a

knowledge of the consequences involved in such neglect,
and done it at a season when such supervision as he
exercised involved the greatest results. He saw it while
cholera was decimating its victims, making wholesale
ravages ; we now see it when frost and cold have purified
the air; when what was a reeking flood of pestilence is
now frozen over ; so that you might walk on it. Some
slight attempts have been made to supply the wants of
the people,—public attention has been called to the
nuisances which here, to the disgrace of our laws, still
pollute this wretched district. The writer we have alluded
to, says,—" The striking peculiarity of Jacob's Island
" consists in the wooden galleries and sleeping rooms at
" the back of the houses, which overhang the dark flood,
" and are built upon piles, so that the place has posi-
" tively the air of a Flemish street flanking a sewer
" instead of a canal; while the little ricketty bridges
" that span the ditches and connect court with court,
" give it the appearance of the Venice of drains."   . .
This is the source of all the disgust with which the visitor
to these dens of wretchedness is inspired. This district,
we have said before, is insulated by a quadrangular *ditch ;*
the very figure of the island tells you that such reservoirs
must be stagnant; and stagnant they are until moved for
a while by the tide, which does not at each rising pour
fresh water into them, but which at intervals alone, twice
or thrice a week, is sparingly introduced, and checked
again when enough is supposed to have been done for the
purposes of those who are concerned in traffic. Mean-

while this circumambient pond is *the common sewer of the neighbourhood, and the only source from which the wretched inhabitants can get the water which they drink —with which they wash—and with which they cook their victuals:* and because habit reconciles men to any anomaly, in the summer, boys are seeing bathing there, though the Thames is not far distant, and offers at least a cleaner bathing-place. Imagination will picture to itself much which we cannot describe, when we point to such a disgraceful condition of being as that entailed upon the denizens of Jacob's Island. We may well blush for the parish which can tolerate such a plague spot,—for our country, whose insulted laws do not at once sweep from the face of the earth such a record of its disgrace. Is it indeed come to pass, that men, women, and children habitually *drink* water whose ingredients decency forbids us to describe?—that with no affected squeamishness we shrink from picturing that on which our eyes have rested, which courts no secrecy, and which is naked and open to all who would inspect it? not carefully fenced off, lest the indignant spirit of Englishmen should doom it to destruction; not carefully guarded, lest perchance some wandering Christian should denounce it as the future city of God's wrath—the Babylon of his country? Is it indeed come to pass, that heavy taxes are wrung from hard-pressed industry, and the poor man divides his loaf with the tax gatherer, and yet no shield is thrown between him and horrors like these? that fierce cabals agitate rival vestrymen, and some patriotic agitator, plethoric

and bloated with good wishes for his country, wields his
thunder, and yet no one is heard to decry these scenes,
till at length a stranger comes and speaks, and men
awake as from a dream, and go and see this new exhibition, and a few guineas drop in for the fund raised to
relieve the poor sufferers, and then perhaps the wound
will be scarred over, till when ?—till it festers in some
outbreak which shakes the nation.

Yet, gentle reader, we shall be told we are romancing.
We say, Go and see. " We then," says the author of the
pamphlet, "journeyed down London Street (that London
" Street we have spoken of before, the best specimen
" of Rookeries, two hundred years old, and upwards).
" In No. 1 of this street the cholera first appeared
" seventeen years ago, and spread up it with fearful
" virulence; but this year it appeared at the opposite
" end, and ran down it with like severity. As we passed
" along the reeking banks of the sewer, the sun shone
" upon a narrow slip of water. In the bright light it
" appeared the colour of strong green tea, and positively
" looked as solid as black marble in the shadow; indeed,
" it was more like watery mud than muddy water: and
" yet *we were assured this was the only water the*
" *wretched inhabitants had to drink.* . . . . . .
" As we stood, we saw a little child, from one of the
" galleries opposite, lower a tin can with a rope, to fill
" a large bucket that stood beside her. In each of the
" balconies that hang over the stream the self-same tub
" was to be seen, in which the inhabitants put the mucky

" liquid to stand, so that they may, after it has rested
" for a day or two, skim the fluid. We asked if the
" inhabitants did really drink the water ? The answer
" was, They were obliged to drink it, without they
" could beg a pailful or thieve a pailful of purer water.
" 'But have you spoken to your landlord about having
" it laid on for you ?' 'Yes, sir, and he says he'll do
" it, and he'll do it, but we know him better than to
" believe him.' 'Why, sir,' cried another woman who
" had shot out from an adjoining room, 'he won't even
" give us a little whitewash.' We had scarce left the
" house when a bill caught our eye, announcing that
" this valuable estate was to be sold. The inmates had
" begged for pure water to be laid on, and the rain to be
" shut out, and the answer for eighteen years had been,
" —that the lease was just out."

What a home for the future mothers of our working
classes ! You may talk of the oppression which preceded
the outbreak of the first French Revolution. Was it
greater than this ? Men, compelled by their occupation
to live within a given circle,—thrust down, oft by poverty, the victims of commercial changes and the alter-
nations to which traffic is subject,—doomed to drag
out their lives amidst scenes like these, as if the close
room and the mixture of sexes were not enough; as if
precarious wages and dear food did not bring their trials,
but that these very Rookeries should be blacker still,
through the infamous neglect of the landlord on the one
hand, and the grasping avarice of the trader on the other.

What purpose does this tidal ditch serve ? Between it
and the river a paper mill is at work ; yet it can scarce
contribute to the power which such a piece of machinery
requires. It would rather seem that the water of the
Thames must do this duty, and that, after having answered such an end, it flowed into this reservoir at stated
times : staves, also, we are told, are laid to season there,
as if no place could be found for this but the source
whence water is supplied for the necessities of human
life. What a place, we say again, for the future mothers
of the working classes—their nature hardened by a long
course of oppression ! For what oppression worse than
this,—to be pinioned down, as it were, to the lowest
conditions under which life can be sustained, their feelings outraged again and again, till every trace of delicacy
is worn out ; and yet a mother's teaching is one, if
not the very first of God's earthly blessings. Our future
working classes to derive their first impressions of the
opening world—their first lessons in divine and human
knowledge, from mothers thus debased ! To live amidst
such miasmata till they connect such poison wells with the
state of being for which they were designed ; or if they
think at all, to be led by the very contrasts of the spacious
warehouses around them to hate the country which gave
them birth, and to trample on the laws under which such
things still exist. Who lives on such gains ? For whom
is the spot which God created made a Devil's world ?
Does Government pay the expenses of the country thus ?
Are hospitals supported thus ? Do we here behold, in

embryo, the funds which strengthen the hands of the schoolmaster ? And thus the specious, oft-refuted sophism, lends its colour to such abuse,—that the end justifies the means. Not even this is the shield and defence of Jacob's Island. From the sufferings of the poor, small capitalists reap a reprieve from honest toil, and build up the income which feeds their indolence, their debauchery, or their avarice. And verily Nature herself hath entered her visible protest against such cruelties, and hath lifted up a voice which speaks to those that will hear.

We are assured by one, who evidently knows the nature of such symptoms, that the brown, earth-like complexion of some, and their sunken eyes, with the dark areolæ around them, tell you that the sulphuretted hydrogen of the atmosphere in which they live has been absorbed into the blood. Scarcely a girl that has not soreness of the eyes ; so that if one of the inhabitants could be taken to a foreign hospital, and there subjected to examination, science would immediately assign the cause of the complaint under which he was suffering— would specify the particular gas or vapour he had been inhaling—and whilst doing so would accurately describe the sort of atmosphere which the patient breathed, though the previous circumstances of the case had never been stated.

Such a description as the one above quoted can only be appreciated by those whose profession leads them often to examine similar cases ; but the most superficial

observer will perceive an unnatural whiteness in the complexion, the scars of scrofula, and the sore eyes of the
children. We are not describing some scene in distant
lands, under a despotic government; but one taken from
a district of what was wont to be called merrie England
—the land of charity, whose plans for the welfare of our
home population are a hundred-fold, and from whose
shores missions are sent year by year to distant colonies.

Now suppose a fire, one of the wasting fires so common to that shore of the Thames, to take place in this
district; and, because the houses are wooden and the
bridges already rotting, it swallowed up this Jacob's
Island in its ravages. We know what a fire is ; how for
a while all aid is impotent, the image of a vengeance
none can stay. Supposing the inhabitants could escape,
a fire would positively be a blessing in which philanthropy
would rejoice, and humanity hug itself. This greatest of
earthly terrors, whose idea suggests desolation, the worst
and fiercest instrument of destruction, with whose name
men connect the immolation of cities, whose wrath consumed half London, entailing on us for the time the
greatest national suffering England ever knew, would be
a gift whose price we could scarce tell, whose healing
influence we could scarce enough appreciate ; and, if the
inhabitants could be removed in time, an earthquake,
which swallowed up this hamlet of the plague, would be
a thing to be remembered with thanksgiving in the
annals of our nation. We read with terror of the earthquake at Lisbon in 1755 ; yet, if we except the loss of

human life, such a visitation here would be a *mercy*. Yet
very, very deep-seated must be the disease for which such
a remedy would be a *cure*—very hard is it to write thus
of any country, especially of one's own. What an
accumulated mass of sin is connected with such doings
and such endurance. How God's laws must have been
put out of sight, done violence to, ere we dare write thus
of any spot in the wide world he has made. With such
ravages as those of fire we connect houseless families—
their household gods laid waste—the memorials with
which men remember their childhood consumed : avarice
groans over property destroyed, and the hordes of capital
wasted : and men stand panic-stricken at the brink of
such ruin, as though the disaster had bereaved them of
the power to think or to do ; and we read of the citizens
repairing slowly, by years of painful toil and at vast
expense, the damages thus incurred, and of the gulph
which yawned during the lives of a whole generation ere
the loss sustained ceased to be felt.

Yet, again, in Jacob's Island such a fire, such wholesale
conflagration, would be a blessing ; it would untie better
than all the lawyers in existence the knots which impede
legislation,—cut through better than even the death of
the owners of these districts the meshes in which such
property is tied up. We should not then wait for leases
to expire, for the capitalist would scarcely value the lease
of charred timber, and crumbling skeletons of what once
were houses ; for gain's sake he would raise, under happier auspices, walls which age alone could acclimatize to

the horrors which now are; and one generation at least be
spared the disgust which at present it endures. Some
opulent speculator might appropriate the ground thus
cleared, and on the foundations of the past rear some
vast superstructure to the genius of Mammon. Better
so than that the poor should pay the penalty of ill-
gotten gains, and suffer, that capitalists should exhibit
to the admiring gaze of their countrymen the pride of
England's wealth. Let us rather, if we yet blush at our
country's shame, repair the injuries which the poor sustain—let us wipe away the blot which all may witness, and write at once the death-warrant of Jacob's
Island.

We struggle for theoretical reforms, and a clever
demagogue shakes the country with his statement of
fancied injuries :—he agitates for privileges which, like
the relics in an Italian convent, are only to be discerned
by the favoured few. If his indignant eloquence must
have vent, let him employ it on wrongs like these.

Yet, let us not be ungrateful ; the caricaturist may
sketch the grotesque amidst the haunts of poverty ; the
antiquarian call up by the aid of their antique decorations
the features of a by-gone age ; the Legislature may banish
to these dens the convicted criminal till his time comes,
without the expense of transportation ; the medical
student may study some strange type of disease amidst the
remaining lazar houses of St. Giles's. Happy age, which
is spared the task of providing for the teeming multitudes
which are yearly added to its population. Happy country,

which denies its well-bred citizens the sight of counte-
nances which might shock their delicacy, and of habits
which might infect the rising scions of a higher caste ;
which girdles vice within a barrier none need pass, and
confines destitution to dens few can investigate,—meanwhile, with a slight change, the words of the poet are
verified in these neglected colonies—

> Ætas parentum pejor avis tulit
> Nos nequiores, move daturos
> Progeniem vitiosiorem.

Chapter VI.

We like to know for what particular offences the justice and the wisdom of England thought proper to consign to dark and comfortless dwellings the working classes for whom religion bids us care, and in whose preservation is preserved a nation's well-being; at what particular era the custom was introduced, whether refractory Barons inflicted confinement in such tenements as a punishment on the commons who supported the sovereign; or whether when cities and boroughs first achieved municipal privileges, they thus tamed the spirit of rude retainers. We cannot thus look into the manners, habits, useful arts, and domestic comforts of an age, without being led to make comparisons between other and our own times;—we cannot trace Rookeries to their source without asking whether the interval was so great of old between the different orders of society; when the gulph widened,—whether the improvement manifest among the wealthier has penetrated to the poorer classes,—whether, enactments in more despotic times achieved reforms which public spirit should now accomplish,—whether with the monopolies granted to towns were associated obligations to their poorer brethren?

Among those districts which bear away the palm of vice, misery, and filth, there is perhaps none more famous than that part of London which lies between the Tower and the Isle of Dogs. There is a particular locality, however, forming part of this Cimmerian region, which may repay our investigation; it may be defined as the district bounded on the South by the Thames, on the West by the Minories, on the North by the Commercial Road, on the East by the basin of the Regent's Canal; this part of the town forms an irregular parallelogram, and is a spot which the sailors much frequent, because it is so near the shipping—it presents, accordingly, many features peculiar to such localities.

Before we describe its present condition, it may be as well to examine the different stages of its growth,—what it was in old times—when and whether it has degenerated from some former palmy state into its present wretchedness.

The district we have described above has, for the last three centuries, been more or less the rendezvous of sailors. If we look at the old map of London, published in Elizabeth's reign, many copies of which are yet extant, the Tower will be the chief object on which the eye, traversing the northern shore of the Thames, will rest. Beyond that fortress the expanse of open country is dotted by a few houses, which are seen here and there—they form, indeed, a short street at the edge of the water for about a mile, but the background is evidently laid out still in fields, with a stray cottage at intervals. The ground on

which Ratcliffe Highway, St. George's-in-the-East, and
Shadwell were built, was then a large and open manor,
spread out in pastures, which at certain seasons were
overflowed, and always therefore abounding in marshes,—
in fact, a sort of Isle of Dogs—for this latter famed spot
bids fair, within a few years, to be covered with warehouses,
steam factories, lead and iron works, and, when drained,
to be the centre of a thriving population. The far-
famed St. Katherine's Docks are erected on the site of a
hospital and convent, dedicated to St. Katherine. This
religious house was founded in 1148 by Matilda, of
Boulogne, the wife of our Stephen. It was not entirely
swept away at the Reformation, but was changed into a
sort of hospital, which still survives in the St. Katherine's
Hospital in the Regent's Park. The remains of this
convent were only removed in 1825, when eight hundred
houses in this quarter were taken down to afford space
for the new docks. Beyond this assemblage of buildings were green pastures, where the citizens practised
the games of quarter-staff, riding at the quintain, bull-
baiting, archery, and other martial sports. Here great
assemblies of them often met : thus, during the rebellion
which was headed by Wat Tyler, we read that Richard II.
rode forth with his councillors and attendants to give
that hardy leader of the commons a meeting ; that this
took place in an open space near Mile End, and certain
concessions were made, which seem to have been recalled
a few days afterwards, when the commotion terminated
by the death of Wat Tyler. Stowe, the antiquary,

writing in 1603, says—" On the East and by the North
" of the Tower lieth East Smithfield, two plots of
" ground so called, without the wall of the city, and
" East from them both, was sometime a monastery
" called New Abbey, founded by King Edward the
" Third, in the year 1359. From the Tower to Aldgate
" ran a long continual street, in place of an abbey of
" nuns of the order of St. Clare, called the Minories,
" founded by Edmund, Earle of Lancaster, in the year
" 1293: many of them died of pestilence in 1515; in
" place of this house of nunnes are builded diverse faire
" and large storehouses for armour and habilements of
" war, with diverse workhouses serving to the same
" purpose. Neare adjoining to this abbey on the South
" side thereof, was sometime a farme belonging to the
" said nunnerie, at which farme I myself in my youth
" have fetched many a halfe pennie-worth of milke, and
" never had less than three ale pints for a halfpennie in
" summer, nor less than one ale pint and a quarte in
" winter, always hote from the kine, as the same was
" milked and strained. One Trolop and one Goodman
" were the farmers there, and had thirty or forty kine
" to the pail. Goodman's son being heyre to his father's
" purchase, let out the ground, 1st, for grazing of horse,
" and then for garden plots, and lived like a gentleman
" thereby. On the other side of that streete, lieth the
" ditch without the walls of the citie, which of old times
" was used to lie open, always from time to time
" cleansed from filth and mud as neede required, of

" great breadth and width, and so deepe that divers
" watering horses, where they thought it shallowest, were
" drowned both horse and man. But now of late times
" the ditch is enclosed, and the banks thereof let out
" for garden plots, carpenters' yardes, bowling allies,
" and diverse houses builded. From this precinct of
" St. Katherine to Wapping in the West, the usuall
" place of execution for hanging of pirates and sea-
" rovers, at the lowe water marke, there to remaine till
" three tides have overflowed them, was never a house
" standing within these forty years ; but since the gal-
" lows being after removed farther off, a *continuall streete,*
" *a filthy straight passage, with alleys of small tene-*
" *ments, or cottages builded, inhabited by saylors, and*
" *victuallers, along by the river of Thames almost to*
" *Radcliffe, a good mile from the Tower.* On the East
" side and by the North of the Tower, lieth East Smith-
" field, Hogs Streete, and Tower Hill ; East from them
" both was the new abbey called Grace, founded by
" Edward the Third, from thence Radcliff by East
" Smithfield, by Nightingall Lane (which runneth)
" South to the Hermitage, a brewhouse so called of an
" hermite sometime being there : beyond this lane to
" the manor of Bramley, called in record of Richard the
" Second, Villa East Smithfield—Villa de Bramley, and
" to the manor of Shadwell, belonging to the Dean of
" Paul's, there hath been of late in place of elme trees,
" many small tenements raised towards Radcliffe. And
" Radcliffe itself hath beene also increased in building

" eastward (in place where I have knowne a large high
" way with fayre elme trees on both sides) that the
" place hath now taken hold of Lime. Now for Tower
" Hill the place is greatly diminished by merchants for
" building of small tenements; from thence towards
" Aldgate was the Minories."

The Rookeries of this neighbourhood, then, are among
the oldest in London. They are *boná fide* 𝕽𝖔𝖔𝖐𝖊𝖗𝖎𝖊𝖘,
built for the habitations of the poorest classes two hundred and fifty years since. Many of the buildings in
this neighbourhood are of wood—for the Great Fire, that
wholesale purifier of these iniquities, did not extend to
the Tower; so that the long narrow streets, with their
branches and intersections of courts and alleys, remain
in a condition little removed from their original form.
The streets are not wider, less tortuous; the alleys are, as
formerly, *culs-de-sac*—the only entrance from the street;
and if the main thoroughfares are uneven, the road
narrow, the houses crumbling with age, with fronts of
every variety, what must the background be? It is
evident, at a glance, that the fire spared this and the
adjacent districts; for the wide thoroughfare of our
Butchers' quarter, Whitechapel, still retain some façades
distinguished by the grotesque carving that remains;
and we know that such external ornaments have not
been in use since the time of Charles II.

This part of London without the walls, then, owes its
origin to the necessities of our growing community of
sailors, and dates its rise from the reign of Elizabeth;

a period very glorious for the English Navy, when Drake, Frobisher, and others, contended with the Spaniard for the dominion of the seas. In those days, the distinction between the naval and the merchant service was unknown, and the victories of Lord Edward Howard and others added much to our commercial enterprise, and increased our commercial marine. It would be worth while to trace the progress of this colony to our own times. It must have increased rapidly, for, in the early part of the last century, the churches of Limehouse, Poplar, Bow, and others, were built; and within the recollection of many, those great emporia of merchandise—the Docks, were formed.

Our business is, rather, to wade through the narrow thoroughfares distinguished by such variety of occupants, and having so many features peculiar to themselves. Go there by day, and every fourth man you meet is a sailor ; you will hear German, French, Spanish, and even modern Greek, spoken by those whose dress at once connects them with our mercantile marine. Some are Negroes, many foreigners,—but the Jersey frock—the souwester, or tarpaulin hat—the pilot coat and pea jacket —the large trousers gathered in tight at the hips—the rolling walk as though the ship was pitching beneath them—the low quartered shoes with large bows, are characteristics of a race, which, whether at home or abroad, are distinguished in a moment from the rest of the population. Public houses abound in these localities : it is difficult to conceive how so many can thrive ;

but they are interspersed with shops also peculiar to such districts,—slop-sellers; from the capitalists, whose ample window is hung round with everything which can catch a sailor's eye, or sound the depths of his pocket, to the small retail tradesman whose stock in trade has exhausted his funds, and who depends almost for bread upon his daily earnings. Ship joiners—ship carpenters— mathematical instrument makers, with their sign-posts of gilded captains peering through telescopes,—provision shops—rope makers—vendors of ship biscuits, even ship booksellers,—ironmongers—dealers in marine stores, are strangely mixed together.

We have said that public houses occur at frequent intervals, and have wondered how they are supported? when night comes, our wonder ceases. These centres of attraction are fitted up with everything which can draw sailors together; there is an ample space upon which the door opens called the bar, in form perhaps square or semicircular, where various beverages are served out as they are called for, and where a motley group of men and women are lounging crowded together, most of the men in the dress of sailors. Behind the bar are large, lofty, well-lit dancing rooms,—the walls of which are decorated with nautical scenes very fairly painted : in one compartment is a shipwreck; in another, a vessel on her beam ends; in another, a vessel in full sail— perhaps a man of war; in another, men are reefing top-sails; in another, there are all the incidents of a stiff breeze; in another, a ship is labouring in a heavy sea with

all the indications of a gale of wind; in another, Greenwich Hospital, or Portsmouth Harbour, Southsea
Common, &c.   As soon as the evening sets in, the gas
is lit, two or three paid musicians take their post at the
top of the room, the floor is cleared, and dancing com-
mences, many of the dancers in fancy dresses, especially
the females; the men too are fantastically arrayed, some
in Indian dresses, some as soldiers, but the mass preserve
their usual costume : spirits are handed round pretty
freely, and in the rear of the dancers are benches and
tables like the boxes in a coffee room.   In some of the
houses professional singers are hired for the entertainment of the company; they sing in character, and a
temporary stage is erected at the end of the room, with
appropriate scenery, which forms a background to the
singer, and gives effect, by its colouring and correspondence, to the subject of the song.

Thus, in one house was sung Russell's well-known song
of the Maniac; the scene was a dungeon, and the singer
had chains on his arms. In another of these dancing rooms
you had Eton College by moonlight ; prospects familiar
to tourists were represented in another.   Several houses
are frequented almost entirely by sailors; mountebanks
are exhibiting their gymnastic feats on the floor, twisting
their bodies into the strangest shapes, or rising from the
ground with heavy weights upon their shoulders.   In
the neighbourhood were several houses of a worse
description; some frequented by the petty pilferers who
abound in London, men, who would steal an eye glass or

a pocket handkerchief; the thimble rig, the card playing, or, as they are called, cardsharping fraternity, and men who sell fictitious sovereigns. The bar was filled with the motley group of men and women; vendors of pickled sprats, periwinkles, shellfish, &c. being scattered amongst the crowd, so that they might wet the appetite of the drinkers by the salt fish which they sold. In the dancing room many of the frequenters of the house were joining, with spirit and skill, in the dance, their partners evidently women of the town. In a third class of houses were professional thieves, men whose living depended upon thefts; they were evidently preying upon the drunken sailors whose ill luck had led them to places with whose abominations they were little acquainted. Women of the town were in league with these men; we were informed that they acted as so many decoys, and when the conversation between the sailor and the prostitute had been carried on to a certain point, the man, with whom she was in league, would come up and abuse the sailor for speaking to his wife; and, after a great deal of acting, the sailor would give a sum of money to be quit of a disagreeable charge. Some there are again who, when they have brought their depredations for the day to a close, resort to the public house, as to a club, where they can meet their confederates; so that each section has its rendezvous, which is, for the most part, frequented by the members only. Even among thieves, division of labour, as political economists call it, is recognised; and a proficient in the higher branches of the art of thieving would think himself degraded by speaking to one who would steal pocket handkerchiefs; and, as there is an aristocracy even among thieves, so they have their separate places of assemblage.

Sailors are proverbially ignorant of the world; they live for years together at sea; and having few opportunities of getting on shore, they never go far inland : whilst they are at sea, their wages accumulate, and they come home with full pockets, more imprudent than children. These houses owe much of their support to sailors, who, from their inexperience, are dupes of the first designing wretches they meet; but there are always a number of dens in the neighbourhood, where the worst evils are rife to which they are exposed. Among the foremost may be enumerated crimps' houses : these are places where the seafaring men lodge when on shore, where they are fleeced and preyed upon by designing knaves; where, when they come home intoxicated, they are robbed of large sums of money. We must devote a separate space to the portrait of the crimp, where he may be sketched as he deserves; at present it is enough to say that in all districts where sailors abound, there are several of these harpies and their lodging-houses—and that of these places there are the successive gradations, from decent looking houses to the lowest dens of infamy where,—if stories told, be true,—even a man's life is not safe, and where it is said, in days of burking, many a poor fellow was made away with. One of these houses was inspected, which seemed a decent specimen of the class;

the landlord was a foreigner, and it was a rendezvous
for French, Italians, Germans, Spaniards, Portuguese,
and modern Greeks. On the ground-floor, there was a
small common room, garnished with prints on nautical
subjects; a very fine macaw (for sailors love parrots like
children) was flapping his wings at one end: this room
was the place where the sailors took their meals; it opened
into an inner chamber which seemed a kitchen, there
were several men here sitting or lounging about, some
drinking; the landlord and his wife were attending on
them, and they were conversing in various languages.
The landlord, though a foreigner, spoke English very
fairly, and also French. On the first floor were three
rooms appropriated as dormitories in which were several
sailors asleep; the rooms were fitted up, like the cabins of
steamers, with tiers; so that there were an upper and
lower range of beds or rather berths, and thus a place
was found for double the number of sleepers which it
would have held if the ·floor alone had been occupied.
On the night in question it was not inconveniently
crowded; though it is scarcely fair to judge by the appearance of the place at an early hour of the night, for
sailors are not very early people, and doubtless, at a later
hour, the rooms would have been more filled :—the payment for the accommodation thus afforded, was 12s. a
week for each lodger; this included bed and board but
not spirits, which were paid for in addition. On the
surface there was little except the dormitory to call forth
remark.

The bare recollection of the use to which some of these rendezvous (doubtless of a lower class than that referred to) had been converted, is enough to make one shudder.

Not far from this place was a house occupied solely by thieves: you entered, through a confined ill-paved alley, a long low house in the side of which was a door opening upon a narrow kitchen about twenty feet in length; the floor was uneven, the walls, long guiltless of whitewash, were stained with smoke; at one end a large fire-place, round which were gathered five or six thieves cooking their evening meal, or lounging on benches. It is often said, that villainy is stamped upon the countenance; if so, the men before us were favourable specimens, for certainly they were not peculiarly ill-favoured; perhaps there was something of the low narrow forehead about some of them, which phrenologists are fond of assuming to be types of the class; but this was far from being universal. Their manner was courteous and civil; they made way, that we should have the full benefit of the fire, and entered readily and with great good humour into conversation. One of their number amused us much by playing off a series of tricks with a cup and ball, in which he evinced marvellous ingenuity. At the upper end of this room was a door, which opened into a small apartment where was the master of the house as it were on guard; he went to bed about two o'clock in the morning, and at that hour he was relieved by an assistant who took his place. A narrow ricketty staircase led

from the larger room to a first floor, in which were twelve
beds in the same apartment occupied by twelve thieves;
the linen was not dirty, and the bedsteads of iron, like
those used in a hospital, and, except that the walls were
more bare and bore the marks of age, the place was very
like a sick ward minus the usual accompaniment of nurses,
phials, lint and ointment. Over this again, on the second
floor, was a similar room, in which fifteen men were
sleeping; the charge was 2d. per head, per night; the
doors were closed at two in the morning, and regular
laws were established for the government of the body
corporate, which seemed to be punctually and precisely
observed—so that there is not only honour, as the proverb
tells us, but law among thieves. A few streets further
on, was a wretched alley branching off from the main
thoroughfare—to which you proceeded by a tortuous
passage; the pavement was broken and uneven, dotted
here and there with pools or puddles of stagnant water,
which seemed to have accumulated and to have been of
long-standing. The houses inclined considerably over the
pavement with their ragged crumbling fronts—the first
story particularly seemed to overhang the ground-floor,
as though it had been originally built so; the roofs with
their broken tiles, the plaster with which some of the
houses were covered peeling off, and the crazy doors by
which you entered speaking of years of neglect. You
entered by stooping down under a low doorway, and on
the right was a small room ten feet by twelve, in which
fifteen men, women and children, slept two or three in a
bed; the men were entirely naked, covered only by bed-

clothes. In a sort of coal-bin, which, because of the
stairs, was in shape triangular, were three more; and
when, as upon this occasion, the door was shut, there was
no opening for the admission of air. In summer, when
that part of the town is full, the rooms are even more
densely populated than at present; policemen tell you,
that sometimes as many as thirty people sleep in one
room. The upper floor was not so full, here also were
the same fetid smell and want of ventilation,—the same
scanty clothing, the same racking cough, the same crying
of children, mixture of sexes, ages and callings, which
are the common features of these 𝕽𝖔𝖔𝖐𝖊𝖗𝖎𝖊𝖘! In the
heat of summer, if policemen may be believed, and they
are not given to exaggerate, the inhabitants of these
houses sleep perfectly naked, the heat enabling them to
dispense with clothing; they think their linen will be
cleaner if they put it aside for the night.

The house alluded to was only one of a series; the
occupants were not thieves but chance comers, tramps,
sellers of different street commodities; many of them,
from their brogue, evidently Irish. On entering another,
the same scene was repeated, excepting that it was not so
thickly peopled as its neighbour; we crossed the road,
and came upon another back street in which were several
lodging houses. In the first of these, in the rooms we
entered, were seven or eight people sleeping, though
there was accommodation for many more; here the
cabin fashion, with its row above row of beds, or rather
berths, prevailed, so that the assertion might have been
easily corroborated; thirty persons might have been here

located in a single apartment. Sheets seemed scarce things; in many of the houses there were no beds, but only mattresses strewed on the floor, and a few blankets thrown over the sleepers. In winter, the occupants may suffer from damp, as many of the floors are beneath the surface of the ground, and the water finds entrance under the doors and through the roof: they can scarcely be cold, for they are packed too close together; and you may well believe the writer in the *Morning Chronicle*, who, a short time since, asserted that 20 cubic feet of air were only allowed in such dens for the support of animal life, though 150 were the quantity required for health. In these lodgings $1\frac{1}{2}d$. per night is the usual charge.

The lodging houses we have described are only samples of the large class which may be found in this neighbourhood. In all places where sailors resort they seem to create such dens; not that they are favourable, as a body, to dirt and want of ventilation; but that they are the prey of a vast number of designing persons, male and female, of the lowest description, who gather round them the moment they are discharged, and who live by preying upon them. Released from the severe discipline and the confinement of a ship, they experience an exuberance of joy; they are like boys let loose from school, their habits lead them to drink, and when intoxicated they are the more easily ensnared. Thus Rotherhithe, Shadwell, Deptford, Woolwich, and Portsmouth, abound with dark courts and wretched alleys, where they who live by the imprudence of sailors are accustomed to reside.

Chapter VII.

We have before stated that the most aristocratic streets have a background of wretchedness,—this at first sight seems incredible. We are too apt to suppose that St. Giles's is the only very poor quarter in London. Artisans, gentlemen's servants, policemen, and others, must live somewhere, and we fancy that they form respectable colonies on the outskirts of the larger squares and thoroughfares. Mews, and other places of a similar description, take off a goodly proportion of domestic servants; still the better class of artisans and policemen are much straitened because of the dearness of lodgings ; the places where they live are destitute of most of the comforts and some of the necessary conveniences of life. Still we do not term their dwellings Rookeries, yet we maintain that few parishes are without a certain number of tenements which it would be difficult to describe by any other name. As a sample of this, let us survey part of the Berwick Street district of St. James, Westminster.

In the time of Charles I. the whole of this district was, as yet, not built upon ; here and there was a solitary house surrounded with fields ; the great thoroughfare, Piccadilly, was just coming into notice, for Lord Clarendon, in the History of the Rebellion, speaks of Mr. Hyde going to a house, called Piccadilly, which was a fair house for entertainment and gaming, with handsome gravel walks with shade, and where was an upper and lower bowling green, whither many of the nobility and gentry, of the best quality, resorted for exercise and recreation. In Knight's London reference is made to a petition, from Colonel Thomas Panton, bearing date 1671, which was read at the board of Privy Council, setting forth that the petitioner having been at great charge in purchasing a parcel of ground lying at Pickadilly, part of it being the two bowling greens fronting the Haymarket, the other part lying on the north of the Tennis Court, on which several old houses were standing; and praying for leave to build upon this ground, notwithstanding the royal proclamation recently issued against building on new foundations within a certain distance of London. In consequence of Sir Christopher Wren's favourable report, Colonel Panton obtained leave to build certain houses in Windmill Street, on the east corner towards the Haymarket, about one hundred feet in front, on the east side of Windmill Street, in the two bowling greens between the Haymarket and Leicester Fields.

In the year 1662, orders were issued for the paving of the way from St. James's north, which was a quagmire, and also of the Haymarket about Piqudillo.

The Piccadilly line of road is said to have formed, at its east end, the line of demarcation between the courtly

mansions erecting in St. James's Fields, and the small
and mean habitations which, in Wren's words, " will
" prove only a receptacle for the poorer sort, and the
" offensive trades to the annoyance of the better inhabi-
" tants ; the damage of the parishes already too much
" burdened with poor, the choking the air of his
" Majesty's palace and park, and the houses of the
" nobility ; the infecting of the waters,—these habita-
" tions so complained of being continued and erected in
" Dogs Fields, Windmill Fields, and the Fields adjoin-
" ing Soho." This then is the first mention we have of
the district now assigned to St. Luke's, Berwick Street.
The property, in this neighbourhood, belonged of old to
Lord Craven. The famous Pest House was erected here
for the reception of those stricken with the plague, where
was what was called a lazaretto, consisting of thirty-six
small houses ; and near it, at the lower end of Marshall
Street, was a common cemetery where some thousand persons were buried during that dreadful pestilence. Out of
Wardour Street, which is the eastern boundary of the
district in question, we are told by Strype, in 1720,
" goeth Peter Street, which crosseth Berwick Street,
" falleth into waste and unbuilt ground ; a street not
" over well inhabited. Here is a small court, but the
" right name is not given. Further northward is Edward
" Street, which also crosseth Berwick Street, and falleth
" into waste and unbuilt ground ; nor is this street over
" well inhabited." Berwick Street is represented as
being on the west of Wardour Street, beginning at Peter

Street, and running northward as far as Tyburn Road ;
it is described as a pretty handsome straight street, with
new well built houses, much inhabited by the French,
where they have a Church ; and near it a Court with a
freestone pavement, called Kemp's Court. About the
middle of the street was a place designed for a haymarket, and a great part of the low ground raised with
some of the houses built piazza-wise. Westward of this
street, says the Annalist, " is a large tract of waste
" ground reaching to the wall of the Pest House, built
" by the Earl of Craven, which runneth from the back
" side of Golden Square to a piece of close or meadow
" ground which reacheth to Tyburn Road."

The district we would now describe was evidently
covered with small buildings towards the beginning of
the last century, though a large space of open ground
was still left unoccupied to the north. A square piece
of stone is let into one of the houses in New Street, on
which is inscribed the date 1704. Thirty years before
this Sir Christopher Wren could complain of the small
streets which were building, and the poverty of their
inhabitants ; and Fielding, in 1740, describes the mob,
whom he calls the fourth estate of the realm, as en-
croaching upon people of fashion, and driving them
from their seats in Leicester, Soho, and Golden Squares,
to Cavendish Square and the streets in its vicinity. The
site of The Rookery we are about to describe was then
in its infancy, covered with mean streets and houses, and
appears, even a hundred years since, to have formed part
of a district which had rapidly degenerated.

The particular spot to which attention is invited is
bounded on the north by Cock Court, so called because
of a low public house whose sign is the Cock; on the
west by New Street, on the south by Husband Street,
on the east by Hopkins Street. There is a mouldy,
smoky, dilapidated air about the whole; some of the
houses have evidently sunk much; others are closed up
with shutters, the windows, in many cases, broken or
mended with paper; some houses marine store shops,
others inhabited by sweeps and costermongers; the usual
number of idlers lounging about, so that should you stop
a minute to make inquiries, a crowd of suspicious looking
characters would assemble, many youths among them
whose age averages from fifteen to twenty; the passages
between opposite houses narrow, the pavement covered
with decayed vegetable matter; Irish, the vernacular
language of the inhabitants. This mass of buildings, so
bounded as we have described, forms a quadrangle; it
will be asked, is the interior or court of this quadrangle
open? To this we answer, that the buildings which are
exposed to view form only the outer lair of the colony
which is established within these precincts. In the centre
of this square, yet lodged in and confined by buildings, is
a large cow-house, in which thirty cows are said to have
been confined at one time, though, on the occasion of
our visit, there were not much more than half that
number: a space in this large cow-house was allotted
to pigs, of which there was a goodly number. When you
look at the area of these buildings, you will say that so
many cows could not be collected together in a space so

confined; strange as it may seem, there are two stories
in this building, the upper of which, as well as the
ground floor, is filled with cows, and they are hoisted up
in a sort of box very much like those used for the con-
veyance of horses by railroads. The stench arising from
this packing of unwieldy animals in so small a space,
and the near neighbourhood of the pigs, may be conceived. The houses in Husband Street flanked this
cow-house, and their back windows looked out upon it.
Between these dwellings of the poor and the place we
have described were a series of excessively small, narrow,
uneven yards not to appearance five feet in breadth, and
this was the only open space allotted them. In summer,
the smell from the cow-house must have been carried
into every open window in the tenements described: if
Husband Street on the south was thus affected, it will be
asked how the dwellers on the north in Cock Court
fared, small as the intervening space between the cow-
house and this northern boundary is? Even this is
rendered smaller by an intervening screen of wooden
houses, the access to the habitable parts of which is by
a covered staircase: the lower floor of this building is
a sort of cellar in which were some rabbits belonging
to the tenants. In one of the houses, the upper part was
occupied by families: a proportion, though small, of
these tenements is let out in lodgings; in a few instances
trampers and nightly lodgers are harboured, and there
is the usual crowding together of inmates common to
Rookeries: by day it is not easy to calculate the number

of persons who sleep there. The houses are not so
crowded as those in Church Lane or Saffron Hill,
and there is not the same amount of squalid misery. It
is said that instances are upon record of three families
living together in the same room : in one room we saw
three or four beds, but were told that they were all
tenanted by members of the same family. The rooms
are miserably small; mere closets, very dilapidated, quite
unfit for human habitation, scarcely safe, below the level
of the ground, with hardly any ventilation; until lately
miserably, if at all, drained, their back parts very close in
consequence of the cow-house we have described; so
that the atmosphere is rendered still more fetid by
the rank odour continually emitted from the animals
confined. Some of the houses were occupied by chimney-
sweepers, several by day labourers—some by men who get
their living by selling baked potatoes. There are three costermongers living in one of these streets, from whom the
potatoes are procured. Under the houses are large cellars,
which are filled with these vegetables, and from which
the tin cans of the vendors are replenished. There are
also several rag shops in this part of the parish, the
cellars being filled to overflowing with rags—which, at
certain seasons, are carted away and sent to the paper
makers. You are struck with the curious appearance of
some of the lower windows in these houses,—old bonnets,
veils, articles of dress, faded indeed, shorn of much of
their original splendour, are exposed as if to tempt those
who pass by; these are unlicensed pawn shops, where

women deposit their wearing apparel, and with the money thus obtained gratify their passion for drinking at the next public house. Sometimes they redeem the goods, yet too often never return to claim them; after a time the goods are sold, though, whether a year elapses, as in the case of pawnbrokers, before the sale takes place, we could not learn. In the streets opening upon the quadrangle to which we have limited our inquiries, are two or three houses where thieves are harboured. Inquests are common in this locality—many persons die by violence. Not long since, three women of the town were residing here, two of them sisters; the youngest died of concussion of the brain arising from a blow she had received from one of her companions in a scuffle. There are several low lodging-houses in Husband Street, where the charge is 3*d*. a night, or 1*s*. 6*d*. a week, Sunday Evening being considered, according to the law adage, a *dies non*, and therefore the lodgers pay only for six nights. The rooms are too small to admit of many sleeping together at the same time, accordingly, eight persons in a room seems as far as we could learn to be the maximum.

It is gratifying to think that an attempt is being made, with what success it remains to be seen, to buy up this block of houses (to speak technically), and on their site to erect model lodging-houses: a Society established three years since in the parish have built some lodging-houses on the opposite side of New Street, which have been tenanted for some months; and, for the special object of erecting the building contemplated, the Society of which

Lord Ingestre is president, has agreed to co-operate with the Parochial Society, and endeavour to accomplish between them the good work, not doubting that funds will be provided for a purpose so desirable*.

* Since this was written, the Committee of the Society have accepted the offer made them, and there is every prospect of the progress of the good work, if funds can be procured for the outlay.

Chapter VIII.

Among the worst districts in London, is the locality near Westminster Abbey, bounded on the north by Victoria Street, (which has displaced a host of obscure courts and alleys,) on the east by Dean's Yard, on the south by Peter Street, on the west by Stretton Grounds. Till the time of James I., this district was laid out in open fields, dotted at rare intervals with a few houses. The old picture of Westminster, in the reign of Henry VIII., represents the Abbey without the incongruous towers added in the last century by Wren. Westminster Hall, the Church of St. Peter, an old conduit, and St. James's Palace, are almost the only objects on which the eye rests. After this era, London extended from Charing Cross towards the Abbey, and a few scattered houses were, at intervals, erected. Stowe, who writes about the beginning of the seventeenth century, thus describes the district to which our inquiries are directed:—" And nowe I will " speak of the Gatehouse, and of Totehill Street, stretch-" ing from the west part of the close. The Gatehouse is " so called of two gates—the one out of the Colledge " Court, towards the north, on the east side whereof was " the Bishop of London's prison for Clarkes convict;

" and the other gate adjoining to the first, on the south
" side, King Henry VII. founded an almeshouse for
" thirteen poor men, one of them to be a priest aged
" forty-five years, a good grammarian, the other twelve
" to be aged fifty years, &c. Neare unto this house
" westward was an old chappel of Queen Anne, over
" against the which the Lady Margaret, mother to
" King Henry VII., erected an almeshouse for poore
" women, which is now turned into lodgings for the
" singing-men of the Colledge. The place wherein this
" chappel and almeshouse standeth, was called the
" Eleemosynary or Almonry, now corruptly the Ambry,
" for that the almes of the Abbey were there distributed
" to the poore; and therein Islip, Abbot of Westminster,
" erected the first presse of booke printing that ever was
" in England, about the yeare of Christ, 1471. William
" Caxton, citizen of London, mercer, brought it into
" England, and was the first that practised it in the
" sayde Abbey, after which time the like was practised
" in the Abbeys of St. Augustine at Canterbury,
" St. Albans, and other monasteries. From the West
" Gate runneth along Totehill Street, wherein is a
" house of Lord Gray of Wilton; and on the other side,
" at the entry into Totehill Fielde, Stourton House,
" which Gyles, the last Lord Dacre of the South, pur-
" chased and builde new, whose lady and wife, Anne,
" sister to the Lord Buckhurst, left money to her
" executors to builde an hospital for twentie poor women,
" and so many children to be brought up under them,

" which hospital her executors have begun in the field
" adjoining."

During the struggles of the Great Rebellion, Sir
Robert Pye, a courtier of the period of Charles I., had a
fine house and garden near this spot, on the site of
which, a few years afterwards, were erected Pye Street,
Duck Lane, Stretton Grounds, and the adjacent alleys.
Orchard Street, too, owes its origin to the same period,
and is supposed to have been built upon the orchard
belonging to this Baronet. Some say it was the site of
the orchard of the Monastery. Of this now degraded
locality, Strype, writing in 1720, says,—" Stretton
" Grounds is a good, handsome, long, well-built, and
" inhabited street which runneth up to Tothill Fields,
" almost against the new workhouse for employing Poor
" People; and hath on the West a passage into the
" New Artillery Ground, a pretty large enclosure, made
" use of by those that delight in military exercises.
" Pye Street lieth between Duck Lane and Great St.
" Anne's Lane, better built than inhabited. New Pye
" Street is a passage from Old Pye Street into Orchard
" Street, a pretty, handsome, new built place. Orchard
" Street very long, with good buildings, which are well
" inhabited. On the North side is a place called the
" New Way, which hath houses on the West side, the
" East being Sir Robert Pye's garden wall."

In Walcott's " Westminster," recently published, it is
said,—" In the New Way, the well-known Sir Robert
" Pye, the husband of Mary Hampden, the patriot's

" daughter, resided where the present workhouse
" stands."

On the 27th of January, 1741, Lord Tyrconnel, in
moving for leave to bring in a bill for the better paving
and cleansing the streets within the city of Westminster,
said,—" It is impossible, Sir, to come to this assembly,
" or to return from it, without observations on the
" present condition of the streets in Westminster,—
" observations forced on every man, however inattentive,
" or however engrossed by reflections of a different
" kind. The filth, Sir, of some parts of the town, and
" the inequalities and ruggedness of others, cannot but,
" in the eyes of foreigners, disgrace our nation, and
" incline them to imagine us not only a people without
" delicacy, but without government—a herd of bar-
" barians—a colony of Hottentots." Such was the state
of the roads, we are told that, when the King's state
coach passed along at the opening of Parliament, the
ruts were so large, that faggots were thrown in to fill
them up.

It would seem that the materials for a Rookery were
accumulating more than 130 years since ;—that, at a later
period, Lord Tyrconnel was obliged to make the complaint detailed above ;—that, from too common neglect,
whilst improvements were made between the Abbey and
the Bridge, the narrow courts and alleys which had
grown up on the western side, were suffered to degenerate,
till, in process of time, they became one of the worst
resorts of thieves and prostitutes in the Metropolis.

A colleague of the author's, the Rev. Mackenzie Walcott, has kindly placed the following memoranda at his disposal. Mr. Walcott has shown great research in his " History of Westminster," and this contribution to the present work must prove interesting.

" A considerable portion of the ' City of Westminster' lies under high-water mark: New Tothill Street, $3\frac{1}{2}$ inches; the road by Mr. Elliot's brewery, $11\frac{1}{2}$ inches; and Palmer's Village, $12\frac{1}{2}$ inches. A creek of the Thames entered also at the river-end of the present Manchester Buildings, flowed into the St. James's Fields, and, turning southward, at the line of the modern De la Hay, Princes's, and Dean Streets, and again eastward, by Great College Street, formed the precinct of the Abbey or Thorney Island. At the time of the compilation of the Doomsday Book there was a village of Westminster, with arable land, and pannage in the woods for swine, gardens and cottages of the tenants of the Monastery. So low and unprotected the river banks continued to be even in the reign of the later Stuarts, that King Charles II. remonstrated with his Parliament on the quantity of water which surrounded the palace of Whitehall. The floor of Westminster Hall and the upper part of Millbank Street have been far more recently flooded by the over-flowing of the Thames. In 1791, Privy Gardens, were inundated with a ' slimy river,' and boats plied in Palace Yard. The names of Downing and Fludyer Street, fix the dates of their erection. Until the middle of the seventeenth century, King Street did not boast a brick

house, although the principal thoroughfare to the House
of Parliament; when the royal carriage passed through it
on state occasions, faggots were thrown into the ruts.
The lanes in the vicinity were infested by thieves and
cutpurses: among a list of such proscribed houses in
the reign of Elizabeth, furnished to the Prime Minister,
we find one in the Palace, two in the Sanctuary, one in
Tothill Street, and one close to the Abbey. Palings of
considerable height were erected in Palace Yard, to fence
off the passengers from annoyance by mud thrown up by
the carriage-wheels. ' Dirty Lane,' a miserable narrow
outlet, occupied the site of Abingdon Street. Petty taverns
clustered round the Houses of Parliament till very lately.
Along Millbank, was a row of houses facing the river
only ; a range of willow trees bordered a walk by the side
of the Thames, frequented by the London apprentices
even in the present century.   On the site of Black Dog
Alley, was the Abbot's pleasance ; from it to the Thames
eastward, extended the Hostry-garden of the monastic
Guest-house.   Bowling Street, derives its name, from
the Benedictine's bowling green ; and Orchard Street,
from their fruit garden. Wood Street, in 1720, was a
narrow alley composed of old boarded hovels.   Barton
Street and Cowley Street were built by the great actor,
Booth. A vine-garden, in 1568, it appears occupied the
site of Vine Street.   North Street was begun in 1728,
and St. John's Church in 1721.   Smith Street, about
the same time. Tufton and Marsham, and St. Peter's
Streets, in the early part of the seventeenth century.

Palmer's Village, and the Pye Streets somewhat later.
' Artillery Place,' recalls to our recollection the butts
for archery set up in Tothill Fields, the expenses of
which were constantly defrayed by the Churchwardens of
St. Margaret's. Fairs and duels often occurred in that
area, which space afforded abundant harvest for cattle.
In the time of the plague and the civil wars, it was made
a burial ground : the ' Five Houses ' stand on the site of
the ancient lazaretto. A maze and a bear garden also
found a place in the fields. Vincent Square, the Peniten-
tiary, and Vauxhall Bridge, were erected in the present
century. But the lower parts of the fields were little
better than a mere marshy swamp. Gardeners, famous
for their cultivation of melons, inhabited the ' neat
' houses,' so called, from the ancient manor of ' Neyte.'
Snipes have been shot on these grounds in the present
century. In 1631, the Broadway Chapel was built on waste
ground. The Tyburne was divided into three streams,—
one flowed down the Horseferry Road, and afterwards
became the boundary of St. Margaret's and St John's
parishes ; one into the scholars' pond ; and the third
down College Street, discharging itself by the Abbey
Mill : from the last branch were supplied the brooks and
runnels of Orchard Street and Duck Lane. A few
pretty villas, in the reign of Elizabeth, were built along
the banks of St. Anne's Lane, Pye Street, and Duck
Lane ; very few houses were yet built in Petty France or
York Street ; and extensive gardens were attached to
those in Tothill Street. The miserable Almonry has

only recently disappeared, owing to the construction of
Victoria Street.   That desolate prison, the neighbouring
Gate-house, was demolished in 1776."

" It seems to have been the heritage of Westminster, by
the force of custom, after the institution of the Sanctuary
and the formation of its ' Thieves' Lane,' to become the
shelter and resort of lawless characters, who find a fitting
home in the dirty, narrow, uncleansed streets,—its
miserable, undrained, dilapidated courts and alleys,
reproduced and rebuilt time after time with the determi-
nate purpose of receiving only the degraded and outcast
of the population.   The accumulations of filth in the
courts without an outlet—the absence of water—the
crowding of people—the contamination of vice and
idleness—the filthy stenches—the boarded rooms not
weatherproof—the despair of improvement and better
situation—and the facilities offered for sinking yet lower,
by low and numberless beer-shops and pawnbrokers,
contributed thoroughly to demoralise the population.
In the wretched New Pye Street, at high noon on a
fine day, young thieves might be seen playing at cards,
gambling on the public footpath.   The Middle-man here
has been in the habit of erecting tenements, formed upon
the sites of old gardens or yards, and providing access to
them only through the front door of what was once the
main house ; hence the production and reproduction of
hideous stifling back lanes and courts, worse than the
close garret, or over-crowded attic was before.   Then
these places, too often slightly built of wood coarsely put

together, crazy and destitute of every requisite for the maintenance of decency and cleanliness, are divided out by preference among weekly lodgers. What wonder if there be squalid misery and all the excessive sorrows of poverty, if in vain they struggle against the impurities of situation, and the uncleanliness of an air that breeds a constant malaria, and is the first place in which cholera, pestilence, fever, and every malignant disease appear! Added to these causes of wretchedness is the natural lowness of the ground, which requires the utmost resources of science to obviate its inevitable results; flooding cellars, densely peopled, with loathsome streams accumulating in the gutters and kennel—stagnant refuse waters emitting abominable smells—and noxious vapours increased by heaps of garbage by the road-side;—and we have to reflect, that within the short space of one century, during which we boast, that we have made the most wonderful advances in civilisation and science which the world has ever known,—these monstrous evils have grown up. How long shall they continue? yes, how long? Demolitions of Rookeries will only enhance the present suffering of their late occupants now daily driven into more compact wretchedness, unless there be, at the same time, improvements made in the dwellings which they are about to inhabit! While we admire the royal grandeur of the splendid palace of Westminster, and the newly completed front of Buckingham Palace, which will shortly be connected by a street, to be provided with every accessory of refinement after the most

improved methods of modern science, and be the residence
of wealth and power ; let us cast a thought upon those
who have been rendered homeless by this great design.
The Roman, the Maltese Knight, and the Saracen con-
structed vast aqueducts to supply their cities.   In every
foreign town a sparkling fountain throws up its jet of
abundant waters : our wells in old days were famous for
their clear streams : we want water now for draught,
washing, cleanliness.   Let humanity apply every resource to neutralise the ills that attend an over-crowded
neighbourhood : while it relieves the faintness of hunger
and takes off the rags of poverty, let it take away also
the recklessness of destitution, fostered by those receptacles of want and disease, those lazarettos of spiritual
sickness, and channels of immorality,—the putrid lane
and festering court, swarming with every provocative to
vice, with dismal crowds prowling about to beg and steal,
and destined to premature death, or to fill workhouse and
gaol, sinking down through misery into crime.   Let the
layman have a care for the body of his brother, and speed
on the work of those who have, through rebuke and
difficulty, and sometimes peril, in the name of their
Blessed Master, for years toiled to lighten the darkness
of that ignorance, and have, single-handed, gone forth to
seek and to save the lost."——[*Thus far, our Friend.*]

Turning out of the New Victoria Street, on the second
street on the left hand, you come at once into a densely
populated neighbourhood ; running at right angles to
this street is the famous Pye Street—a long narrow

thoroughfare, intersected by various subordinate alleys, some of them worse than the parent causeway; the road is thickly strewed with decayed vegetables, and there are a number of young men and boys, from fifteen to twenty years of age, lounging about in groups—a great proportion of whom are juvenile thieves. At the west end of the street is a large Ragged School, held in two or three rooms, which were originally obtained for the purpose of a reading room, — these apartments are crowded with the children of the district. Passing eastward, you come to a cross street, which is called Duck Lane, dividing the rest of Pye Street from the upper part in which the school is situated. Duck Lane is portioned into low lodging houses and the resorts of thieves, where chance lodgers are harboured at about 3d. per night: there were the usual open doors—creaking stairs—broken railings—mouldy walls, with the whitewash pealing off—strings across the room with linen hanging to dry—worn-out bedsteads, with a scanty supply of clothing—grotesque, or old fashioned prints—old women cooking vegetables for dinner,—and here and there, in different rooms, a stray wolfish-looking dog. At night alone could you give a guess of the number harboured in a single room; until lately, especially in summer, they were crowded in certain periods of the year: but the Legislature has lately passed an Act, limiting the number of persons who can occupy each room in the house, apportioning a certain number of square feet to each individual. The character of the district may be gathered from the callings exercised by certain of the inhabitants we visited. In one room, the floor of which seemed to be below the level of the house, was a man with a consumptive wife and several childen, who was employed making mats, his children handing him the straws as he platted them together ; his address was good, though the furniture, the decayed and imperfectly mended floor, the scanty fire, and the ragged clothes of wife and children, indicated severe poverty. His history was this :—In early life he lived with his uncle, who was a corn dealer in Berkshire, and had been, it would appear, in a fair way of business ; misfortune came, (whether owing to speculations in the corn trade, or to the fluctuations to which that trade is subject, was not stated,) and the poor man was ruined ; having been bred to no trade, he was obliged to take up this occupation, as that which most readily suggested itself to him as a means of livelihood. The next case which was offered to our notice was of a very different kind :—In a low narrow room were seated, at about ten o'clock in the morning or a little later, an old woman, the mistress of the house, and two young men ; they sat on low stools crouching over a small fire : against the wall was pasted a printed notice, which defined the number of persons who might be lawfully harboured in a room of such dimensions as that in question ; the old woman complained bitterly of the interference with her perquisites. There was a peculiar look about one of these men, which induced us to question him as to his occupation : he had been bred a sailor,—had been at the battle of Navarino, of which he gave us a graphic account. He had been at Sydney, Calcutta, and various foreign parts, but at length had deserted owing to the following circumstance, according to his version of the story :—One day, he and a messmate observed a hamper with twelve bottles of brandy invitingly open upon deck—they could not resist this, and accordingly stole a bottle ; whilst drinking this, they were discovered by one of the mates of the vessel, who reported the circumstance to the captain, and our informant was duly sentenced to three dozen,—this led him to desert. He afterwards made some voyages in the merchant service; and having observed a great deal of jugglery in India, the feats of which he extolled as far superior to any thing of the kind in Europe, he became a necromancer, as he called himself, in which character he exhibits at different places, and thus obtains a livelihood.

In this neighbourhood are located street musicians ; some in the dress of highlanders, with bagpipes; some with other instruments, whom we meet so frequently. There too are the smashers, or coiners, who assume so many different dresses,—in the morning habited as cab men, in the afternoon as countrymen,—to personate a new character in the evening. Many of these men are, upon occasion, pickpockets. At right angles to Pye Street is Anne Street, which again is intersected by a variety of courts, among which is James Court. In this veritable *cul-de-sac* live many low prostitutes, and

poor Irish. In one of the rooms was a poor Irish widow
with some small children ; her history was melancholy,
while, at the same time, it threw light upon some,
among the many, causes of Irish emigration. She and
her husband had lived in Cork during the fearful pestilence of 1847, or the Skibbereen fever, as it may be more
properly called. She had seen her brother-in-law, his
wife, and three children lying dead on the same day ; the
fever attacked her, but not fatally. Soon after this, her
husband had taken a pipe from another man who was
smoking it, and, two days after, an ulcer formed in his
throat which terminated in his death. The lone widow,
upon this, was persuaded to emigrate to England by her
son, who came over for the purpose of accompanying her
in a cheap steamer ; this youth earned his livelihood by
carrying dust, unloading dust-carts, &c. The old woman
spoke in very kind terms of the assistance she received
from a Protestant Clergyman, a Dr. Graves; with all
the warmth of the Irish character which endears them
so much to those who know them, she pronounced a
glowing benediction upon his head—" May God give
him a bed in heaven, and sure, why should he not !"

Running up again parallel to Pye Street, is Orchard
Street ; the fronts of many of the houses in which, as
well as the wood-work within, betoken the opulence of
their former inhabitants, whom tradition represents to
have been persons of rank. In one lodging-house, in
this street, we are informed, on good authority, that there
were sixty double beds ; so that, in one house, a large

one it is true, 120 persons had slept in a single night:
behind it was a spacious yard; and the cellars were rooms
common to inhabitants, in which several men were taking
their meals; in the yard at the back, were some dogs,
and men lounging about. It is said, that the occupants
of this house are not very select: there was a melancholy
contrast between the carvings over the door and the
elaborate front, and those who now tenanted the house;
suggesting to us the change which in a hundred years
hence, may come over some of the most fashionable
localities in London.

We are indebted to the kindness of Mr. Walker, the
City Missionary in this district, for permission to make
the following extract from a valuable pamphlet published
by him :—

" In giving a description of this district it will be
" necessary to look back to what it was twelve years
" ago ; and whether looking at it in its physical or moral
" aspect, it required little penetration to perceive that it
" was a spot long neglected. I have described it on a pre-
" vious occasion as being one of the most wretched and
" vicious districts which blot the map of the metropolis,
" —a busy nursery of vice and crime, and the very focus
" of a kingdom's worst criminality. Neither White-
" chapel nor St. Giles's could vie with it in the scenes
" of depravity it could exhibit. It was not always a safe
" matter for a stranger to pass through it : if he did so,
" he would hardly be induced to pay it a second visit.
" The district contained 190 houses, which appeared

" incrusted with the filth and smoke of generations.
" Wretchedness and ruin appeared on every side. Its
" population amounted to upwards of 700 families, or
" rooms occupied with about 3000 souls. Among these
" were 500 couples living in an unmarried state, besides
" as many homes destitute of the Word of life. Wherever
" you turned, the inhabitants were to be seen, in groups
" of half-dressed, unwashed men and women, loitering
" at doors, windows, and at the end of narrow courts,
" smoking, swearing, and occasionally fighting ; and
" swarms of filthy, naked, and neglected children, who
" seemed well trained to use languages as profane, and
" do deeds as dark as those of their parents.

" The cock-pit in the district, and the penny theatre
" in the neighbourhood, besides a few other buildings
" for purposes too dark to be recorded here, were the
" only training-schools for this class of the population.
" Young and old were alike left to grow up and pass
" away from time into eternity, without one to point
" them to ' the Lamb of God which taketh away the
" ' sin of the world ! '

" It is scarcely necessary to say that this district is
" occupied by a criminal population. How could it be
" otherwise ? The midnight burglar, the pickpocket,
" the coiner, and the passer of counterfeit money, seemed
" to have their head-quarters here. These alone, with
" fallen females, occupied one-half of the district; and
" the remainder was possessed by beggars and hucksters.
" Of lodging-houses for travellers there are twenty-four,

" and of public-houses there were seven. The courts in
" the district were the principal scenes of vice. A de-
" scription of one will suffice as a specimen of the others.
" New Court contained twelve houses, with six rooms
" in each. I have seen and known as many as seventy-
" two persons living in one of these houses; and I
" recollect, in the course of three months, sixty-nine
" young persons being transported, and one executed at
" Newgate, out of No. 2.

" I might go on describing the streets and courts of
" the district; but, after all I should write, it would give
" a faint idea of what I have witnessed. I have seen
" upwards of forty policemen beat out of Old Pye Street,
" by the inhabitants, while attempting to take a thief."

Before quitting this district, we must not omit to
mention an admirable establishment set on foot by the
Earl of Ellesmere, Lord Kinnaird, and others, in Peter
Street, where, in three houses, are 117 beds, the charge
made for each of which is 3d. per night. At the back of
these houses are a series of cottages for families, which,
having been recently erected, are not yet fully inhabited.
In this establishment is a sitting-room for the lodgers—
an excellent kitchen, washing-place, &c., and all the
rooms are well aired and ventilated. The superinten-
dant, who seems a shrewd clever man, is a Mr. Archer,
part of whose life has been spent at sea. He appears to
have established a very satisfactory state of discipline
here, if we may judge from a cursory view. It must
not be forgotten that rent, rates, and taxes are very

high in that neighbourhood.   The receipts taken in the
shape of rent for a year are £.389 5s. 6d.

	£.	s.	d.
Salaries, house, expenses, &c. . .	139	0	11
Bills, rates, taxes, &c.	66	9	10
	£.305	10	9

The expenses would not have been so high but for
the alterations and improvements made in the course of
the year.

Chapter IX.

Of other Rookeries we may not speak. We will not pause to describe St. George's-in-the-Borough, with its back courts, where the refuse of Ireland vegetate ; or Kent Street,—the thieves' district,—which years since drew forth the indignation of the topographist; or Pearl Row, St. George's Road, Southwark; or Red House, Old Gravel Lane, Borough ; or a lodging house for thieves at the back of Holborn, where 100 thieves are to be seen, at eleven o'clock at night, on an average, six sometimes in one bed ; or the lower part of Bell Street, Paddington, for the lower class of thieves, such as coster-mongers, &c. ; or the courts and alleys leading out of Tooley Street, City, all the courts inhabited by Irish thieves, &c.; or Rents Buildings, York Street, West-minster, inhabited by pickpockets and juvenile thieves ; or many others which will suggest themselves to the reader.

Sufficient has been said to set at work those who are willing to labour in the cause, to show what Rookeries are, to stimulate us to remove them.

The condition of such colonies is not to be wondered at, when they, who have no visible means of subsistence,

are numbered by thousands! Criminals pass every year
through the metropolitan gaols, by tens of thousands;
there are criminal districts in the metropolis, districts
the hotbeds of particular crimes, so that one parish is a
school for coiners, another for burglars, another for
shoplifters, another for horse stealers; parts of the
metropolis, if mapped out by a moral geologist, would
present as many varieties as a district in which the surface was in one place clay, in another chalk, in another
limestone, in another gravel, and the like.

It is not generally known that more than two millions
are maintained by the charitable resources of the country,
or during their penal confinement. That many of these
might be restored to independence, if you could rouse
them from the moral torpor of despair; that Rookeries
hide the listlessness of departed hope, and the indolence
of broken hearts. Compelled to herd with the worst of
his species, because he cannot afford better lodging, the
honest artisan is tempted to forget the lessons of his
youth; and, forced into precarious occupation, because
his stated trade has failed him, he soon adopts it as his
own. Do you think that vice alone is the parent of
degeneracy, or that social evils result only from the recklessness of the poor; that recklessness itself is never the
offspring of ill-paid labour and exhausted industry; that
sickness has never thrust the ardent from the place his
toil had won, or even change of fashion cast a blight
upon the skill by which he earned his bread?

And yet think not we are unthankful for the charities

so liberally dealt out through this land; the sick are visited, the maimed and the cripple healed, the houseless sheltered, the prostitute reclaimed, the orphan housed, the idiot cared for, the blind taken in. Schools there are, waiting only for the sanction of a better system to instruct the nation; Hospitals, where skill is tasked and science lends her aid; Prisons, where a wise effort would reclaim those whom justice punishes; and, last of all, a Poor Law, whose shelter each may claim, not as by favour, but by right.

Yes, the energies of this noble country need only to be roused, her eyes opened to the wretchedness she well might relieve. We want not so much larger resources— for indiscriminate relief creates more poverty than it dispels—but rather a better distribution of the resources we possess. We want fellow-feeling spread over the surface of the country, not confined to particular classes; we want those, who at heart are just and generous, to look into the anomalies they have often sanctioned unconsciously among their own tenants, and to do that justice to their own dependents, which the stranger, if he claimed it, would receive at their hands. We would that the country should be awakened, not to enact some new Poor Law, or swell the resources on which the existing one depends; we would diminish rather than increase the rates—they more than double the amount at which they ought to be assessed. Up to this very time, and with all our experience, the problem has not been solved—whether a Poor Law does not create much of the poverty it

relieves ? We would deal a death-blow to begging by
giving scope for honest toil, and raise men to independence by the pride which comfort gives,—by a sense that
labour earns the blessings which a father's love claims
for his offspring.

We may rail against 𝕽𝖔𝖔𝖐𝖊𝖗𝖎𝖊𝖘 as we will; we may
club together to put them down ; yet selfishness, when
chartered, or when not denounced by law, will be too
powerful even for the strength of the many. We write
no verdict against voluntary effort,—but, has it answered
the purpose of legislative enactment ?   Have the efforts
of Dissenters and of Churchmen combined provided for
the educational or religious wants of the mass ?   Yet
rivalry has not been wanting,—the fierce conflict of
opposite interests,—the traditions of our Great Struggle,
in which the King was slain, and the Church dismantled,
have bequeathed a portion of their bitterness to these
times ; religious zeal and religious strife, two of the
strongest feelings of the human mind, have not accomplished an end for which both contended, though on
different grounds. Let the law, then, denounce Rookeries,—the law which the people may evoke, and which
the Legislature, the echo of the people's voice, will
enact ; which the righteous energy of a Russell would
gladly sanction, the far-sighted prudence of a Peel assent
to, and the indignant eloquence of a D'Israeli demand.

We may judge what we ought to do, by considering
what has been done. The Great Fire had scarcely spent
its ravages, ere the nation was roused, even under the

sensual indolence of a Charles, even after the exhaustion of a civil conflict, a grievous plague, and a devouring scourge. She arose as a giant to repair the damage which thousands had sustained, and remove the relics which the wretchedness of former ages had bequeathed. How many Rookeries yielded up the ghost amidst the flames, or gave way before the destroyer, history stops not to tell,—she is concerned only with the larger streets and the more public edifices which were consumed. Yet it would do the lawgivers of these times good to peruse the injunctions which were laid down for the rebuilding of the City ; how, when men had just thrown aside a form of government which a successful revolution achieved, they laid down minute laws, whereby, if the liberty of the subject was wronged, his life was extended and his comfort secured.

Did we wield the rod of correction, for which our fingers tingle, this should be the wholesome sentence we would pass upon the indolence of law makers :—They should be confined within the precincts of the British Museum, till they had learned by heart the rules issued and sanctioned for the rebuilding of the City ; they should thumb old Seymour again and again ; and, under a self-correcting memory of the discipline, be once again restored to write the common sense and the common English of former times. Then Rookeries would disappear, not because an Act proscribed cellars, yet forgot to enforce the law it had enacted ; but because, when the sentence of their death was pronounced, men were there to see it carried out.

Still, let us not speak only of existing Rookeries. Could you lay an injunction upon the builder—could you check his labours for the next thirty years, Rookeries would still be formed, and streets rapidly degenerate ; bankruptcy, change of fashion, annual migration and emigration, decay, the adaptation of dwellings to the purposes of a public company, obnoxious settlers, change of habits, rise of new trades, would transform decent dwellings into 𝕽𝖔𝖔𝖐𝖊𝖗𝖎𝖊𝖘. Yet a law should be hallowed, not only by a sense of its use and its benevolence, but by the presence of officers;—they are the visible forms of justice, and they would check these transformations ;—they would vindicate the claim of the poor to the air, the light, and the water, which come direct from God. In their presence you could not confine two families to one room ;—you could not make a crumbling den pay the rent which a decent house does not require;—you could not mix without regard to sex the members of different families;—you could not break down with impunity the line which divides the artisan from the felon ;—at their bidding, dustmen would do their duty, and water-rate collectors remember the meaning of value received.

This is, however, a small part of their work,—population increases, and the working classes have not yet bowed down at the altar of Malthus ; marriage is still popular : the limits of the town will soon overleap the boundaries our fathers set, and London engulph within its circle the fields where childhood yet plays ; buildings will arise, whose architects have taken a wholesome lesson from the errors of their forefathers; and luxuries, which the unhappy Past knew not, be the inheritance of a future generation. Let us look well to it, that Rookeries do not mar our satisfaction, when the delighted eye wanders over splendid squares, and churches of mediæval riches. Let not the abode of luxury be flanked by a back-ground where vice riots, allied with squalid misery,—and the palace of the merchant stand in strong contrast with the hovel of him who is the factor of that trader's wealth*.

We live in an age when heroes and hero-worship are alike gone by; our merchants are not Howards, our patriots, Hampdens : still, if the large sacrifice be denied, let not the tithe which justice asks be withheld ; the law we want might still wield a useful power,—Rookeries, at least, would cease to be built afresh, and perhaps those which exist would die out, for want of congenial companions ; they would soon be limited to certain districts, which the poor would in time avoid, and thus languish because their occupation was gone. As the town increased, we should be comforted, because its anomalies declined ; and crime be on the wane, because deprived of its hiding-place,—some future Agar Town would be spared the pest which clung to it, and an infant Hampstead learn not its mother tongue from the groans of the poor.

We confess, then, that rules are wanted to confine the evil within its present limits, if not at once to stay

* Since the First Edition was published, much has been done by the Bill to regulate Lodging Houses.

the plague, yet we fear the encounter. Interests, large
and many, we say, are mixed up in this system ; we
shall have to fight the battle separately with each,—they
only who have warred against the selfishness and traditions of mankind know the toil before them. Is it,
indeed, so ? We doubt it ; the landlords whose interests
are at stake in these Rookeries, are not very many,—we
speak of the *landlords, not the middle-men ;* nor are
their profits so large ; for the excess of rent paid by the
tenant rewards the trouble and swells the gains of those
that intervene between him and the owner. Many, then,
must be the houses, and extensive the plot of ground
they cover, before an income swells into the dimensions
which make it powerful, and through which the owner
wields an influence to create alarm ; the country magnate,
whose interest you would evoke, and whom you fear to
offend, owns whole streets ; and thus, though his ground
produces treble the amount it yielded a century since,
the size of all the Rookeries combined, forbids that
there should be many who thus unconsciously deal in
things forbidden. You might provoke the hostility of
some few, you would not dare the opposition of a large
class, were Rookeries at once swept away.

This is, however, the lowest line of argument which
we ought to be ashamed, in the face of higher motives,
to adopt. Many pocket rents they scarce know from
what source, because their fathers did so ; their steward
is ignorant of the miseries of those whose landlord is his
master, and it only needs to point out the sufferings their

carelessness has entailed on others, at once to end it; or, if they still persist, shame must do what conscience cannot, and the law enforce what private interests forbid.

Yet individuals are not alone to blame; these houses suffer from other annoyances, which the law has entailed on them; and which, if you pass an Act of Parliament to-morrow, to humanise within a given time all the landlords of London, would still remain. Nearly eight hundred houses, in an aristocratic district of the Metropolis suffer from want of ventilation,—so that the political satirist has been found a true prophet, when he wrote—

> " One for a tax upon the wind,
> Pitt only taxed the light,
> And one for an excise on mind—
> The intellectual sight."

Many windows are stopped up, that the landlord—I beg his pardon, the middle-man—may escape the heavy pressure of the window-tax * ; yet here, according to the well-known adage, the raven escapes, and the dove suffers. The houses in these districts have about them signs of a not venerable antiquity; they retain all past discomforts, and are destitute of all modern improvements; they transmit the evils without the virtues of the age, whose type they are, burdened with the taxes " which blissful Eden knew not." Shifting sashes are seldom found; and, to use the words of a report on this

* Thank God! since the publication of the First Edition, the Window Tax has been abolished.

subject, "modern means of obtaining a supply of atmo-
" spheric air, and producing ventilation, are scarcely
" known, and very little appreciated by the poorer
" classes." A country gentleman, of moderate income, one just trembling on the verge of squirearchy—
one who is gradually working his way into that estimable
corporation, has his house, containing three or four
sitting rooms, seven or eight bed-rooms, his laundry, his
drying ground, his coachman's cottage, his ornamental
and kitchen-garden, piggery, kennel, stable, &c.—each
a distinct province. Now, suppose population to be
quadrupled—an invasion to take place, his house to be
garrisoned, as many homes were in the Civil War, and
suppose him and his family limited to one room,—
linen to be washed there, dried there—victuals to be
cooked there, eaten there—family to sit there, sleep
there, read there, dress there, and you have some faint
idea of the discomforts of a poor man's dwelling. But,
says Sterne, " darken the little light which remains,"
reduce the three windows to two,—bring the piggery,
stable, and kennel, within ten yards of the house, and
even then what is it to A Rookery ? You say we are
supposing a case well-nigh impossible ; that, even if it
were so, the trial would be so much the greater, in
proportion to the habits, education, rank, previous
means of the person so affected. Do you think that
no decayed gentleman has ever been obliged in dens
like these to hide a broken heart,—that ruin among this
class is so very uncommon ? Those who have visited

Rookeries have known too many parallels ; but yet, concede that we have referred to isolated cases,—ask yourself, is the distinction between the small proprietor, and the well-ordered mechanic so vast, the gulph which separates them so profound, that the one should be surrounded by most of the luxuries which the individual can enjoy,—the other be destitute of most of the necessaries that life requires ? Should this be so, when, if the mechanic be ingenious or fortunate, he may live to see his son High Sheriff of the county ?

We are not blaming any one class ; our aristocracy are not savage tyrants, they are English gentlemen,— kind, generous, delighting not merely to relieve the wants, they encourage the sports, and promote the happiness of their tenants ; our merchants are not penurious traders, they are an open-handed, open-hearted race ; the bane of all this is thoughtlessness, and a clinging to old traditions.

Amidst the homes of the aristocracy, Dorsetshire labourers are generating a plague, and Dorsetshire poverty has raised the county to the bad elevation of the prime nursery of crime. And the porters, mechanics, labourers, the very shopmen of the Metropolis, waste out their lives amidst Rookeries whose social discomforts demoralise their minds, whose polluted atmosphere ruins their health. Men are not worse than their fathers,—are they better ? We have averred that the gulph is daily growing wider which separates the higher and middle ranks from the working classes. Grant, if you will, that the wages of the working man are not in proportion lower than they were a hundred years since,—still, the population is larger, competition greater,—for then emigration was an evil which men tried to check. Goldsmith, in that model of political wisdom, *The Traveller*, laments over the countryman leaving the home of his fathers, as though the country were deprived of something whose services it might need. It would be difficult to prove that Rookeries were crowded then as now, and the middle class knew not a tithe of the comfort they now enjoy. We wonder not that luxury should increase with wealth; such has ever been the rule, though refinement in luxury has been also the first symptom of a state's decay; yet, when a particular class remains stationary, and in broad contrast with the advancement of all else but itself, then there is danger—then there is a sore in the nation's body which, would she live, must be healed.

And these very evils, whose remedy we ask, or whose removal we cry out for—what are they but the abuse, the perversion, or the withholding of the very commonest, cheapest blessings which God has given to man ? Blessings, to supply which, it costs us nothing ;—the air comes fresh from heaven ; the light, science can neither create has nor destroy; the water, whose beds the Hand above has hallowed, which He has inlaid with a cement, the natural receptacle of the stores they contain, those stores being inexhaustible, would flow spontaneously did we open a channel for it; once sink the well, and it will ever keep running; once unclog the avenues you have choked up, repeal the *abuses you* have made, and Nature will itself supply our wants. When a Committee appointed by a parish of note, went their rounds, they declare that, among the eight hundred houses they visited, " not " one single instance was found of a continuous supply " of water by Water Companies; and, although there " did not appear to be an actual want of the article, " yet the supply being intermittent, and of short dura " tion, does not maintain a sufficient quantity in the " various, and, sometimes, very limited, receptacles found " in poor dwellings, to meet the requirements of houses " crowded with families, and to enable the occupants to " assist in promoting health by cleansing their persons " as well as frequently washing their linen, and scouring " the rooms they inhabit." Yet, small as is the supply, even then it is not pure; an analysis would prove that it has collected many impurities in its transit; its reservoirs are badly placed, and the pipes frequently in juxta-position with the sewers, so that the supplies of the one and the outpourings of the other have been sometimes mingled.

A gentleman hires a house—the landlord at once taking care that it shall be well lit, supplied with water and with air; does the roof show signs of leakage when some August deluge sweeps away a house or two in Middle Row, the landlord repairs it; has the water been turned off during the non-occupancy of the house, the landlord issues his sign-manual, and obedient water-rate collectors turn on the supply. It is part of the owner's duty to provide, not merely that there should be water for all the purposes of cleanliness and comfort, but that the cisterns which supply it, and the pump from which it is drawn, are in working condition ; that no giant nuisance shall rear its head in the vicinity—that no haunts of immorality should pollute the neighbourhood. Should the unconscious tenant enter upon a house, forgetting to make these inquiries ; should he take a house upon trust, supposing that it was furnished with the comforts and free from the annoyances we have mentioned, and yet, after all, find he was deceived, the law would throw its ægis of protection around him, would compel the landlord to supply the comforts that were wanting, to remove the evils complained of, or else that his tenant should be released from his agreement. Such suits as these we have supposed are known to every lawyer, and numberless are the instances in which a respectable jury, instructed by those judges whom it is the high boast of England to rear, has granted the protection which the claimant had a right to ask.

But were redress cut off in this quarter, do you think that no other means would be adopted to bring the landlord to his senses ? The tenant would most probably quit the house, at some expense to himself perhaps, and at some annoyance, but then the place would be marked as a plague spot; it would not, as in the year of the fatal epidemic 1665, be lettered with the red sign which kept the neighbours at a distance, still it would be quite

as much shunned; it would have the bad name attached
to it; other landlords in the neighbourhood would exalt
the merits of their respective tenements by contrast
with the condemned one, or, if the annoyance were one
which infringed the laws of morality, would readily join
in removing that which tainted the character of the
district.

We have already then disbursed sums quite sufficient
to remove the annoyances and evils of which we complain. We assert, again, that in this country there is no
want of generosity,—of readiness to pay reasonable
imposts. Who can doubt this, when the rates of one
parish for sewerage alone in twenty-two years, amount to
£.565,000 ? Nevertheless, there is a sad want of management, of that prudence, economy, watching of details, &c.
which characterises the expenditure of private individuals.
We want an Act, compiled and carried out by practical
men, who have added this principle to their present
conventional morality,—that the man who cheats the
government, or a corporation, is as great a scoundrel as
he who cheats the individual. After railway exposures,
some will say this is too much to expect,—we hope not,
for the credit of the country. Yet, what is the conclusion
we draw from these statements,—is it not the old conclusion, we have before stated, that, if there were no
middle-men between the landlord and the tenant, many
of the evils denounced would cease to exist ?

There would be responsible persons at hand, men
made responsible by the appearance of their names in

leases and agreements, to set in order these abuses. Men who could at once be appealed to—dealt with by law—exposed for contumacy. It is the present system of letting which is in fault, which the Legislature must amend ere the evil is dealt with at its root.

Before we conclude our labours, we must describe the method now pursued of letting out lodgings to the poor, as well as the means by which rents are collected, because we are satisfied that very few know,—even some of the landlords themselves may be ignorant of the process,—for ignorance alone can account for their apathy or give a shadow of justification to their neglect.

Chapter X.

We have considered Rookeries hitherto as means of demoralising the present generation. We fear them for what they are,—beds of pestilence, where the fever is generated which shall be propagated to distant parts of the town,—rendezvous of vice, whose effects we feel in street robberies and deeds of crime,—blots resting upon our national repute for religion and charity. Still they are dangerous, not so much on account of what they are, as what they may be ;—they are not only the haunts where pauperism recruits its strength—not only the lurking-places, but the *nurseries* of felons. A future generation of thieves is there hatched from the viper's egg, who shall one day astonish London by their monstrous birth. Suppose these haunts to increase, as poverty and distress ever have a tendency to do, in the proportion of two to one to the growth of the labouring classes, and what a prospect have we before us! The colony of Van Dieman's Land is a penal settlement ; the number of its population 60,000, half of them convicts. Did you ever, gentle reader, attend a public meeting, or read a report of the state of things which prevails there,— of the desperate immorality which, to name, would stain

our pages ? Can you contemplate the acting of such
scenes here ? Huge chimeras of crime, embracing in
their outstretched arms districts not yet polluted,—fresh
supplies of the labour and industry of the country dragged down to this loathsome pit,—fresh scenes of our
country's nurture going forth, trained in such schools,
to bear the name of England ! Such a leaven, eating
gradually into the heart of that race from which we
recruit the trade, the agriculture, the army, the navy of
Great Britain. Vice making some further inroad, and
crime not content with its present per centage.

Among the more prosperous and thoughtful of the
working class, marriage is a state on which prudence
holds its council, and the future lifts up her mirror, and
contingencies are considered,—the family that may be,—
the expenses that must be ; and thus the higher you go
in the scale, the fewer these unions,—the less produc-
tive the classes by which the strength and numbers of
the people are best recruited. But the denizens of
Rookeries know not prudence,—the future suggests no
fears, because the past speaks of no comforts,—the present of no hopes ;—they marry ; their condition, they
argue, cannot be worse, it may be better ; or, if marriage,
as in very many cases, is dispensed with, concubinage is in
its stead, numerous broods of children are reared around
them, to hand down at once their features and their
habits. If a man in these haunts could dismiss the idea
of a wife, yet he likes a companion, and wants a servant to cook, to wash, and provide for his comfort.   He

supplies this want in the mother of his children. In the classes above him, men would rather want the comfort than support the burden of a partner, that partner, too, with the family she may rear in the distance. We may look, then, for a superabundant increase of the Rookery class, with no corresponding growth of the industrious labourer, unless you check such increase by salutary laws, which strike down the nests, not where men, but rather human abortions, are produced. Grave must be the fears of the thinking man when he views the swarms of children who people the back alleys of London,—when he thinks that each of these must be clothed, fed, and supported, and ought to be thus supplied by the wants of a class daily becoming, in proportion, less than it was. What new scheme shall we—shall the next generation, put forth, to provide for the wants of its teeming millions? Yet we need not anticipate, rather let us look at things as they now are. We were wont fondly to imagine that childhood's innocence was something more than figure; that manhood goaded by want, learned strange trades, and plied strange traffic, but childhood at least had yet to imbibe poison; crime must wait, thought we, till the powers of mind and body are developed, ere it can grasp its victim. It was reserved, perhaps, for the Rookeries of our day not to rear a few anomalous instances, but whole gangs of juvenile delinquents; to send forth children trained to be adepts in wickedness; these poetic innocents calculating chances of discovery, watching times and seasons for theft,—conversant with the habits, scru-

tinising the weak and unguarded points of those by
robbing whom they must thrive,—taught noiselessly to
do their deeds of darkness, not singly, but in gangs,
where concert aided the theft, where numbers made it
difficult to trace the delinquent ; so that hours, days
must have been spent to make them adepts in their
calling,—oaths of fearful import administered to bind
them to silence,—laws enacted to regulate these bodies
corporate,—the wires carefully adjusted along which the
electric fluid passes, if we may be allowed the figure,—
schools, in a word, formed, whose task-book is the
Newgate calendar. No one who knows Rookeries will
doubt this. A case occurred some time since, which
came under the writer's observation. A man and his
wife died in cholera ; their only child was known as a
boy given to petty thefts ; he was very young—there was
hope he might be reclaimed ; he was placed with a
respectable widow, to whom a sum was paid for his
board ; in the day-time he was sent to school ; he had
not been long with her before she missed some plate ;
she searched more minutely, and found out the extent of
her loss : a series of depredations had been carried on,
and her little stock of valuables was sensibly diminished.
Some of the articles were afterwards recovered from the
pawnbrokers, where they had been pledged. The boy
was taxed with the theft, the poor widow, from mistaken
humanity, not wishing to proceed against the offender ;
he confessed the theft, yet soon ran away from the
tutelage under which he was placed, returning at times

to annoy her. When she remonstrated with him, he said, "You had better take care, there are forty of us, " and, if you offend one, you may calculate upon being " annoyed by all." She was at first inclined to treat this as an idle threat, till some boys insulted her, called her names, and upbraided her ; when she learnt that the youth who had been under her protection was really one of a juvenile gang, called the forty thieves, who were concerned in petty thefts in various parts of the metropolis. It is no uncommon thing for boys to stay out all night, and, when they return, not to be able to give a satistory account of themselves. Though their parents are honest, there is little doubt that they themselves have been entrapped by designing criminals, and made the instruments of nefarious practices. Thus the poor are often disgraced by their own offspring, who have fallen under the evil influence of some professor of wickedness. Boys are easily tempted by some bait suited to their years,—are initiated into the unhallowed mysteries of the craft,—are taught to deceive by plausible excuses the vigilance of their parents. A poor man is bereaved of his wife by disease,—is left with young children, his trade being one which takes him much from home; he leaves his children under the guardianship of a neighbour who has children of her own, and can feel no particular interest in the welfare of another's offspring. In the very Rookery which he inhabits are people of questionable occupation,—old and juvenile victimizers. What a tempting speculation, to make these poor mother-

less children—such at least as are old enough—the
means of carrying out their iniquities! These harpies
know the occupation of the father,—daily experience
teaches them to calculate the moment of his return,—
his habits are no secret, the dispositions of his family
easily ascertained,—they are tempted, in their ignorance,
by a bait they cannot resist, and enter gradually on the
course of crime. The writer has known more than one
such instance, and has had reason to be thankful that
Refuges for the Destitute afforded an asylum for those
thus early betrayed. Too often—hard as it may seem
to write such things—female children, in haunts like
these, have fallen victims to the gross passions of abandoned men, when their tender age would have seemed to
have put such dangers out of the way, and when their
very ignorance was the cause of their fall. And recollect, the arrangements of Rookeries foster such things.
When distinction of sex is practically ignored, can you
expect decency to survive? When the sexes are thrown
promiscuously together, do you wonder at paradoxes in
immorality? When vice bears with it little disgrace, can
you expect the blush of shame? and where exclusion
from society is a penalty which cannot be carried out,
do you look for the virtues which are the growth of
mingled fear and self-respect?

And some speculator will talk in set terms about the
danger of interfering with capital, as though this capital
by a native elasticity adapted itself to the necessities of
those over whom its influence extended; much in the

same way in which a novel machine feeds the steam engine with just so much and no more coals than it requires. Verily men must not have faith, but credulity,—reverence for great names, and the sway of large firms, who will believe it. Confide in this, and the Stock Exchange shall discourse sublime morality, and the Bourse endow a lecturer to declaim against avarice. Confide in this, and the kitchens of the Mansion House shall glow with the fires which cook the dinners of the poor, and the rafters of Guildhall ring with cheers from the denizens of St. Giles.

What shall we say to the juvenile depravity of Rookeries ? We do not deny that emigration will do much to thin them. New Zealand may invite them, a moral oasis in the social desert, climate, scenery, natural productions, large tracts of land uncultivated,—a second England to be peopled,—breathing time and breathing room afforded for our people for centuries to come. Yet has this scheme of emigration ever been taken up by the nation as a national duty or engagement ? Have the poor rates been applied, in the shape of an annual per centage, to forward such schemes ? With thousands willing to go, have you opened a vent for them in this direction ? and if you had done so, is there no consideration due to the tens and hundreds of thousands who will even then be left behind ? Some will tell us that the poor might be lodged within the same area as at present, and yet Rookeries be swept away. In Edinburgh and Paris you have houses six or seven stories high ; such seems also the

rule in Antwerp and the old Flemish towns; thus, where
ground is dear, room is economised; the appearance of
the dwellings thus elevated is much more picturesque,—
height ever adds to the magnificence of buildings, and
even on the lowest ground, a change in this direction
is desirable; but who shall measure such advantages
with increased space and good ventilation? In the
lodging-houses in St. Pancras, the tenants do live on
flats, to speak technically, and thus each family has
three separate rooms at its disposal. We may not forget,
whilst on this subject, the benevolent scheme proposed, by which labourers should be lodged in colonies
distant ten miles from the Metropolis, to which they
should go and return by railroad. Could such a proposal
be carried out, and we pretend not to know how far it is
feasible, their families would have the benefit of fresh
air, country scenery, and all the invigorating influences
of a rural residence; the pressure upon London would
be relieved; the bloated rent-rolls of Rookery owners
shrink again to their fair proportions. Nor would the
time consumed in the journey be an object; many
labourers pass quite as much time on the road between
their lodgings and their work, as would be taken up in
the rapid transit of the steam carriage. Yet, with all
this, there are certain trades which necessarily confine
the operatives to the spot where their work is obtained;
shoemakers, tailors, carpenters, perhaps, must be within
call,—must have rooms where they can work, though it
would scarce be correct to state that they could not ply

their calling without absolutely living on the spot. Amidst the many ingenious devices of the day, there is room for a plan which would obviate this necessity. Now, supposing the panacea discovered, you would still have a large poor population around you—some from choice—some from indolence—some from habit—some because it was unavoidable, clinging to the metropolis. So that Rookeries would still be an object for legislation, and juvenile delinquents still call upon the resources of wisdom and benevolence. People are apt to be sceptical about this lamentation of ours over the early lost, and think we exaggerate in order to swell a page or point a paragraph. The following is an anecdote taken from the journal of one who conducted a Ragged School :—

" Finding it impossible to get the children to attend
" our school in the forenoon, we determined upon
" changing our hours to half-past six in the evening.
" We commenced our new plan on Sunday, November
" 26th, when we had upwards of two hundred children
" and youths in attendance. Under all circumstances
" their behaviour was good during the greater part of
" the evening. About ten minutes to eight o'clock,
" however, there was a signal given by some of the boys,
" and instantly there was a move in all parts of the
" room and a rush made to the staircase. The super-
" intendent was amazed at this proceeding ; recovering
" from his surprise, however, he darted across the room
" and was just in time to catch the last one ere he
" reached the door. Twenty-one had already made

" their exit. The boy who was caught struggled hard
" to get away and loudly cried, Let me go! let me go!
" But, holding him fast, the teacher replied,—When you
" have told me what this plot means you shall. I want
" to go to business, said the boy. Business, why it is
" Sunday night. Never mind, you let me go, continued
" the lad. The superintendent still held firm. Well,
" I'll tell you the truth sir, do you see it is eight o'clock.
" The teacher looked at the clock and nodded assent.
" Well, sir, we catches them as they comes out of church
" and chapel. A policeman now entered. Where, said
" he, did you get these boys from? *they are every one*
" *of them convicted thieves.*"

Where, then, are these Ragged Schools situated? for
whom are they provided? Are not National schools
sufficient for the population? British and foreign
schools, and other seminaries, for the working classes?
Why these ragged schools, whose name conveys something offensive? They are situated, then, in Rookery
districts. Your Bethnal Green, St. Giles's, Saffron Hill,
Minories, Bermondsey Rookeries recruit their numbers.
The back streets and courts behind Westminster Abbey,
the Berwick Street district of St. James's, though the
school there rejoices in a more euphonious appellation,
fill these receptacles. 𝔅𝔞𝔫𝔦𝔰𝔥 𝔕𝔬𝔬𝔨𝔢𝔯𝔦𝔢𝔰, and Ragged
Schools will be remembered in the chronicles of the
past. They are so called because the children are ragged
and dirty; a marked line between them and the offspring
of the working classes. They pay nothing for their

schooling; the penny a-week, which in national schools keeps up the decent pretence of money paid for value received, is here unknown; the poverty or recklessness of their parents denies it. The working man would be annoyed if told that his child was educated by charity; his just and honest pride be wounded. Yet the lowest of the Rookeries know not this feeling; it is something Utopian, excluded by the stern and rigid poverty or the degraded condition of the parent. His child, he thinks, will there learn to read and write—will be out of the mother's way in the day time—cannot as yet be more profitably employed; and thus, as it cost him nothing, he concedes as a favour the permission to educate one whose welfare should be his dearest wish. We say not it is always so. Doubtless in the worst Rookeries there are some capable of, and still longing for, better things, and no nature is so entirely corrupted but that a lingering feeling of remorse may still be left behind; yet our Ragged Schools seek first to obtain pupils such as these, and were devised for the lowest of the population.

Begging goes hand-in-hand with juvenile theft. Children, by the softness of their voice, the smallness of their figure, the innocence attributed to their tender age, are popular as mendicants. If the satirist of antiquity could say that we groan, as by the instinct of our nature, when the funeral of a young child passes along the streets, we cannot hear the cry of distress on the lips of the young, or see its tokens in their face, without emotion; so that infants have been hired by beggars who had none of

their own, to aid the appeal made to the pockets of the
charitable. Thus our Rookeries are the refuges of mendicants, who there divide the gains of the day. In a
town in Scotland, whose population is not much above
fifty thousand, upwards of two hundred children were
supported solely by begging ; the police knew that they
lived on alms or thefts. Their condition was sad, and
great the annoyance they gave to the inhabitants. When
these children were at length convicted of some petty
theft, they were removed for a few days or weeks to gaol,
and here methods for their reformation were adopted ;
yet so short was the time for which they were confined,
that the regimen adopted had not time to display its
powers, or work its changes on them. They rapidly fell
back upon their old habits, till, after being imprisoned
again and again, they were at length transported.

To such a class our Ragged Schools supply the best
antidote at present devised ; yet whilst Rookeries remain
as they are, it must be up-hill work. This class must be
attacked by a combined effort ; all the elements of reformation blended into the plan proposed for their relief.
Rookeries there still will be, whilst Rookeries are recognised as legal habitations, into which even the schoolmaster of a ragged school cannot penetrate, and from
which, when entrance is obtained, he cannot drag a
tenth part of the younger inhabitants; and they who
are brought forth are liable to a variety of calls which
check his efforts, and impede his schemes for their improvement. How long will he retain these children ?

Will their attendance be regular or at intervals ? Will the parents put no impediments in their way ? Have you calculated to what extent the lessons learnt at school are neutralised by the examples of the home ? Recollect, these children eat, drink, sleep in the rooms their parents inhabit. In their sports they mingle with their neighbours, several of whom go to no school. They need education we know, for the returns of prisons show how few of the felons have been humanised by early training. Some cannot read or write at all. Some even know not the name of the Saviour of the world ! Few can read and write with accuracy ; so that, if education were still an untried remedy, it would be worth the trial. But should not the Government carry out, in connection with the condemnation of Rookeries, some scheme for the general education of the poor ? Private schemes are cramped for want of funds. The design should be tried on a grand scale.

Are you aware, gentle reader, of the snares laid to entrap these children—that they learn vice at penny theatres, which, in their cases, supply the desire felt by most of us for dramatic entertainments ? Are you aware that several sweetmeat shops exist in the neighbourhood of Rookeries, where children are enticed to gamble for the tempting articles exposed on the counter ?—that one mode of carrying on such practices, is this :—A doll is fixed to a board, the body of which is hollow ; through the head of this figure a marble is passed, which, after circulating through it, falls into one of the many holes

made for it in the board beneath ; these holes are numbered, and accordingly as he exceeds or falls below a
given figure, the youthful gambler wins or loses?   At
first sight such a practice seems comparatively innocent;
but too often, from the thirst for gaming in this small
way, children rob their parents.   Here, again, is felt the
want of a public prosecutor.   It is difficult to get any
one to give evidence in these transactions ; the children
do not like to do it, their parents shrink from it, and the
shopkeeper carefully shields himself as much as possible
from detection.   How many are the children nurtured in
Rookeries, driven from their home by the cruelty and bad
conduct of their parents—orphans, neglected children,
and others.   What becomes of them ?   They are taken
into workhouses ; and notwithstanding the care of those
who have charge of such institutions, they are not
adapted either for the instruction of the young or the
reformation of the old.   The schoolmasters of such
institutions are seldom carefully selected, often very
ignorant men ; and the paupers too often try to demoralise the children whose age is considered mature enough
to allow them to mix with the adults.

You have your model prisons in the Isle of Wight,
your Millbank penitentiaries ; but you forget that more
than half the mischief is done before the boy is admitted
into these institutions.   He has gone through a training
which has implanted what you must now root out ; it is
scarcely needful to tell you that the latter is the more
difficult task of the two.   Crime must have some sweets,

some attractions, if, as is too often the case, people worship Jack Sheppard and Turpin as heroes; and romance has been called in to gild their career, and novels have been written whose chief interest is in the traditions respecting them which have been revived to please the present age. These children have been already tutored under a system in whose annals these worthies are hallowed; and you have to grapple with the propensities already excited, rather than to mould and frame the virgin mind, so to speak, into the shape you wish. Your efforts are indeed most laudable, and God forbid that, with the beautiful teaching of holy writ before us, we should deny either a place for their repentance, or blot out the hope of their reformation. Why not at once put forth a comprehensive plan which nips the evil in the bud?—why not get for yourself the first hearing in the child's mind, by teaching him before that mind be warped to crime? Instead of establishing more penitentiaries, raise schools suited to the class whom they must train; call to your aid practical men—the magistrates, the inspectors of police, and others—who by daily experience know the habits of these children. Strengthen their hands as you might do, by providing nurseries for those over whom their too prophetic eye sees hanging disgrace and ruin. When the father has paid the penalty due to the injured laws of his country, and is transported, don't let his children be left to the tender mercies of his companions, but have the school ready to receive them; let them there be fed, be clothed, be taught—taught whilst the recollection of what their fathers were shall kindle the diligence and awake the caution of their master. Suppose an onslaught made upon Rookeries—model lodging-houses built, till rents were lowered, and the disciples of Mammon found that to build proper dwellings paid for the outlay—even then you would want schools for the poorest class; the national schools would not meet the case of the destitute; these very establishments are stunted through want of funds,—the nation is not yet half awake to the greatness of the mischief already done through want of education, nor to the still greater dangers in the prospective. We *must forget our sectarian differences,* if we would dare call ourselves any longer a Christian people, and save the nation from ruin; and if the Government cannot get these sections of the Christian body to unite, may the day come round when a general system of training is enacted in spite of them.

Suppose 𝕽𝖔𝖔𝖐𝖊𝖗𝖎𝖊𝖘 𝖉𝖔𝖔𝖒𝖊𝖉, but half the evil is crushed, if a plan is not set on foot for the well-being of the junior members of these fraternities. Do all you can, and there will still remain behind a great amount of poverty, recklessness, and crime; lay every Rookery low within the bills of mortality,—interdict them under the severest penalties, and still you will have room enough for all your wisdom and all your benevolence. The habits which Rookeries have stamped deep and burnt into the nature of those who dwelt there would still cause you anxious thought, though we might then hope that the crime of our land would not compel us to invade peaceful colonies, or to force rebellion upon our distant dependencies.

Under the most favourable circumstances, the time

allotted to the education of the poor is too short,—two or three years being very often the utmost extent which circumstances allow of; for in many trades children are soon useful. In the trade of brick-making young children are often employed, and during the summer months earn considerable sums. The poverty of their parents too soon withdraws them from our schools; their education half finished, and many of them going out into the world scarcely able to read and write.

How great, then, must be the drawbacks with the class we have described above; where they do not go to the school, but where the school must come to them— where they must be coaxed for a time from the Rookery land into the rooms open to receive them; coaxed, perhaps, when hunger indisposes them to learn—when parents forbid them to leave the house—when persons round about them are on the watch to bribe and ensnare them. Boys love play and hate work; training alone makes them quit the sports congenial to their age and disposition, and devote a portion of their time to learning. Parental authority must back the arguments of the teacher, and second his efforts on their behalf. In Rookeries, no one forbids the children to waste, in sports or other less harmless occupation, the precious seed-time of life.

Whilst Rookeries still are—whilst any of those remain who were bred amidst their purlieus, there must be Ragged Schools; but with what especial care should they be organised, if suiting themselves to the wants of those for whom they are intended. No ordinary stretch of wisdom or benevolence will satisfy the call made on us. We should remember that 𝕽𝖔𝖔𝖐𝖊𝖗𝖎𝖊𝖘 will furnish our pupils. The habits 𝕽𝖔𝖔𝖐𝖊𝖗𝖎𝖊𝖘 generate must be eradicated ; and, as our sectarianism has not descended to this level—as different bodies of professing Christians have not yet began to quarrel respecting the *doctrinal* teaching of ragged schools, and are content to proselytise birds of a higher flight, let Government with intuitive discernment seize the happy moment, occupy the vacant ground ; for once, whilst the clamour is hushed, devise some plan of its own for teaching sound religion and useful learning.

It may be very well in the face of all this to plead that the miserable condition of Rookeries is owing to the habits of the labouring population ; that the sum of money spent in public houses bears a large proportion (we forget the exact amount) to the poor rates of the country. Are there no Rookeries, then, in foreign cities where drunkenness is rare,—do not wretched and dear dwellings produce recklessness and disgust, which, in this country, vent themselves in intoxication rather than cabals, factions, and insurrections ?

Men, even in the higher orders of society, whose homes are not comfortable, seek other resorts, though not confined to a single room, and use stimulants too, though not always such as produce inebriety. But the reading room, and the society to which the purchase of intoxicating liquor *is not the passport*, supply a refuge in the one case, which in the other the tap-room alone affords.

We want a large, comprehensive, national remedy.

We must have an Act of Parliament. Let it discard as much as possible that technical language which renders so many of these documents inoperative; let it be compiled by practical men. Let nuisances, 𝕽𝖔𝖔𝖐𝖊𝖗𝖎𝖊𝖘, fever courts, *et hoc genus omne,* die the death; let them be replaced, not by shops for the tradesman, but by dwellings for the working man; let the number of inmates for each house be fixed, the due supply of water regulated by some provision which shall bring Water Companies to their senses; let each family have a sitting-room and at least two bed-rooms. This may be done not merely at little cost, but at a remunerative outlay; it has been proved by those lodging-houses which have been lately erected in St. Pancras and other parts of the Metropolis. On the adjuncts to such colonies we will not dwell, there is here a noble field for ingenuity, philanthropy, and religion; our space only allows us thus generally to allude to the subject. We do not say that the Legislature has done nothing, doubtless there is great opposition to contend with; it is obliged to wait for the impulse of some popular movement to display its energies rather than volunteer a measure to meet the difficulty; but it has not done well what it has done. In 1845 an Act of Parliament came into operation, which forbade henceforth that any kitchen should be inhabited which had not an area of seven feet to each window. making also many other judicious regulations, and vesting some powers in the parish officers. Doubtless for a time these pauper landlords were alarmed, their province

invaded, their gains abridged,—but only for a time.
Why ?   Because the poor themselves were bribed to
connive at infractions by the supposed cheapness of
kitchen-lodgings,—the parish officers, instead of being
required to make periodical visitations, or keeping a
person whose duty it was to do so, were obliged to wait
till their interference was called for.   We know how
much the old adage is acted on, that an Englishman's
home is his castle—there is then a difficulty in getting
access to houses—the jealousy of the landlord, the
independence of the lodger, is soon aroused, so that it is
scarcely possible to make the necessary inquiries ; paid
informers would find it difficult to ply their calling here,
and the efforts of the philanthropic are of course futile.
It is only when disease breaks out, that the surgeon
called in finds how the law has been broken, and for a
while remedies the evil; even then there are difficulties
in his way—he must lodge a formal complaint, the
parish must take the matter up, indict the refractory,
and be at some expense to enforce the law; and after
all there is no guarantee that, when the tumult has
subsided, the landlord and lodger alike shall not return
to their old practice.

Nor must we forget the nature of English legislation.
When some giant evil has at length broken bounds, the
cause of the oppressed is taken up by the public, it gets
into the newspapers.   Our countrymen bear long with
an evil, shut their eyes to it, till at length they have no
excuse for sleeping any longer; all at once a chorus of

different, yet, on this occasion, accordant elements strikes
up,—local meetings, leading articles, pamphlets, parlia-
mentary agitation, lend their aid. Ministers listen atten-
tively to the voice of their countrymen, and make an
effort to remove the nuisance complained of. An Act is
passed in all good faith, yet couched in cumbrous, technical, old-fashioned language, which errs precisely where
it ought to be most direct, and is clear when clearness is
not wanted. The evil is lessened, but not destroyed;
frequently some new Act is needed to make up for the
short-comings of its predecessor; the hotbeds of the
Rookery system were for a time invaded,—they have
risen again after the panic in ranker luxuriance.

In any reform proposed we have to encounter the cry
of interfering with the liberty of the subject. The poor
have gone on very well as things were—they desire no
change. We are humanity-mongers. That *laissez faire*,
that unreadiness to act only in great emergencies, is the
bane of the English character, it will impede us. Yet
recollect, at one blow rotten boroughs fell; the Corn
Laws, backed by the most powerful aristocracy in Europe,
are no more; let us then take courage. All legislation
is, to some extent, an interference with this liberty of the
subject; still it is that interference which a mother exercises for the welfare of her offspring, which the doctor
wields for the recovery of the patient. This same Palladium is fearfully misconstrued, an Ægis too often used
to destroy rather than protect the stronghold of those

who resist all interposition; the practical absurdity of
such a theory has ever been too powerful for its adoption; we do interfere, are always interfering, sometimes
most dangerously, witness the Window Tax; sometimes
suicidally, witness the National Debt; sometimes to the
perdition alike of taste and comfort, witness the Building
Act, or at least some of its provisions : the very republican calls for interference, knows it is necessary, sacri-
fices his favourite theory to it; and shall you hesitate,
when a nation's character and a nation's safety are at
stake ?

Now, suppose that we throw up our cards in despair ;
because every inch of ground won from the selfishness
or indifference of the mass is won by protracted struggle.
Suppose even good men should be staggered—like the
late renowned Dr. Arnold—that tired of a continual anta-
gonism, they grew weary of the contest, disgusted by the
selfishness, borne down by the opposition of the interested—and yet his sympathy ended with a life, alas!
how short, and he died like the warrior, with his face to
the foe, in knightly harness donned for a noble contest?
Yet, if we dared to appeal to lower motives, there is
much to encourage us in improving the dwellings of the
working classes. The lodging-house lately established
it St. Giles's finds that it can give each man a separate
bed, a place to cook his victuals and wash his clothes in,
a common room, where he may read and converse with
others, for 2s. 3d. a week—that such a charge remu-

nerates the proprietor. In St. Pancras parish, the apartments let at 5s. a week consist of a bed-room, sitting-room, and kitchen ; and the scheme is organised by a company, who have shares, and who consider it as a profitable investment, inasmuch as it yields them five per cent. ; so that, supposing the plan to be carried out, and an adequate trial given to it, the annuitant would consider one of these societies a better means of investment than the funds.

The Soho model lodging house is in Compton Street, in the parish of St. Anne ; it is a commodious establishment, making up one hundred and twenty-five beds, divided into two classes ; the front bed rooms (seventy-five in number) are let at 3s. 6d. a week, and the others at 2s. 6d. Attached to this institution are baths and a reading room.

The working classes do not seem hitherto to have appreciated the advantages here afforded them, as, during the first year of its course, the last mentioned establishment has unfortunately not been well filled. Some time must elapse before the comforts which it affords are fully acknowledged; yet surely a place like this, which offers each man a separate sleeping room—a kitchen where he may cook his food—and a bath where he may wash,—should meet with every support, and find favour in the eyes of those for whom it is especially intended.

In one instance where lodging-houses have been established, it is believed that the owner is an eminent builder, who has erected them for his workmen, and who lets them at a remunerative price; though for size, cleanliness, and cheapness, they are most favourably contrasted with the usual dwellings of the poorer classes.

Shall it then be said that we shrink from the task which humanity imposes, when it finds favour in the eyes even of the capitalist?

Chapter XI.

Before we can devise a remedy, many questions will be proposed; these we must answer. We must know under what particular evils the working classes suffer because of high rents and wretched dwellings, before we shall have placed Rookeries in their true light,—before men will regard them, as they really are, the pregnant causes of varied ills. We may begin the inquiry by asking under what landlords such traffic exists; some one must be much to blame; men cannot thus be traded with as though they were corn, molasses, indigo, or any other marketable article, without some grievous neglect of duty,—of fair dealing, we had almost said,—in some quarter.

Some of the most densely-peopled localities in London are owned by men of great property and high rank,—some of the most wretched streets in the metropolis, if you went deep enough to find the real owner, swell the income of an opulent speculator who has bought them as a good investment. In many cases they are the hereditary estates of some country magnate, who maintains upon the proceeds his costly establishment of hounds and horses ; some, again, belong to Corporate Bodies, Public Charities ; some to Deans and Chapters, to endowed Schools—in short, they are owned by various landlords, whose occupations are of every description. Some of them have been in possession of their present owners' family for two or three hundred years; others have been more recently acquired.

You ask,—Are these landlords the recipients of the 5s. a-week per room or story, as the case may be? do their stewards superintend the repairs, take the rents, levy distresses, in the name of their masters? In most cases they do not. Originally, the landlords only leased the ground on which the houses were built for a term of years; two hundred years since, great part of the West End of London was in fields; cattle strayed—and it might be said in the words of the poet,—

" Passimque armenta videri
Romanoque foro—et lautis mugire Carinis ;"

the owners let out plots of ground for building at so much a foot for ninety-nine years; at the expiration of these leases, the ground and the houses erected on it came into possession of the family, and the descendants of the original owner found themselves enriched.

In some cases, the property is encumbered with long leases; so that the heir succeeds to an inheritance, with the wholesome control he ought to exercise over his property alienated for half his life. A Middle-man has bought a long lease, the father, or grandfather of the present owner having received a fine as a premium; such binding hand and foot of the landlord's duties as well as his interests, is indeed too common. Men enter upon these covenants, because such is the rule which all follow under similar circumstances ; which legal advisers recommend, which present necessities render prudent, —much in the same lax and inconsiderate way in which oaths were administered in the last century, without thought or reflection on their terms or obligations. The system of long leases and heavy fines is unjust, fatal to improvement, checking all reform, and giving a charter to the errors of our forefathers ; if it could be abolished, Rookeries would decrease. But suppose the landlord to manage his own property ; the collection of rents from many of the tenants of these Rookeries would be difficult, tiresome, and from their very number expensive. It would not sound well to hear that some man of influence had distrained upon one of these hewers of wood and drawers of water ; the necessary communication between landlord and tenant would be next to impossible, — in short, without tasking the imagination, we can readily suppose some method of obviating these impediments would be invented. And most injurious has that system been, which, to save trouble, litigation, and notoriety, has been put in the stead of the natural relation between the lessor and the lessee, which has broken a bond honourable to the one, invaluable to the other. As things are now, we have a large class of Middle-men even in the mildest form the case admits of; in many instances, the houses are let out, and under-let again and again, so that there are several links between the owner and the occupier—the latter perhaps not knowing the name of the former. No one supposes that a middle-man sees any abstract beauty in long rows of dingy houses, or that there is anything peculiarly elevating in the occupation of letting lodgings. The man who by heaping manure upon land doubles his produce, may have at the same time food for thought; he may bring chemistry to bear upon his art if he be learned in Liebig, and every acre bear an increased crop; nevertheless, few will be hardy enough to argue that love of Science is kept alive, although a love of Gain may be pampered by quartering the greatest number of human beings within a given area, so that every square foot should yield an increased rental.

There is, then, the strong motive of gain in these transactions! The middle-man supposes that he shall be more than indemnified for his trouble by subdividing these tenements into floors, or the floors into single rooms; and if such an occupation be lucrative, competition will increase in the same ratio; there will be several middle-men in the field whenever a Rookery is to be let, the ground landlord will have no difficulty in disposing of his houses. The only questions with him are, who is the highest or the most solvent bidder; this very competition puts money into his pocket. From what source, then must the middle-man, who ultimately obtains the lease, be indemnified for the high price he has paid? He must wring it from the hapless poor who tenant the apartments which he lets out! they are the real victims. Thus, a carpenter will be a candidate

for a number of houses which are to be let; these
houses will be very much out of repair, and the landlord
unwilling to lay out the money to make them tenantable;
the carpenter considers that, at a very small expense,
he can render them habitable; he takes the property on
a repairing lease, and repays himself by the rent he
exacts. Or suppose, as is often the case, that the first
middle-man, the actual tenant, dislikes the trouble of
collecting rents, he underlets these tenements to middle-
man No. 2, as we will call him for the sake of distinction.
No. 2 is himself a working man, more thrifty, more
cunning, than his brethren,—he has gained the ear of
No. 1,—is in some degree connected with him, pleads
plausibly in some way or other, induces No. 1 to give
him what we will call an under-lease. But who is No.
2 ? One who has been for some years the victim of the
system he is now about to administer; on whom at
length the conviction has flashed that he has been
egregiously silly to pay rent, where he might not only
live rent free, but put something into his pockets besides.
He enters upon his new trade, he finds that the interests
of the tenants have been habitually set aside. You can
scarcely expect this man, with the recollection of his
wrongs—the force of custom strong upon him, with his
imperfect education, with that absence of religious or
moral restraint too, which is so fearful among the working classes—you can scarcely expect him to be more conscientious or more feeling than his brethren. He will
grind others as he has been ground, prey upon his

species as he was preyed upon; their loss will be his
gain; he will indemnify himself at the expense of others
for years of oppression. He often does this unconsciously
—as by mere force of habit, because others do it, because
it is the rule; he is not by nature an unkind man; for,
after all, the English are a generous people, not unsym-
pathising, but adopting the creed which prevails; not
reasoning about it, well nigh unconscious, and quite
forgetful that it is wrong, looking at it as a trade, considering his gains payment for his trouble—only doing
to others what they would not scruple to do to him.

Yet this man wields a fearful power: he can turn out
his tenants at a few days' notice, his caprice or his
resentment guiding him; he can prevent them from
obtaining other lodgings, for the next landlord will
come to him for their character. This man wields a
power which the best and wisest might shrink from
exercising, which is environed with difficulties, so that
many a conscientious man would dread it, lest he should
be betrayed into injustice or oppression. And this, our
Middle-man, has been the victim, though now to be the
victimiser. Think what a catechism he has imbibed—
under what a system he has been trained! Does not the
heart insensibly harden, as we read of persons long
immured in prisons, who have at length lost the sympathies of their kind? Does not some such process go on
within one thus oppressed?—His nature is transformed;
just as men, looking at vice for a long time, by degrees
forget it is hideous, begin to sympathise with it, so that

it becomes, at first, bearable, then pleasing, at last, in-
dispensable; as habit, so metaphysicians tell us, is that
facility which the mind acquires in all its exertions, in
consequence of practice. Suppose a man of indolent
habits, to become a Middle-man — one fond of low
pleasures and debauchery; this occupation furnishes an
excuse for the neglect of his business, whilst, because other
aids are withdrawn, he is thrown back upon the gains to
be obtained by sub-division of the property he controls.
If thus to sub-let be a source of profit, is not this of
itself an argument against the system? Is not the poor
man *the* victim? Does it not show that, if men would
reflect, they might lodge the poor both better and more
cheaply than at present? Should the *tenant* be called
on to pay for each separate link between the landlord
and himself? Just examine this system :—take a house
which, because of its size, its dilapidated condition, its
want of a yard behind, and the scarcity of its accommo-
dations, would be dear at £.25 a-year; by this system its
first tenant pays somewhat more than £.30 and a per
centage of taxation;—this house contains ten rooms,
these are let out at an average of four shillings each
per week, in other words £.104 a-year; but deduct
from this bad debts, which may be supposed to be
many,—take the general average, at which these are calculated, at 25 per cent., there will still be a surplus of
about £.78. Is not this monstrous, when you consider
the class of society from whom, and from whose ill-paid
and precarious labour, these rents are levied? Is it not

fearful ? Shoemakers and tailors, perhaps, who, during
the season, earn good wages; yet who have an interreg-
num of five months in the year, during which trade is
almost at a stand still.

Take an instance of the evil which has come under
the writer's observation during the last few days. Some
years since a journeyman shoemaker came to London ;
he got work, but it was precarious ; he was a cunning
man, and was soon employed by an unhallowed fraternity,
as what is called, in cant terms, a " smasher," or utterer
of base coin; his trade of shoemaker, at which he continued to work, was a good cloak; he amassed a little
money; from tenant he became middle-man of the house
in which he lives, he was fond of drinking, and disliked
work; his new " trade" was more profitable, less tiresome,
still he was not satisfied ; he joined with this occupation, the task of collecting rents. He is now broker and
middle-man, his original calling is neglected, and he
lives upon exaction. Whilst his tenants are able to pay
he exacts a heavy per centage ; when they are in arrear,
and their goods seized, he plies his trade and swells his
gains.

Take another instance. A decent old couple occupy
two rooms on a first floor in a low and dirty street,
where the sewerage is extremely bad, and where there
were several cases, (two fatal,) of Cholera during the
prevalence of the epidemic. The old man had lived in a
family of rank, and but for the rascality of trustees,
would have had a handsome competence, instead of a bare

annuity. Like many of the domestics of the nobility, he has acquired a courtesy of manner and regard for cleanliness and comfort, and thus he is desirous to rent two rooms instead of the usual single apartment. For these two rooms he pays 8*s*. a week, more than £.20 a year—in the country, he might get a pretty cottage and garden for the same sum. The person who lives under him, and has female lodgers, pays the same for the same accommodation. The kitchen is let out, and the third floor, with a workshop at the back, to separate tenants; the house is a small one. In the neigbourhood of St. Pancras, houses occupied by professional men are often let for £.45 per annum; they have ten rooms, and all modern comforts about them. These two individuals whom we have named, pay nearly as much for scarcely half a small house in a bad situation.

We do not find the evils of middle-manship peculiar to our country or our times, for it is instructive to call to mind that some of the great social disturbances of ancient Rome may be traced to the same source: the patricians having obtained large grants of conquered lands, rather than be at the trouble to cultivate them, leased them out to their clients or dependents, who again wrung a large revenue from the labours of those who really tilled the soil; these men were scantily paid—were always in debt; the client could enforce payment by the harshest punishments, and hence the famous assemblage of the people at the Mons Sacer—the seditions of the Gracchi—and many other tumults which shook the State.

Much remains to be said in explanation. We admit
that the wages of the tenants are precarious, their employment fluctuating; must not then the losses of the
Middle-man be greater than we have allowed ? It may
be very well to say that men would not be so anxious
to get leases if they were not lucrative; and the gains
be much less than we have supposed, though quite
sufficient to tempt cupidity. In answer to this, we can
only say the Middle-man has his remedies, and they are
many. He ejects the insolvent; yet this insolvent must
be lodged, and therefore goes to some other locality;
before he can get a room he must pass an ordeal,—
Where did he come from ? Why did he leave his last
quarters ? Can he get a recommendation from his last
landlord ? Can he show any resources wherewith to pay
his rent ? Is he a decent and orderly person ? If he
has children the difficulty is increased, for Middle-men
have a Malthusian horror of children, though, in most
cases, they are the adjuncts of the poor.

Are not these so many checks upon the poor, all
tending to make them careful in their payments ?
But suppose all these terrors fail, there is a very
Cerberus in the background. It would seem to be
enough that the tenant is at the mercy of one who was
once a tenant himself, and who knew well a tenant's
wants, the diseases to which that body is subject, their
several little lets and hindrances,—the tricks and cus-
toms,—in short, that one, a member of a body corporate,

should understand the wants of his own corporation. There is in store for the refractory, a minister of no ordinary wrath—*The* BROKER!

You will urge that, in rooms scantily furnished, there is little for him to seize. Should the poor man, on whom the distress is levied, get free from his embarrassments, he cannot repurchase even that little, except at double or treble the price which has been put upon it by him who seizes. Bedsteads and bedding are costly things too, even to the poor. Again you will say,—Is not the broker obliged to submit the goods seized to auction— to give an account of their sale? Is he not precluded from bidding himself? We believe the law runs thus : but how often, we would ask you, is this law obeyed, which may be so easily evaded? Where the poor man so often forbears further inquiry, — where this inquiry may be so easily eluded, — where recourse is so seldom had to the magistrate; and where, even with the best intentions, it is so difficult for the magistrate to unravel the complications of the affair; where magistrates undoubtedly are favourable to the poor, yet are checked and hindered by laws in which there are so many loopholes?

We need scarce allude to the case of Jones so recently reported in *The Times*, and which created so much sympathy; and that ready instrument of iniquity, the Palace Court, which, now that our English spirit of fair play is roused, has fallen to the ground, as most obstacles are wont to do before the excited mettle of our countrymen.

How easy it is for the broker to swell his expenses—

how difficult to tax his bill—even when inquiry is made; and too often the recklessness or ignorance of the tenant forbid it.

An execution is put into a dwelling—a broker's man quartered in the premises, as the first step, at five shillings a day, with certain attendant expenses—an endeavour is made, for a time at least, by the tenant to compromise, to borrow the money, or otherwise to meet the demand. It is futile. The furniture is then seized, the rent paid by its sale, whether that be nominal or real ; the expenses of the process swallow up the surplus. We said that the broker is forbidden by law to buy the goods upon which he distrained—but ask if it ever happened that the broker was not at the same time a dealer in furniture —kept a shop for second-hand goods, so that his trade of broker was only a sort of subsidiary adjunct to his real occupation ? Is not the connection obvious between the goods seized and the goods exposed in the shop ? Suppose a *bonâ fide* sale to take place—and we cannot doubt that such is commonly the case—how easy it is to get a second party to bid for these goods, and then to hand them over again to the broker.

There are not wanting kind Middle-men—there are not wanting, on the other hand, refractory tenants, whom it is difficult to eject, even when the rent owing by them is forgiven upon the stipulation that they leave the house. It would be wrong to represent the injury as being all on one side ; no doubt there must be remedies to check dishonesty, a fair means of redress for those who seek it fairly, the landlord must be protected as well as the

tenant, and moonlight flittings are not so obsolete that
we can dispense with protection. Tenants here and
there will set landlords at defiance, and cling to the fancied
security of some unwritten law. Still, we must not take
refuge in these individual cases. We have shown what
powers a broker has—how easily he may abuse them,
what temptation he has to do so—and these are fearful
engines in the hands of a vindictive, an angry, or a
covetous man—fearful stimulants to those who would
uphold the system we decry.

Many of these brokers, at best, are harpies who prey
upon legalised food. A Christian would loathe such
a trade—would shrink from it in disgust. It must demoralise those who exercise it, deaden their sensibilities,
and sear their hearts. Vultures of the body social
preying upon ruin, fattening on the carcasses of nobler
beings, gorged by the distresses of their brethren, they
live and thrive amidst scenes of sorrow which would
poison another man's existence—seize the bed upon which
consumption reposes—and, as the writer of this paper
knows, the agonies of childbirth have been enhanced by
the bare boards upon which the patient lay, as she
brought her offspring into the world.

The middle-man and the broker are common to all
Rookeries; each district has its peculiar evils. This
will be evident from what follows.

We mentioned crimps as among the different harpies
who are let loose upon the sailor when he comes home

from a long voyage; and, when describing the district
bounded by Shadwell and the Thames, stated that it
was much infested with these nuisances. We promised
to state, at length, what crimps were. Nominally, they
are keepers of lodging-houses where the sailors live :
really, they make their professed trade a pretext for
plunder. When a ship, coming up the river, has got
as far as Gravesend, it is boarded by these lodging-
house keepers, each of whom has three or four satellites,
who have have come down from London in a boat; they
directly commence bidding for lodgers among the sailors,
much in the same way as touters do when you arrive in
a foreign port from England. They will go up to a
sailor and say, "Where are you going to lodge ?" If
he is not already engaged, they will persuade him to go
to their lodgings. Thus each crimp will get five or six
sailors, of whose luggage he will possess himself and take
it with him into the boat; they will then bring their victims
with them to London. It is generally understood that
sailors are not paid upon landing;—their wages have
accumulated during the voyage, and thus, within a
fortnight of the arrival of the vessel, a considerable sum
due is paid to their crew by the owners of the vessel;
the crimps speculate upon this. No sooner has the
sailor seen his luggage, as he would call it stowed away,
than he feels thirsty,—wants to borrow money,—applies
to his landlord for a loan upon the strength of the sum
to be received within a few days. Sometimes, from
various circumstances, the crimp himself is not able to

OF LONDON. 187

supply the wants of his tenant; he at once, therefore, resorts to a Jew, tells him of the sailors he has been able to ensnare, and borrows a sum in proportion to the demands of the lodgers he has obtained. Part of this sum is lent out to the sailor, who, as a matter of course, spends it in a public-house. When he has become intoxicated, he borrows more, or perhaps buys half a gallon of spirits of the crimp. All these sums are duly entered to the sailor's account; large interest is charged on the sum borrowed, sometimes 5s. in the pound; false entries are the rule, a quart of spirits is often entered as a gallon,—a loan of 5s. represented as 10s. or even more. Should the sailor remonstrate, the answer is ready,—"You were " intoxicated when the money was borrowed."

Connected with these crimps are low prostitutes; a drunken sailor has often been robbed of all that he has, perhaps several pounds, and then turned out with only a few rags on him. In the days when so many victims disappeared by burking, crimps' houses were more than suspected, and many a poor sailor was enticed into these dens, and never heard of again. Slopsellers are frequently leagued with crimps, Jews especially. Articles of clothing of the very worst description are furnished to the sailors at a price which the very best cloth they could purchase would hardly justify. The fortnight during which the sailor has been living on credit elapses—he is to receive his wages. He goes to the ship-owner's office—the crimp meanwhile has watched him narrowly—he knows to a fraction what his debtor will receive. Sometimes, under the guise of a friend of the sailor, he enters the office with him, but some ship-owners will not permit this : he besieges the entrance, or hangs about the street in which the house of business is situated. When the sailor has received his money, his landlord and he adjourn to a public-house and call for a private room. The public-houses in this district are not models of well-regulated establishments ; so that the score is paid, they are not very particular, not bound to inquire too closely into the character of those who frequent them. Thus the conference between the sailor and his creditor is not likely to be interrupted. The bill is produced. Suppose the sailor has received £.12 as wages, and the bill to be paid, much to his dismay, has unconsciously swelled to £.8,—much is put down to money lent when he was intoxicated, much to spirits which it is impossible he could consume, much to clothes he never bought, or wore. Suppose he agrees to the demand, the crimp will even then try to swell the bill till he has not left above a pound to the share of his victim. Should the sailor turn restive, he is coaxed, or threatened, sometimes even set upon by the crimp and his deputy, who obtain by violence what they cannot get otherwise. It will be said, now, at least, after going through such a purgatory, the sailor is free. Far from it ; not even when reduced to his last shilling, does he cease to be an object of gain to these harpies. His money spent, he must go to sea again. He is driven to the docks, where he obtains a berth in a ship, but he

wants an outfit. Again, then, he has recourse to a Jew,
or a crimp. You will ask what security the sailor can
give? He draws a sort of promissory bill on his new
employers, called an advance note : for this the Jew
advances about half, or more, of the value, according to
the bargain made. It is true, that the money-lender, in
this instance, runs some risk. The sailor may leave his
vessel at Gravesend, and then, of course, the note of
advance is lost ; but if he does not escape, the following
process takes place. When the ship is fairly clear of the
Land's End, the pilot quits it ; just before he leaves,
the ship's company is mustered, their names are taken,
and the list thus made is sent up to London ; the money-
lender then knows that his advance is secure. Within a
month, he presents the bill, which is paid as a matter of
course. He runs some risk, and there is some delay,
—the money-lender amply indemnifies himself for this,
exacting a terrible per centage for the accommodation
afforded to his victim. It will naturally occur to us,
that even sailors, at times, will tax exorbitant bills,—
many of them may be bad accountants, many of them
imposed on when intoxicated, many threatened into
compliance ; but sailors are proverbially a bold and
hardy race. Suppose the charges made are so barefaced
that even these thoughtless beings resist it, there is still
a remedy for the extortioner. There is a clique of low
attornies, probably men who are called hedge-lawyers in
the country,—some have certificates, some have not ; by
long practice and native cunning, they entangle their

victims in the meshes of their profession, and manage, by
a show of law, to obtain the greater part of the iniquitous
charge for their infamous clients.   They who escape the
toils set for them are the exceptions; and the crimps
make so good a harvest, that they can afford to lose in a
solitary instance.   The humanity of a British public
is at length slowly beginning to awaken, and, in the
establishment of Sailors' Homes, to provide a few receptacles for the large class of men, to whose services this
Empire owes so much of its blessings and it greatness.

Having endeavoured to sketch the crimp, we should
not be justified in omitting some notice of the tally-man,
whose gains must be obtained at the expense of the
working classes, and who would only encounter the
risks he runs by making the solvent members of the
community pay for the deficiencies of the less scrupulous.
The tally-man, then, is the London traveller of some
large linen draper, who obtains orders for the house to
which he belongs, and, in some instances, collects the
money due to his master.   A few houses in this and
other trades keep men whose only duty it is to get orders.
These men come into some neighbourhood inhabited by
the working classes, ascertain the character of a certain
number of the inhabitants, and then obtain orders from
those who can be depended on.   It will be asked how
the information is procured?   In many ways ; the Middle-
men can generally give it : they know who pays most
regularly ; can tell whether a workman is sober, honest,

careful, solvent; they can inform the inquirer how long the person, to be trusted, has lived in his present residence, and this is a very fair criterion, because it shows that his payments have not been very irregular, and that he is to be depended upon. Such information may be, to a certain extent, paid for,—they who want and they who give it adjourn to a public house, where the tally-man treats his informant, and soon, directly or indirectly, draws from him all that is necessary to be known. The characters of those who have long resided in a neighbourhood are soon discovered ; and even should a working man with his family leave one parish, he is soon tracked to another ; if he be in regular employ, he cannot live at any great distance from the shop where he obtains his work ; if he have a family, he cannot suddenly transport them to a country town—if he should do so at all, timely notice is sure to be given of his intended removal, the Middle-man will generally take care of that, the removal will be talked of, and it will get wind in some way. The tally-man, thus secured against loss, then calls at a certain number of rooms in a particular house, at a certain number of houses in a particular street ; sometimes he merely takes orders for certain articles of dress, more frequently he carries a pack upon his back which he opens, and the contents of which he displays in the different rooms : the vanity and love of dress in his female customers are soon kindled. A gaudy shawl, a flaunting silk dress are not without their charms—but then the money is not forthcoming ;

he begs them not to distress themselves about that, he will give credit,—he will take weekly payments. Few of us can resist such a temptation as this ; present possession, distant payment, are powerful charms to conjure with : the shawl is obtained ; it is hinted that, without the dress to match, the general effect will be spoilt—the dress is added, and a sum is set down to the unlucky customer, which amply repays the credit given. Generally one-third of the real value of the articles is added, nominally as the proper price, really, as the interest for time and risk. Sometimes these tally-men have with them pieces of cloth, and when the unconscious husband returns home at night, he finds a new pair of trowsers awaiting him, the cloth of which has been obtained by the same means as the dress, and an old pair of trowsers has been the pattern by which the new have been made. The tally-man departs ; but regularly, as each week opens, is he seen with the demand for the instalment due ; if it is not ready, he must be propitiated with a new order,—if the money be forthcoming, an exorbitant rate of interest is obtained for the accommodation.

The following case came under the writer's notice last summer. A working man and his wife were residing in a street filled with lodging-houses. The working man was industrious, and there is reason to believe, regular in his payments ; he had married a widow, whose only son was a sailor : the sailor returned, generally after a year's absence, about Midsummer. On this occasion, he remained longer at home than usual, having determined to marry a young girl in the neighbourhood. Marriages with sailors are great events—at least, so thought the young man and his mother; and they were of opinion that the forthcoming marriage should not be celebrated without a flourish of trumpets. The mother, though no longer young, retained much of the vanity of youth; recourse was had to the tally-man, and a shawl, in which was a mixture of colours which might have pleased the Great Mogul, and a dress to correspond, were carefully selected. The poor woman had long been in a precarious state of health when, unknown to her husband, these things were procured: before the wedding took place, she died. The young couple waited ten days, and then were married. The father-in-law of the bridegroom returned home; the bill for the funeral of his deceased wife awaited him; this he provided for by obtaining the money from a loan society, and thought that his expenses were at an end. What was his surprise when, a few days afterwards, he was informed by the tally-man of the debt contracted and the demand awaiting him. The shawl and dress were useless, what should he do with them? He exchanged them, at great disadvantage, for some clothes which he wanted himself, and then sat down to work out the debt as well as he could, satisfied that, for many months to come, his neck would be under the yoke.

The tally-man system is not confined to London or

large towns. A relative of the author assured him it
was one of the greatest pests of agricultural districts.
When this gentleman paid his wages weekly to his
labourers, the person, through whom the money was sent
to the men, complained that he could never get even a
shilling in change; that when the Saturday night came
round, the money of the labourer was always spent, and
yet sometimes the man had sold a pig, or taken some
garden-stuff to market, or, in harvest-time, earned higher
wages than usual. The gentleman asked how it happened, that men receiving 10s. a-week all the year
round, and having a cottage and garden, should be so
poverty-stricken? The answer was, they were in debt to
the tally-men. He then recollected that he had observed
some very pretty crockery-ware in his own lodge, on one
occasion, and had remarked the taste displayed in it.
Upon inquiry, he found that it was obtained from the tally-
man, and still unpaid for; that his labourers had been
tempted — almost driven, by the importunity of this
itinerant vendor, to purchase goods, and then pestered
and hunted for months to pay the exorbitant charge
made. He directly ordered that these harpies should
henceforth be prevented from setting foot within his
gates, and that any labourer from that time dealing with
them, should be discharged.

The agents for houses are called "barkers:" it is supposed that they have a certain per centage upon orders
received. Sometimes, when they sell tea, or other

articles of food, it is conjectured that they give credit
on their own risk, much in the same kind of way as is
done in country places, where the grocery cart comes
round once a week. The agents are sometimes furnished
with printed bills, describing the articles sold, with the
prices affixed. When the goods sold are not paid for
within a given time, a summons is served on the
defaulter. The tally system is also carried on by coal
merchants at the beginning of winter. One man assured
us that thus he was charged 5s. per ton more than the
market price of the best, for very inferior coals. One of
those who have supplied us at different times with valuable information assured the author, that credit given by
tally-men to married is always refused to single women,
because there is no husband who can be answerable for
the debt. He says there is only one remedy, and that is,
no recovery of the debt without the husband's promissory note. He thinks that tally-men form a committee
amongst themselves; for when he was in their power, all
except his creditor seemed to shun his house; when the
debt was paid, he was immediately beset.

In this sketch, we have referred to loan societies.
The working classes often require loans; this is not to
be wondered at when men of large fortune are frequently
much pressed for want of ready money. If a working
man marries, he must furnish the single room in which
he lives; he can scarcely do this, even at the cheapest rate,

for less than five pounds, and he will want a new suit of clothes ; or, suppose his wife confined, he will incur a considerable expense. The death of any of his household will again require a large outlay—for, much to the credit of the very poorest be it spoken, they do not like, they cannot bear that their relatives should be buried at the parish expense, the workhouse coffin, and the paid mourners seem to insult the friend they have lost. They go then to the undertaker—still, he must be paid, or have the best guarantee for payment. What shall the bereaved husband do in this extremity ? He has recourse to the loan society. He gets some one to be security for him, and obtains the necessary sum. You will naturally ask, upon what terms ? He must come provided with a security, obtain a form of application, and return it properly filled up. The solvency of his surety is then inquired into, the candidate for the loan having paid a preliminary fee of two shillings ; which, even should he be unsuccessful in his application, is not returned to him ; it is supposed that trouble incurred in the inquiry, and the form which is supplied are worth the sum paid. For the sum thus borrowed, the debtor is required to pay five per cent., the term for which it is borrowed being, in no case, more than one year ; the interest is at once and on the spot deducted for the whole period over which the loan extends ; this having been done, the principal is to be paid off (supposing for instance, £.5 obtained) at the rate of 2s. a-week, if for twelve months ;

—3*s*. a-week, if for nine months;—and 4*s*. a-week, if the loan is for six months. Persons who omit any weekly payment, are fined a half-penny on each shilling. Should a week pass, the surety is immediately written to, and if the whole amount due, or such part as the directors think proper is not paid, proceedings are taken. If the weekly payment be not made on the day and at the hour specified, the secretary writes a letter to the defaulter, for which, a charge of 4*d*. is made ; and, should the security refuse to pay the amount borrowed by his friend when called for, in case of default, he will not be accepted as surety in any future loan. If a borrower should remove from the place where he lived when the loan is granted, and omit to send notice to the secretary, he is fined one shilling. As each weekly payment is made, 2*d*. is charged under the head of rent of office—thus, if a man, borrow £.5 and pay the debt off in the course of a year in addition to the interest, he will also be called on for 8*s*. 8*d*. ; a charge in every way most unfair.

Some of the rules laid down, are perhaps necessary for the security of the society ; but no one will contend that this applies to all. What can be more unjust or even contrary to law, than to require the payment of interest before it is due ? What would a borrower say—if when a sum of money was advanced on property, or even when remittances were obtained on a bond, the mortgagee, or the lender at once deducted a year's interest? again, the sum of 2*s*. paid at the onset, is unjust. We subjoin a scale of charges framed by the society, from whom we have taken it :—

SCALE OF INTEREST AND RE-PAYMENTS PER WEEK.			
LOAN OF	FOR SIX MONTHS.	NINE MONTHS.	TWELVE MONTHS.
	s. d.	*s. d.*	*s. d.*
£.5,	Interest . . 2 6 Re-payments 4 0 per Week, and 2*d.* per Week for Rent of Office, Se- cretary's Salary, &c.	Interest . . 3 9 Re-payments 3 0 per Week, and 2*d.* per Week for Rent of Office, Se- cretary's Salary, &c.	Interest . . 5 0 Re-payments 2 0 per Week, and 2*d.* per Week for Rent of Office, Se- cretary's Salary, &c.
£.10,	Interest . . 5 0 Re-payments 8 0 Rent, &c. . 0 2	Interest . . 7 6 Re-payments 6 0 Rent, &c. . 0 2	Interest . . 10 0 Re-payments 4 0 Rent, &c. . 0 2
£.15,	Interest . . 7 6 Re-payments 12 0 Rent, &c. . 0 2	Interest . . 11 3 Re-payments 9 0 Rent, &c. . 0 2	Interest . . 15 0 Re-payments 6 0 Rent, &c. . 0 2
£.20,	Interest . . 10 0 Re-payments 16 0 Rent, &c. . 0 4	Interest . . 15 0 Re-payments 12 0 Rent, &c. . 0 4	Interest . . 20 0 Re-payments 8 0 Rent, &c. . 0 4
£.25,	Interest . . 12 6 Re-payments 20 0 Rent, &c. . 0 5	Interest . . 18 9 Re-payments 15 0 Rent, &c. . 0 5	Interest . . 25 0 Re-payments 10 0 Rent, &c. . 0 5
£.30,	Interest . . 15 0 Re-payments 24 0 Rent, &c. . 0 6	Interest . . 22 6 Re-payments 18 0 Rent, &c. . 0 6	Interest . . 30 0 Re-payments 12 0 Rent, &c. . 0 6

These instances will show the price an unfortunate, or unthrifty man has to pay for a trifling accommodation, and the iron terms by which he is fettered.

The working classes are beset with other annoyances. Porter is the common beverage with them, just as *vin ordinaire* is in France; but it is retailed to them at a price too small to allow of it being fit for drinking.

This porter is a compound. Suppose it comes from the brewers in a proper state, it is compounded anew before it reaches the customers. With the porter, working men tell you, is mixed what they call *dash;* some infusion, whether liquorice or something else, is poured into it, and thus deteriorates the liquor of many of the public houses, and some even of what are called the gin palaces. Large brewers' firms are the real possessors ; the landlord is only a *locum tenens* during the pleasure of his masters. Whether those who drink it be correct or not respecting the ingredients of the porter, there is no doubt that it is not what it ought to be and might be, perhaps would be, if free trade extended to the cheaper French wines. As meat is a luxury which many families only taste once or twice a week, they buy it in small quantities, and thus are obliged to take what they call odds and ends, because they cannot afford to buy a joint. And they deal at small shops for grocery— shops where sugar, starch, grocery, soap, bacon, butter, &c., are sold ; the tea, coffee, and sugar procured there are notoriously of the worst quality, because it is not worth while, in large shops, to sell less than a pound of tea, and the working classes buy it often in ounces.

Against these and many other annoyances, a great cry is often raised, and the interference of the Legislature is demanded. It is difficult to convince men badly educated, that too much interference on the part of our law-makers would be injurious, and that the remedy lies nearer home ; but until a better system of education has taught men when and how to combine, and for what purposes, it is useless to expect an adequate remedy. Otherwise, a combination which bound men only to deal at shops where a genuine article was sold, and to buy large pieces of meat by putting into one fund the earnings of two or three families, would seem a most obvious cure for the evil complained of.

It will be said that the evils we have described belong more properly to artisans than to the inhabitants of Rookeries. It would be nearer the truth to say that they suffer most by them, as the latter are, in a great degree, rendered callous; but as even they must eat, drink, and be clothed, and as some of them at times obtain loans, it cannot be affirmed that they are exempt from the injuries we have described.

Another evil still remains, on which we would say a few words, and that is the present system of leasing. In some cases, property is practically alienated, as we have before stated, for many years, in consequence of the granting of a long lease, in which there is no clause restraining the tenants from applying the houses let, or the ground built on, to improper purposes. A bad use may be made of property under any circumstances; yet, when this takes place in the case of a short lease, the remedy is at hand: the lease is not renewed, and the evil is at an end. This very circumstance may be held in *terrorem* over the heads of those who would misapply the powers with which a lease invests them. These are not the only objectionable sort of leases: corporations possess property,—especially ecclesiastical corporations, where the following rule prevails,—when a lease has terminated, it is not renewed at an annual payment commensurate with the value of the land or houses ; a small rent is substituted, and a large fine, in ready money, paid down for this privilege, or rather robbery of the next generation. This prevails, or rather did prevail extensively in the property of cathedral chapters. A clergyman was appointed to a stall at fifty years of age for instance, and property belonging to his stall fell in to the amount of £.500 a year ; the lease was not renewed at this annual payment, but at £.200 a year, and then a sum of £.2000 was paid at the same time. If the figures here given are not correct, still they will be accurate enough to give us a notion of the system pursued. With such transactions, the famous Ecclesiastical Commission has, to a great extent, done away ; but not in all cases. We believe the Chapter of Westminster is an exception, the number of canons there has been reduced, and their salaries diminished ; and even there the mode of payment adopted, differs from that generally in use in other chapters. The Dean and Chapter of Westminster did not and do not, we believe, receive a fixed stipend as at St. Paul's ; only a proportion of the income of the chapter property, say a sixth or a tenth each, as the case may be. They then are still interested in the old system of fines; and we believe we are correct in stating, that this has not been done away with. Thus they will, at times, receive a large fine, which increases

the income of a particular year at the expense of suc-
ceeding years, and, consequently, are as much exposed
to the temptation of renewing leases without inquiring
into the manner in which the lease was used, as their
forefathers. We should be glad to find that we were
mistaken in supposing the old plan still to be in operation ; there is, however, room to believe it still remains
unchanged.

The present Dean and Chapter have exerted themselves, in conjunction with the Westminster Improvement Commissioners, to get rid of several abominations
which disgrace the neighbourhood of the Abbey. The
new Victoria Street has thus nearly obliterated the land-
marks of the famous Almonry ; yet a description of the
purposes to which part of that property was converted,
may bear us out in attributing the growth of Rookeries,
and the spread of vice and crime, to long leases, or the
renewal of leases with a fine.

It was affirmed by one who well knew what he said,
that, in 1848, there were in the Almonry alone twenty-
four brothels ; all these houses were then the property
of the Dean and Chapter ; most of them had been so for
many years. The oldest inhabitants tell you their
fathers represented the district to have been in the same
condition as far as their memory extended, or as far
as any traditionary account went back. In Orchard
Street district, abutting on the Almonry, there were
thirty brothels. In the same district, gangs of thieves
and coiners resided, in fraternities of three, five, ten, or

twenty; most of them living unmarried with women, and having families of children, breeding up for prostitution and roguery.

There were a series of courts leading from Pye Street to this district, one within the other, approached from Pye Street, through a narrow archway; these were filled with coiners and thieves; at the back of these, opening upon the Almonry, was a small outlet. On one occasion a surgeon was sent for, to visit a dying thief, and had some difficulty in getting into the court; for the entrance, *mirabile dictu*, was blocked up by a donkey with panniers, which were so large, that with the utmost difficulty was the animal thrust into the confined space which served as an entrance into the court. This device was used to impede the police, who were expected to visit the court in quest of a thief. Time was thus given for his escape through the outlet at the back, while they removed the impediment. This property, if not belonging to the Almonry, runs in its immediate neighbourhood. The condition of the district at large is the best protest against renewals of leases on the terms described above.

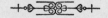

Chapter XII.

We may not be able to scare away these evils for ever; we may mitigate them, we may provide against their frequent recurrence! we may narrow the circle in which they can occur; we may do away with middlemen — and there are few, we believe, who pretend to the rank of gentlemen or the dignity of the Christian, who as landlords or agents would evoke the law under circumstances such as we have stated, or sanction the *abuse* of enactments already too severe. The broker, confined within proper limits by statutes which were founded upon present experience, would have less temptation to overleap his bounds, and his occupation would languish when he was called in only in cases of confirmed obstinacy or reckless frauds. They who used their power would use it wisely, because an act of cruelty would recoil with a force proportioned to the station of him who perpetrated it.

We do not anticipate, under a better system, a Saturnian age; but let us not rest upon that stronghold of indolence, that, because we cannot do all we wished, we must fold our arms. There are several degrees between the serf of Russia and the servant of England, though both, perhaps, be capable of improvement.

And here we shall be pressed again by the assertion, that the working classes are prone to drunkenness—that if they can find money for this purpose, they could find better lodgings. Comparisons will be instituted between the comparatively sober character of the French and ourselves—Alison the historian be quoted, to show that the Northern nations are more prone to intoxication than those of the South. It will be said to be the fault of our unmercurial climate, rather than owing to social neglect. Strange, this—that thirty years ago the vice was prevalent among all classes of society, and is now banished from only the lowest. Does that prove that climate is in fault ? Do you wonder, as we said before, that the hard-worked mechanic escapes from the only room where he and all his family eat, drink, and sleep, to the public-house ? when, either as a refuge from domestic disagreeables, or because he can enjoy the society of his own sex there : the rich and powerful joins the club, and spends there much of his time.

Suppose we allow, for the sake of argument, that drunkenness is at the root of these social evils, that this places the working classes at the mercy of middle-men; to this refer bad ventilation, unhealthy drains, want of water, crowded rooms, and the like. Admit this monstrous fallacy,—yet Father Matthew has laboured long and well,—many are his disciples, many who never touch intoxicating liquors—some from constitution or habit

averse to them, some from prudence, some from religious
feeling.   Is there such a marked social difference, as
confessedly there is a moral one, between the drunkard
and teatotaller ? the lodgings of the one doubtless are
more cleanly than those of the other, yet not more spacious, the supply of water not more copious ?   The sober
man must wait the issue of a long course of prosperous
industry, must change his grade in society before he
changes his social condition.   Grant that all these evils
are the offspring of drunkenness ; yet why is he who is
exempt from the sin, not exempt from the effects of it,
why does he suffer for the vices of others ?

Has any attempt been made, in connection with better
lodgings, to elevate the tastes, and open sources of in-
tellectual amusement to the working man—for recollect
Mechanics' Institutes are calculated for the *tradesman*,
not the *mechanic* ? You cannot stroll through the Champs
Élysées in Paris, in the evening, without remarking groups
collected to see some mountebanks perform a vaudeville ;
bands playing, fountains dancing in the setting sun,
picturesque cafés, lend an interest to the scene.   At the
same hour in England, walk down the Blackfriars Road,
and before dingy brick houses, at the side of a dusty
road, are artisans besotting themselves with beer ;—which
is the more innocent amusement, the Frenchman's or
ours ?

The tenants of the Rookeries are bowed down by
heavy toil ; work too often gluts the market, too often
deserts it.   During the season, a Court Ball will set at

work many thousand hands, if you consider the division of labour in the making of a single shoe; and very thankful are the artisans for these opportunities; yet how many nights as well as days are devoted to work ? This perhaps could not be entirely avoided. George IV. was not a model of moral purity, nevertheless, many workmen bless his memory for the impetus he gave to trade. It is of very great moment to the workman, that he should get work on any conditions; it is the duty of the employer to render the task as easy as possible, and masters are little careful to save trouble. Sunday, instead of being given to rest and devotion, is the scene of labour. Persons leaving London, from pure thoughtlessness never give an order till the last week before they quit town ; how many of their fellow creatures are deprived of their night's rest that it may be executed !

Yet men so spent by continued labour should have opportunities of relaxation, not merely parks, but places where they can play cricket, or any other manly national amusement. There should be cheap libraries for the studious, and the seven months during which trade is slack in town would give time for study, and beguile many an hour spent in questionable relaxation.

Some one will say we are straying from our subject. We might, perhaps, in this place, speak a word about the necessities of the poor during the seasons when work is slack; then, it is well known, recourse is had to the Pawnbrokers. We do not accuse these tradesmen of injustice; the interest they may levy is fixed at twenty per cent. ; at first sight this appears enormous, but then many of the articles are perishable, they suffer much by fraud ; and, on particular occasions, Saturday night for instance, such is the rush to the Pawnbrokers, that they are particularly liable to make mistakes.   If they advance money on any articles which have the Government mark, they are fined heavily, and these are often offered to them at night, by way of bait ; undoubtedly many of them make large fortunes, and many of them fail.   The more intelligent among the Pawnbrokers, tell you that they really lose money in selling the pledges not redeemed by the poor, though they may make it by the interest charged on those which are taken out again.   The real source of their profit, is the large loans advanced to persons of rank and influence, upon security of plate, jewels, deeds, &c.   Would it not be better to establish some Loan Societies (the *Monts de Piété*, of Paris, are an instance of this), where the interest required was only sufficient to pay the expenses of working the Society ?

Up to this point, we have done little more than show the general evils of 𝕽𝖔𝖔𝖐𝖊𝖗𝖎𝖊𝖘,—the lets and hindrances, to which these bodies corporate are subject. Because, in truth, there is an hideous sameness between St. Giles's, Saffron Hill, Minories, and other haunts of the destitute or the abandoned ; there are, however, in some districts, peculiar trades in operation, which add to the ills to which this kind of flesh is heir. 𝕿𝖍𝖊 𝕽𝖔𝖔𝖐𝖊𝖗𝖎𝖊𝖘 of the Mile-End Road, Lambeth, Maiden Lane, Paddington, and others, recognise no sanatory discipline, other than that of their class,—yet are environed with nuisances peculiar to themselves. In one district, the air is polluted by the decomposition, or boiling down, or perhaps both, of dead horses,—the unfortunate creatures degenerating from a carriage horse to a cab hack, passing through the intermediate stages, by gentle gradations, are at last consigned to the care of what is called in cant terms a "knacker," and having been quickly put an end to, are boiled down for glue, or their remains turned into some other profitable use. The stench from such a Necropolis, or colony of the dead, is dreadful,—must feed disease, and, when fever breaks out, aid its ravages! In another locality, tan pits spread an unwholesome odour, taint the sewerage of the neighbourhood, and add much to the mortality. *The Times* newspaper, during the late epidemic, noticed a petition emanating from the Archbishop of Canterbury, and other householders in Lambeth, praying that bone crushers be henceforth forbidden to ply their trade in that neighbourhood. The memorial stated that the epidemic then raging in Lambeth with unprecedented severity, was aggravated by the miasma generated from the decomposed bones.

If the late pestilence did no more than lay bare the nuisances of the Metropolis, and spur our lagging energy to agitate for their removal, it had its end. Just as a wasting malady discloses to the patient's observation symptoms of other deep-seated diseases, which otherwise might have lurked in his system unobserved,—so the

Cholera settled down upon some plague spot, where everything was at hand to feed it and extend its ravages, and thus laid bare the inward sores of London. Within a given circle hundreds sickened,—science quailed before it, it struck down right and left the doomed victims; —baffling the usual arts of the physician, it drove him to a new analysis; he became a disciple of the sanatory science,—at length discovered, in some reeking sewer, or licensed pest-yard, the source of the disease, and endeavoured to cope with a new adversary, now happily dragged from his hiding-place. Gas works, too, already begin to line the southern bank of the river; copperas works, white-lead works, and other factories, are established in dangerous vicinity to a crowded population; and recollect that large houses are scarce in these localities; Rookeries, indeed, spring up all around, or small streets little better than these; for the workmen employed in large numbers, must live near the scene of their labours.

In other neighbourhoods, accumulating dust heaps take a pyramidical form, and too often surrounded by rows of small cottages, on the outskirts of London; because the Metropolis, ever stretching out its arms, each year embraces some new plot of ground, engulphs some small suburb, encroaches upon some outskirt, and thus the dust-heap, which of old marked the limits of our great Babylon, becomes the centre of a district. You will say that the necessities of the citizens create these several depôts, that London must be lit, and that the other trades, of whose exercise we complain, are called into being by our wants. It would be difficult to prove that necessity involved their exercise in the very neighbourhood of the Metropolis; if suburban cemeteries are being put in the place of London graveyards; suburban factories, in many cases, might do the work now carried on in Lambeth, Mile-End Road, Maiden Lane, and Bermondsey. Large establishments connected with the crape trade are found at Enfield, Ponder's End, and other places, at some distance from London; and some branches of trade are carried out at least ten miles from the Metropolis.

Yet, suppose that we could not help ourselves,—that we were compelled by very need to endure the presence of these establishments, are we compelled to build Rookeries in their neighbourhood? Would it not be better to allot a certain district to those who carried on these trades?—to have a factory suburb, in which these works might be erected, where they might blend their several odours, and perhaps by blending, neutralize; but that no dwelling should be erected near them? That they, whom choice or necessity compelled to work there, when the night drew near, might escape to a purer air, and return refreshed, because they had breathed for a while a better atmosphere.

Is this Utopian, an advance little to be expected from this Mammon-worshipping generation? Is it a task a dictator alone could accomplish,—meet for the iron rule of a despot,—or, are we looking forward to the

golden age of a millenarian ?   Shall we ask some
sterner plague to teach us our duty, or wait till
Science has found that even trade cannot ply her full
energies under such a system ?   Are we wholly utilitarian,
and not in a large sense even this, rather the victims of
paltry selfishness, with the cunning of the small trader,
not the ample foresight of the lordly merchant ?

Other countries have done their wondrous works—
raised trophies to the science and the humanity of their
age,—Shall we be last in the race ?

Our streets are disgraced by the sufferings of overdriven bullocks, savage butchers belie our national character; accidents occur ; the animals, maddened by heat,
or overdriven, turn restive, attack those passing by,
gore those who cannot escape.   This impediment to our
traffic, this injury to our fellow-subjects, still remains.
Smithfield is a pest to the neighbourhood, disgusts the
eye, offends the nose, brutalises the mind*.   Gentle
reader, you are perhaps in happy ignorance of what are
called vested interests, corporation monopolies,—the licence to trade, to the injury of the many, to the benefit
of the few.   Hallowed age defends these precincts ; some
quaint allusion of Ben Jonson, Beaumont, or Fletcher,
would lack interpretation were the place and the memory
of Smithfield blotted out.   Our fathers walked in shoes
which pinched their feet ; shall we, their degenerate off-

* We must again remind the reader that this was written in 1850 ;
since then, the knell of Smithfield has tolled ; although Paris, with her
five *abattoirs*, has not taught us how to turn the event to good account.

spring, forego the penance?—are we better than they? The cholera seems to have interposed, if not to settle, yet to moot anew the question of removal. And who is there that does not blush for his country as he looks on the *abattoirs* of Paris; the order with which every thing is managed, the different departments into which the establishment is divided, the ample space around it? And recollect the slaughter-house near Montmartre is not the only one, though the most frequented;—four or five different *abattoirs* are placed in different parts of the city.

Yet the Islington Cattle Market, judiciously arranged, is covered with weeds—the victim of a giant monopoly.

Intramural burial-grounds are already doomed; many of these had long offended public decency, and their removal was long cried out for; sensible of the evils of such receptacles within the walls, several of our larger parishes have, for the last fifty years, possessed cemeteries in the suburbs, although these suburbs have since been incorporated within the Metropolis.

The attention of philanthropists has lately been called to the cow-sheds, of which there are so many in London —in the very heart of the city too : few nuisances are greater than these; the animals, fed upon improper food, give milk scarcely fit for use,—their sheds reek with an abominable odour; and not long since the public mind was disgusted with an account of cows kept, we believe, in Whitechapel, in underground sheds, where, for a long time, they never saw the light of day. This was scarcely so bad as the nuisance pointed out in our sketch of the Berwick Street district, where a cow-house, surrounded on all sides by buildings, harbours not only on the ground, but even first floor, a large number of cows and pigs. Such intramural dairies should surely be removed, if we wish that the Rookeries, in the midst of which these are situated, should be reformed.

We said, in the earlier part of this work, that the most aristocratic parishes are not without their back-ground of wretchedness ; that they have their 𝕽𝖔𝖔𝖐𝖊𝖗𝖎𝖊𝖘, though not always such dens of destitution as those of St. Giles's. In a pamphlet addressed to the inhabitants of St. James, Westminster, by the Hon. Frederick Byng, in 1847, is the following statement :—

" There are in the parish,—

    14 Cow-sheds,
    2 Slaughter Houses,
    3 Boiling Houses,
    7 Bone Stores,
    1 Zincing Establishment."

It then proceeds :—" Two of these sheds are situated " at the angle of Hopkins and New Streets (𝖗𝖊𝖆𝖑 𝕽𝖔𝖔𝖐- " 𝖊𝖗𝖎𝖊𝖘), and range one above the other, within a yard " of the back of the houses in New Street. Forty cows " are kept in them, two in each seven feet of space. " There is no ventilation save by the unceiled tile roof, " through which the ammoniacal vapours escape to the " destruction of the health of the inmates. Besides the " animals, there is, at one end, a large tank for grains,

" a store-place for turnips and hay, and between them a
" receptacle into which the liquid manure drains, and
" the solid is heaped. At the other end is a capacious
" vault with a brick partition, one division of which
" contains mangold-wurzel, turnips, and potatoes; and
" the other a dirty liquid, called brewers' wash, a por-
" tion of which is pumped up, and mixed with the food
" of the cows."

A report, after many other details, drawn up by Mr.
Anselbrook, a medical practitioner, concludes :—

" From the above-mentioned facts it is obvious, that
" much of the milk sold at the West End of the Metro-
" polis is elaborated in the udders of animals unnaturally
" treated, and kept in an atmosphere impregnated with
" gases detrimental to common health."

The slaughter houses alluded to, we are told, are in
the vicinity of the cow sheds. Many of the animals
slaughtered there, help to swell the mass of diseased
meat which is sold to the poor, nominally cheap, but
doubly dear, as cheating them of the expected nourish-
ment, and robbing them of their health. The extent to
which this practice is carried, may be judged of from a
statement made by a slaughterer, that he took annually
£.200 from one man for slaying diseased cattle.

The working classes have much to complain of here ;
they will tell you, if you ask them, that their poverty
compels them to purchase their meat in small quantities;
that they pay quite as much as the rich for a pound of
meat, and yet, because they cannot buy so much as a

joint at one time, are compelled to take the refuse at retail price, for which otherwise the butcher would have no sale.

The rate of mortality in three districts of an aristocratic parish, is thus given from calculations made.

" St. James's Square .... 1 in 90
   Golden Square .... 1 in 36
   Berwick Street .... 1 in 42.*"

Yet we complain that convicts increase,—that they are the country's bane ; the colonies reject them ; the counties where penal establishments are reared loathe them. Have we ever tried to remove the evil by social cures ? Bigotry, peculiar to our island, denies a system of education to the wants of our countrymen ; one day jarring sects may wrangle over a corpse, for dear food, scanty lodging, imperfect training, are eating deep into the hearts of our brethren. The system of education may come, but too late : the affections of the people long estranged, may no longer respond to the call.

We admit then, I hope, that these Rookeries are a disgrace to our age ; that they have sprung up in part from neglect, in part from the tide of fashion setting in another direction ; that unless legislation check them, by fixing the number of inmates to a house, according to the number and size of its rooms, such things will always be. Our selfishness may be alarmed by fevers there

---

* *Vide* Pamphlet, by a late Churchwarden. I am not violating confidence—I have the Author's sanction for attributing it to the Honourable Frederick Byng.

generated, and thence wafted to wealthier streets; our humanity may be shocked by this very slight and imperfect sketch, which aimed, not so much at a statistical account of 𝕽𝖔𝖔𝖐𝖊𝖗𝖎𝖊𝖘, as at a description of their effects, which has been, perhaps, rather an historical essay than a sanatory report.

All, however, agree in this—the remedy is difficult. Though *why* should it be thought so? Why not hope better things of our national character—generous in the extreme, kind, sympathising, charitable?—of our land, the hospitable refuge for distressed foreigners; the rich spending much of their incomes in a wise benevolence, the merchant and the noble often vying in generous ardour to surpass one another, in the number of their charities; most men thinking they are bound to do something for the poor, many giving a considerable portion of their income in charitable donations, notwithstanding the many private claims upon them. Would to God they would consider this vast social question! that they would superintend their own property, instead of committing it to needy Middle-men, and leaving to their tender mercies the dearest interests of their poorer brethren : they little know or think how much misery is caused by their neglect and even ignorance, their subservience to bad custom and unhallowed tradition; so that, because the Fathers did wrong, the sons cannot emancipate themselves from the paternal trammels. Therefore working men tell you, in tones of the greatest earnestness, that they had rather have any landlords, than men

from their own class, whose natures have been changed
by a long course of oppression.   And what shall we say
to those who are the owners of large factories, makers of
steam engines, &c., men who employ commonly at one
time five or six hundred workmen, some double or even
treble that number ; if these men were sensible of their
duty, would they not form little colonies, in which those
employed by them would be decently lodged, with some
attempt, too, at innocent relaxation, when the business
of the day was done ?   Is it just or right thus to bring
together large bodies of men, merely to wring from them,
at a certain price, a certain amount of labour, and then
to consign them and their families to Rookeries ?   Are
not the consequences in the prospective fearful, with our
teeming population and increased intelligence ?   Is it
not the grossest selfishness, or the most criminal indifference, thus to treat men as draught horses, or beasts
of burden ?   And shall we be checked by a homily, on
the danger of interfering with capital ?   What is capital
to the value of men's bodies and souls ?   Can they be
put in competition by the Legislature ? although, if we
spoke to individual avarice, we have little doubt to which
side the balance would incline.

   Is not Brotherhood the very essence of Society—all
freemasonries living by it, all corporations proceeding
upon this as a foundation,—all religion teaching it, the
savage feeling its need, and civilised man for ever forming new combinations ?   And yet, how is it set aside in
establishments such as these ?

Since these pages first saw the light, pestilence hath ridden, like the Angel of Destruction, upon the tainted gale! Well nigh 15,000 victims have fallen beneath him! What human hecatombs! How many fissures gape where his foot hath trodden,—how many widows and orphans pine beneath the stroke! Yet, where did he do his work?—Amidst the dwellings of the rich, where wealth could soothe disease, and tax the powers of science in its aid,—where, if Death left aching hearts, and yawning voids, it left not poverty to aggravate domestic sorrow? Were these homes laid bare? No! seldom. But where want, scanty food, and confined cabins, fostered disease,—where the cesspool found no vent for its Stygian tide,—where open sewers generated noxious vapours,—where crowded courts and pent-up masses beckoned the destroyer. Is this mere declamation?—Lambeth, at once a poor and a crowded district,—Rotherhithe, the centre of a squalid population,—Fleet Street, named from the stagnant ditch which it conceals, were the spots where Cholera was most virulent.

St. James's and St. George's felt its influence, and many were the sufferers; yet the deaths bore no proportion to those of less-favoured parishes,—and there, too, the disease was confined to the dwellings of the poor, few of the wealthier classes sinking under its effects.

Fifteen thousand victims, taken chiefly from the labouring classes of the Metropolis;—Liverpool, too,

Manchester, Leeds, Bristol, Hull, Plymouth, each has its
tale of woe. Is not this the signal to be up and be
doing ? Who can tell the amount of suffering entailed ?
—Who but those who witnessed Cholera in the 𝕽𝖔𝖔𝖐𝖊𝖗𝖎𝖊𝖘 𝖔𝖋 𝕷𝖔𝖓𝖉𝖔𝖓 can appreciate its malignancy ?—Not
that the patients were uncared for,—not that surgeons
denied their aid—most fearlessly, most ardently, did
the members of that noble profession labour in behalf
of the plague-stricken ; all that Science, all that personal
energy could do, the surgeons of London did. Nevertheless, how could they cope with disease thus suddenly
fatal, passing rapidly into the worst stages,—where bad
diet and ill-ventilated dwellings had broken the patient's
constitution ! How hope to stay the ravages of the
destroyer, where the train already laid waited only for
the fire to kindle it ?

Since the great Plague, one hundred and eighty-four
years ago, a mortality so extensive has never been
witnessed in the Metropolis, as that which occurred
during the present autumn*. An able pamphlet has
been published by Dr. Webster, in which he mentions
the ravages of the pestilence in districts abounding with
Rookeries, and where, too, the Rookeries are of the
worst kind.

" In Lambeth parish, the deaths by Cholera were
" 1570, during the last six months ; the ratio was, there-
" fore, 1 in every 91 inhabitants. In St. George's,
" Southwark, where Cholera proved fatal to 811 indi-

* We must again remind the readers this was written in 1849.

" viduals, one person died in every 64 of the population ;
" whilst, in Bermondsey, with its tan-pits, glue yards,
" tidal ditches, and other local nuisances, injurious to
" the health of the labouring population resident in that
" insalubrious part of London, not less than 704 per-
" sons died by Cholera, so that the very large proportion
" of 1 in every 56 inhabitants became victims to the
" pestilence. But even this excessive mortality was
" exceeded by the numbers registered in the parish of
" Rotherhithe, where 1 death from Cholera actually took
" place in every 38 inhabitants."

Dr. Webster then proceeds to point out a most singular
exception to this fearful mortality. We do well indeed
to dwell on it. "Although Cholera proved exceedingly
" fatal for several consecutive weeks throughout the
" neighbourhood, Bethlehem Hospital, with its nume-
" rous population, remained perfectly free from it,
" although situated in a district otherwise unhealthy in
" reference to the recent epidemic. At this royal hospital,
" having a constant population of about 700 individuals,
" comprising upwards of 400 lunatics, besides the
" juvenile inmates of the House of Occupation, officers,
" attendants, &c. ; whilst there are weekly admissions and
" discharges of patients and others, whereby, during the
" last six months, perhaps 1000 persons have resided
" within its walls, not a single case of Cholera has
" occurred, during the entire year, nor indeed pre-
" viously. The ventilation of the Hospital is excellent ;
" the utmost attention is paid to cleanliness ; the food

" is wholesome, plentiful, and regularly served; and
" there is an abundant supply of pure water throughout
" the whole establishment, alike for baths, washing, and
" cooking. A very deep Artesian well, reaching to
" below the chalk, supplies the water required in the
" establishment, of which a steam engine pumps upwards
" of twenty gallons a minute into the numerous reser-
" voirs on the roof of the building."

What a homily this upon 𝕽𝖔𝖔𝖐𝖊𝖗𝖎𝖊𝖘! The Hospital,
in the very centre of the plague, insulated from its
effects, because well drained, ventilated, and supplied
with water; because well furnished with those very
comforts which Rookeries want, as though this fearful
mortality was inflicted on us solely through the agency
of Rookeries,—they the *foci* of the disease, the rallying
points, beckoning its attacks,—I had well nigh said
decoy ponds, so that if they had not been, we might have
been passed over comparatively unscathed; they, meanwhile, like the conductors which were placed to attract
the lightning, and almost to confine it to themselves.

Bethlehem Hospital is not the only place which has
enjoyed an immunity from Cholera. Bridewell, some
of the prisons, and other well-regulated public institutions have been spared. The felon, whose crimes have
outraged his country's laws,—the lunatic, whose existence
is a burden, are preserved; the mechanic, whose labour
supplies our wants and luxuries, expiates the neglect of
others by his life.

Chapter XIII.

We cannot conclude without a few reflections upon the results of the evils we have considered. The mass of the working classes, not only in London but our great towns, are wretchedly lodged, the distinctions of sex confounded,—a system sanctioned which overthrows all the decencies of life and fosters immorality. Are you surprised after this that women are thought marriage-able with damaged reputations? that previous offences against chastity on the part of the woman are lightly regarded, not considered a subject of reproach? that men degenerate—love of truth, the foundation of all morality, grows weak—that they become indifferent to religion, that they rail against Divine and human laws, as though both were answerable for the ills under which they suffer? that infidelity is rife among the male part of the working classes? that lecturers in different parts of the town fan this discontent, endeavour to root out their attachment to Divine or human ordinances? that, under the cloak of lectures on science, their political grievances are magnified, our system of government decried, and men's worst passions roused by the invectives of artful dema-gogues? that schools are established for the rising gene-

ration in connection with these hot-beds of sedition? that
on the Sunday Chartist orators harangue? that there is
a sullen feeling of discontent brooding among our working classes? that they lack the power, not the will, to
overthrow the institutions of the country? that for several
years pamphlets of a revolutiouary character have issued
from the press? that sedition and blasphemy have formed
a close alliance, and that men are banded together to
upset the religious as well as political establishments of
the country? We say not that they have made great
progress, for our national character is on the whole fond
of order, averse to commotion, patient long, and bearing
much, yet these things should not be forgotten. We say
not that the disposition of the nation at large is revolutionary. We are, perhaps, more secure against such
attempts than any nation in Europe; but of what nature
is our security? Some will say our safety lies in our
army faithful to its trust; is this a proper ground for
security in a nation whose form of government is popular?
Has not the liberal party, ever since the times of Cromwell, lifted up its voice, at first against the establishment,
ever since against the increase of a standing army? have
they not professed to regard a large military force as
fatal to the liberties of the country, and is it right to
rely upon the fidelity of our army alone, as standing
between us and popular disturbances?

Yet some will say that our middle classes, not our
army, are the Palladium of the country; that the moral
and physical force of an intelligent, wealthy, loyal,

powerful middle class, is the best defence of our country. We are not inclined to question this; we will admit, if you will, that, if there had not been a soldier in the country on the famous 10th of April, 1848, we could have stood our ground. Nevertheless, *The Times*, not usually the organ of alarmists, conceived that we were preserved from an outbreak, because the Liberals held the reins of government, and the sympathies of the middle classes were with them. Would the result, think you, have been different had ministers persisted in carrying out their plan for an increased Income Tax? Thus you reduce our liability to popular commotion, to the chances of support afforded to our government by the middle classes. But suppose a case where this influential body was divided, indifferent, sullen, disgusted — not, we admit, a very likely case, considering the property at stake—and suppose also any unforeseen combination to arise, and recollect we have had too many such in Europe during the last few years, the stability of our institutions would be endangered, though they might be tough enough to work through the convulsion; new elements have been brought into the field, and we must expect new combinations.

So thought Dr. Arnold, a man whose mind was essentially an historical one; and so thought Lord Byron, whose poetical works were accompanied with notes indicating much foresight and discrimination. In one of these notes, appended to the four-volume edition of 1829, he thus writes :—" The Government may exult

" over the repression of petty tumults; these are but
" the receding waves repulsed, and broken for a moment
" on the shore, while the great tide is still rolling on,
" and gaining ground with every breaker." So thought
Wilberforce, no mean judge,—so thinks his eloquent
and far-sighted biographer, Sir James Steven, who
thus records the misgivings of that celebrated phi-
lanthropist:—" Wealth," says he " such as avarice had
" scarcely pictured in her dreams, was accumulated in
" the centres of mechanical industry; and the higher
" class of English society, commercial as well as noble,
" revelled in a sumptuousness of living, for which a
" description or an example could be found nowhere but
" in the fabulous East. Yet, behind this brilliant
" spectacle, his prescience saw the lowering of that
" storm, the approach of which is now confessed by the
" forebodings of every thoughtful man in Europe; his
" meditations and his discourse continually pointed to
" the still widening gulph between the two extremes of
" English society ; he mourned over the coming conflict
" between vice, ignorance, poverty, and discontent, on
" the one hand,—and selfishness, sensuality, hardness of
" heart, and corruption, on the other—between our
" loathsome cellars and our luxurious palaces."

Whilst these Rookeries remain, there must be something rotten in the state of Denmark ; and we cannot
forbear to recollect that some of the greatest convulsions
which have shaken Europe at different times have had
their origin in social discontent. We say not that the

popular indignation has always triumphed, or that the
stability of the governments under which these seditions
occurred has always been sacrificed ; we merely indicate
the source whence they arose. A review of some of
these will not be an unfitting conclusion or moral for the
present work ; if it be nothing else, as an historical essay
it may interest many.

In reading history, few things strike us more than the
historical parallels which so frequently suggest themselves. Certain phenomena distinguish a particular
reign, period, or century ; certain peculiar features
characterise an epoch, give it an idiosyncrasy, and these
features belong not to one country, but are rather
common to several nations, so that men speak of the
European mind being engaged in a particular object, or
the fortunes of Europe as affected by a series of events
in which each nation had a common interest. We do
not mean to say that as, in the decline of the Roman
Empire, you have first a series of convulsions which
uprooted all the ancient institutions of the Empire, then
an age of conquests, then an age of chivalry, then
succeeds the feudal age, then the age of charters and
municipalities, then the age of revivals, then the age of
popular risings, and the like ;—but that the history of
different nations is connected together by closer bonds,
and more intimate associations than these, and that the
coming events of a future generation have been typified
in the experience of times gone by. Thus Europe, not
a single country, has been the scene of several distinct

convulsions, which have modified, changed, and, at times,
uprooted forms of government and political conditions;
there is a wonderful similarity between the progress of
popular discontent and its outbreaks, whether we consider the history of the fourteenth or the eighteenth centuries; such revolutions have not been confined to any
particular country, they have extended throughout the
whole range of modern civilisation, as though several
nations had only one pulse, which beat with a like throb-
bing.   Thus a particular age has been marked by great
commotions, and these have extended throughout a great
part of Europe, instead of being confined to a particular
nation.   Thus, again, the same features of popular discontent and outbreak have been reproduced after the
lapse of centuries, as though certain changes in the
history of our quarter of the globe must succeed one
another in regular order, and after a certain time.   We
do not wonder that such an impulse should extend itself
in an age of intelligence like our own,—the press, the
railroads, steam-ships, and constant exchange of information, knit nations together, and the account of what
has taken place in one country soon finds its way to that
of its neighbours, yet the simultaneous movement of the
European mind has not been confined to our times, it
has been discernible for many centuries.

Another parallel cannot escape him who reads history
in a discerning spirit.   Two kingdoms have alike suffered
at the same time from popular commotions; although
these commotions, originating in very similar causes,

have not had in each case the same results, still the
parallel does not fail us even here. One nation has
passed through a particular trial earlier than its neighbour, but the latter has not escaped the probation.
Similar incidents to those which distinguished the political fortunes of the one have been repeated, after the
lapse of more than a century, in the annals of the other.
Thus Charles I., upholding the remnants of the feudal
system, perished in 1649—was succeeded by a military
dictator—a restoration followed ; and his son, who had
not profited by the misfortunes of his father, was exiled
within forty years of the death of Charles I. Louis XVI.
fell beneath the guillotine in 1793 ; within forty years
his brother was driven from the throne, the nation in the
interval having experienced a dictator's rule. In both
cases the first revolution was sanguinary—followed by
civil conflicts, coerced at length by the successful head
of the army ; in neither case did they who were brought
back to the throne of their fathers, learn or forget anything in exile. The second revolution was of a much
milder character in each kingdom than its forerunner,
well nigh bloodless, and the monarchs who succeeded
those that were banished connected closely with the royal
family, and coming in with a promise of large popular
concessions ; and had the life of William III. been
spared as was that of Louis Philippe, it is not improbable that he would have passed the remnant of his days
in exile, for he soon lost his popularity. The reign of
his successor was cut short by the political intrigues

which weighed on her spirits,—was disgraced more than
any period of our annals by political rivalries and party
tactics. Thus Blenheim was to England a barren field ;
the triumphs which saddened the closing years of the
Grand Monarque neutralised by the jealousy of a faction,
and two formidable insurrections made the foundations
of the throne rock ere many years had passed.

But the parallel we are most interested in, is that
between the popular commotions which disturbed the
reign of Richard II. and the contemporary disturbances
of France and Flanders.   During the latter part of
the reign of Edward III., the father of Richard, the
first symptoms of revolt against the hardships of the
feudal system began to show themselves in France.
The peasants felt themselves aggrieved—the unhappy
state of the country during the wars with the English,
no doubt aggravated the distress of the peasantry—they
assembled together in large numbers, headed by a peasant
whom they called Jacques Bonhomme. They attacked and
plundered several castles of the nobility, under pretence
of avenging their wrongs ; their numbers soon increased
to six thousand.   Old Froissart tells us that, at length,
after several successful expeditions, they were attacked
and defeated by the royal forces, " yet that, at this time,
" they were so much increased in number, that, had
" they been altogether, they would have amounted to
" one hundred thousand. When they were asked for
" what reason they acted so wickedly, they replied they
" knew not, but that they did so because they saw others

" do it, and they thought that by this *means they*
" *should destroy all the nobles and gentlemen in the*
" *world.*" Froissart habitually passes over the social
inequalities of the times, and makes light of the slaughter of peasants and others of this class, being only alive
to the chivalrous influences of the age, the daring of
knights, the heroism of princes. There is no doubt
that these assemblages of working men were provoked by
their poverty, and a sense of the injuries which they
sustained at the hands of their feudal landlords. This
insurrection was the first protest made by the peasantry
against the feudal system, yet so little were they ambitious of political privileges, that they were generally
called into the field to aid their lord in his struggles
with the municipal towns.

Not many years after this the famous Wat Tyler
insurrection broke out in England. Froissart tells us,
" that the evil disposed in Kent, Essex, Sussex, and
" Bedford, (although he admits that they were much
" injured,) began to rise, saying, they were too severely
" oppressed ; that at the beginning of the world there
" were no slaves, and that no one ought to be treated as
" such, unless he had committed treason against his
" lord, as Lucifer had done against God ; that they had
" done no such things, for they were neither angels nor
" spirits, but men formed after the same likeness as their
" lords, who treated them like beasts ; but they had deter-
" mined to be free, and, if they laboured or did any other
" works for their lords, they would be paid for it."

Their leader, a priest named John Ball, thus addressed them :—" My good friends, things cannot go on well in " England, and never will, *until every thing shall be in* " *common,* when there shall neither be vassal nor lord, " and all distinctions levelled ; when the lords shall be " no more masters than ourselves. How ill they have " used us, and for what reason do they hold us in " bondage ? Are we not all descended from the same " parents—Adam and Eve ? and what can they show, " or what reasons can they give why they should be " more masters than ourselves, except, perhaps, in " making us work and labour for them to spend ? They " are clothed in velvet and rich stuffs, ornamented with " ermine and other furs, while we are forced to wear " poor cloth ; they have wines, spices, and fine bread, " when we have only rye and the refuse of straw, and if " we drink it must be water ; *they have handsome* " *seats and manors, when we must brave the wind and* " *rain in our labours in the field ;* but it is from our " labour they have wherewith to support their pomp. " We are called slaves, and if we do not perform our " services we are beaten, and we have not any sovereign " to whom we can complain, or who wishes to hear us " and do us justice. Let us go to the king who is " young, and remonstrate with him on our servitude, " telling him we must have it otherwise, or that we shall " find a remedy for it ourselves. If we wait on him in " a body, all those who are called slaves, or are in " bondage, will follow us in the hope of being free.

" When the king shall see us, we shall obtain a favour-
" able answer, or we must then seek ourselves to amend
" our condition."

To this period belong the well-known lines which were
the rallying cry of the insurgents :—

"When Adam delved, and Eve span,
Who was then the gentleman?"

This extract sufficiently shows the spirit of this great
rebellion, which was not put down before many ravages
had been committed.

Froissart, speaking of the great Flemish Rebellion,
about the same time, after relating the defeat of the
Commons, under Philip Van Artavelde, sufficiently
explains the cause of the war, when he adds, " This
" event was very honourable to all Christendom, as well
" to the nobility and gentry; for, had these *low bred*
" *peasants* succeeded, there would have been unheard of
" cruelties practised, to the destruction of all gentlemen,
" by the common people, who had everywhere risen in
" rebellion."

Mr. Hallam has an interesting note appended to his
sketch of this period in his "History of the Middle Ages;"
it is as follows :—

"The Flemish Rebellion, which originated in an
" attempt, suggested by bad advisers to the Court, to
" impose a tax upon the people of Ghent, without their
" consent, is related in a very interesting manner by
" Froissart, who equals Herodotus in simplicity, live-
" liness, and power over the heart. I would advise the

" historical student to acquaint himself with these
" transactions, and with the corresponding tumults at
" Paris—they are among the eternal lessons of history;
" for the unjust encroachments of courts, the intem-
" perate passions of the multitude, the ambition of
" demagogues, the cruelty of victorious factions will
" never cease to have their parallels and analogies,
" while the military achievements of distant times afford
" in general no instruction, and can hardly occupy too
" little of our time in historical studies. To the
" example of the Gantois (or men of Ghent), Froissart
" ascribes the tumults which broke out about the same
" time in England as well as in France. The Flemish
" insurrection would probably have had more important
" consequences, if it had been cordially supported by the
" English government. But the danger of encouraging
" that democratical spirit which so strongly leavened the
" Commons of England, might justly be deemed by
" Richard the Second's Council, much more than
" a counter-balance to the advantage of distressing
" France."

We need scarcely, *en passant*, refer to the very serious
commotions which took place in the reign of Henry VIII.,
a similar peasant insurrection having broken out about
the same time in Germany, in which the famous Gotz
von Berlichingen, of Goëthe, distinguished himself so
much. Speaking of this peasant war, Menzel tells us,
—" The condition of the peasantry had greatly dete-
" riorated during the past century. The nobility had

" bestowed the chief part of their wealth on the church,
" and dissipated the remainder at court. Luxury had
" also greatly increased, and the peasant was conse-
" quently laden with feudal dues of every description,
" to which were added their ill treatment by the men-
" at-arms, and mercenaries maintained at their expense;
" the damage done by the game, the destruction of the
" crops by the noble followers of the chase, and, finally,
" the extortions practised by the new law offices, the
" wearisome written proceedings, and impoverishment
" consequent upon law suits. The German peasant,
" despised and enslaved, could no longer seek refuge
" from the tyranny of his liege in the cities, where the
" reception of fresh suburbans was strictly prohibited,
" and where the citizen, enervated by wealth and luxury,
" instead of siding with the peasant, imitated the noble
" and viewed him with contempt." Much of this was
owing to the extravagant lengths to which fanatics
wished to carry the Reformation, but much also to the
depressed state and great poverty of the peasantry. This
is evident from some of the demands made by them in
the Twelve Articles, as they are called, presented in their
petition for a redress of grievances.

The Second Article is as follows:—" That the dues
" paid by the peasantry were to be abolished, with the
" exception of the tithes ordained by God for the main-
" tenance of the clergy, the surplus of which was to be
" applied to general purposes, and to the maintenance of
" the poor."

The Fourth and Fifth.—"The right of cutting wood
" in the forests, hunting, fishing, fowling. Sixth and
" Eighth.—The modification of soccage and average
" service; the modification of the rent upon feudal
" lands, by which a part of the profit would be secured
" to the occupant. Eleventh.—The abolition of dues
" on the death of the serf, by which the widows and
" orphans were deprived of their right."

In England, the abolition of monasteries had deprived
the poor of their usual refuge in times of distress, and
stung by poverty, goaded by the withdrawal of their cus-
tomary aids, they took up arms to redress their wrongs.
So great was the distress, that the famous poor law of
the 43rd of Elizabeth was enacted for their relief, when
other intermediate measures had fallen to the ground.

The great revolutions of England and France grew
out of financial difficulties; the frequent applications of
Charles I. to his Parliament for subsidies were met by
their determined opposition; and his endeavours to
levy ship money and other duties, the proximate cause
of the outbreak which followed. In the case of France,
however, it was not only the accumulation of monetary
embarrasments, but rather the smouldering discontent
of the masses, which eventually brought on the revolution. Had other causes been wanting, had there been
no struggle between Great Britain and her American
colonies, no encyclopædists, that revolution would have
come. Louis XV. only hoped that the storm would be
postponed till his death, and Lord Chesterfield, forty

years before, had predicted what followed. " In short," he writes, " all the symptoms which I have ever met " with in history, previous to great changes and revolu- " tions in government, now exist, and daily increase, in " France*." Taxes there were, large taxes, but the pea- sants paid them, the nobles were nearly exempt; thus the rallying cry so fearfully distinct, — " Peace to the " cottage, war to the château." You cannot read the history of these times without remarking this.

Arthur Young, the celebrated agriculturist, published an account of a tour made by him just before, and during the period when the revolution broke out. He was a plain practical man, more the farmer than the politician, much better pleased to describe crops, grasses, cattle, farming instruments, and the like, than to moralise over the fate of nations. Perhaps on this account he is a better guide ; he had no very strong political bias towards liberal views to influence him,—no favourite theory to maintain, in what he wrote. On the contrary, he was a Tory of the old school, the decided enemy of reform. He published a pamphlet, in which he dealt roughly with Major Cartwright, Tom Paine, and other worthies of that class ; venting antiquated anathemas against them, muttering venerable grand-papaisms, like others of his day, terrified by the French Revolution, and fearing lest the infection should spread, watching the germs of the Irish Rebellion, and foretelling, from the gatherings and speechifyings of the manufacturing

* CHESTERFIELD'S *Letters*, Dec. 25, 1753.

districts, a similar outbreak in England. He calculates
that in 1789, the year when the revolution broke out,
the rural labourer in France, taking into view the price
of provisions, was seventy-six per cent. poorer than in
England,—that is, he had seventy-six per cent. less of
the necessaries of life than fell to the lot of a similar
class in this country. "With very few exceptions, *their*
" *houses dark and comfortless, and almost destitute of*
" *furniture,* their dress ragged and miserable, their food
" the coarsest and most humble fare."

In addition, says Mr. Alison, to an indigent peasantry,
France was cursed with its *usual attendant — a non-
resident body of landed proprietors.* This was an evil
of the first magnitude, drawing after it, as is always the
case, a discontented tenantry, and a neglected country.

Arthur Young, writing in 1787, says that, " in Mont-
" auban, the poor people seem poor indeed, the children
" terribly ragged—if possible, worse clad than if with no
" clothes at all ; as to shoes and stockings, they are
" luxuries. In another place, he speaks of meeting with
" a poor woman, who told him that her husband had but
" a morsel of land, one cow, and a poor little horse ;
" yet he had forty-two pounds of wheat and three
" chickens to pay as quit rent to one Seigneur, and one
" hundred and sixty-eight pounds of oats, one chicken,
" &c., to pay another, besides very heavy tailles and
" other taxes."

" In one district, all the women and girls are without
" shoes and stockings, and the ploughmen at their work

" without shoes or sabots or feet to their stockings ; the
" poor people's habitations are miserable heaps of dirt,
" —no glass, and scarcely any light, but they have earth
" chimnies. And, in another place, on the borders of
" Brittany, husbandry not much advanced, the people
" almost as wild as the country, and their town one of
" the most brutal filthy places that can be seen ; mud
" houses, no windows, and a pavement so broken as to
" impede all passengers, but ease none." You cannot
read the journal of this eminent agriculturist without
meeting with remarks in every chapter of this kind,—of
the wretched food and miserable habitations of the poor,
and this, too, when the condition of the farms, and
system of farming, were his more immediate object.
Thus, he says,—" The houses and cottages of wood,
" filled between the studs with clay or bricks, and not
" covered with slate, but tile, with some barns boarded
" like those of Suffolk ; the fields are scenes of pitiable
" management, as the houses are of misery; yet all this
" country—highly improvable if they knew what to do
" with it—the property, perhaps, of some of those
" glittering beings who figured in the procession the
" other day at Versailles. One opinion pervaded the
" whole country (1787), that they are on the eve of
" some great revolution in the government."

Was it not this—the degraded social condition of the
labourer—that made him a tool in the hands of the
anarchist ? Do you suppose that a man—badly educated,
little conversant even with the course of events—became

a political enthusiast, — that he could enter into nice
distinctions between hereditary monarchy and republican
government ?   Is it not, rather, the case of the patient,
sick with an inveterate malady, he gains no relief from
the regular practitioner, and at length, as a last hope, in
the very despair of his heart, resorts to the empiric ?
The working classes had lived in the midst of contrasts
the most appalling : they had seen rents rigidly exacted
and thoughtlessly squandered,—they who resided in the
capital were scandalised by the excesses which marked
the age,—they who tilled the soil of the provinces, felt
that the wealth wrung from their labours was withdrawn
to be squandered by their landlords,—they knew what
the country produced, and how little their share in the
plenty which others abused : the revolution promised a
change ; in that change was hope.   If it failed, what did
they lose ? if it succeeded, they would enjoy their own.
The historical student can afford to smile at such aspirations ; seldom has the wild tempest of a revolution
swept across a land and left anything except the traces of
havoc and desolation ; and the greatest social and political blessings have been achieved by moderate reforms.
But can you teach the mass this ?   Are not the victims
of poverty the victims of recklessness and impulse,
catching at any gratification, however short-lived, which
promises forgetfulness of their woes ?   And, can you
hope to check this, when men vaunt political mil-
leniums, and glow with visions of the plenty which is to
fill the hungry stomachs around them ?

In truth, poverty is a strange thing; the poverty, not
the will consenting, so well brought out by the great
Master of the human heart. At one time it presses so,
that men seem to lose the freedom of the will, and to
resign themselves to the current, not caring where it
bears them, to be content to drift down the tide without
an effort to escape the ruin which is before them : at
another, it makes them the tools of the designing, as
though they lent themselves willingly to the delusion,
hopeless though they knew it to be, which prompted hope.
You may tell him who is the victim of such a condition of being, that anarchy will profit him nothing;
you may prove that the expenses of the state during the
reign of terror doubled the expenditure of the mild
and retiring Louis XVI.; that the conscription under
Napoleon entailed upon the peasantry a burden which
preyed upon them to an extent unparalleled during the
history of France. But men who have been trained
under the discipline, and imbibed the habits which
Rookeries foster, do not reason when their hearts have
been long seared ; and even if they did, there is enough
of real suffering around them; the injustice of the
present system is palpable enough to give a show of
truth to the railings of the demagogue. Old Hooker
could write, about the end of the sixteenth century,—
" He that goeth about to persuade a multitude that
" they are not so well governed as they ought to be,
" shall never want attentive and favourable hearers ;

" because they know the manifold defects whereunto
" every kind of regiment is subject; but the secret lets
" and difficulties which, in public proceedings, are in-
" numerable and inevitable, they have not ordinarily
" the judgment to consider; and because such as openly
" reprove supposed disorders of state are taken for
" principal friends, to the common benefit of all, and
" for men that carry singular freedom of mind; under
" this fair and plausible colour, whatsoever they utter
" passeth for good and current. That which wanteth in
" the weight of their speech is supplied by the aptness
" of men's minds to accept and believe it."

The French peasantry lived in mud hovels; yet around
them rose those glorious old châteaus, some of which are
still standing, the relics of different ages, the strongholds
of power and feudal greatness, the palaces of that golden
age of nobles—the age of Louis XIV.,—all speaking of
riches, and power, and many retainers; pomp and splendour sadly contrasted with the ruined dwellings of the
peasant: and then the duties, whose name was legion,
and laws, some of which, from their severity, would
seem to have been rather the fictions of the romancer,
than the records of history: do you wonder that the
revolution swept, like the blast of the destroying angel,
over the devoted land,—that châteaus were first pillaged,
then given up to the flames, whilst memory would drop
a veil over the excesses which accompanied the havoc?

It will be urged that we are exceeding the bounds we

had assigned to our lucubrations,—that we are concerned
with one form of evil, when popular outbreaks are the
offsprings of accumulated injuries. Still, Rookeries are
seldom tolerated where other evils have been long
banished. They would cease to be, were landlords
mindful of the duties property entails—were they who
pay their share in the taxation allowed a fair share in the
councils of the nation. Rookeries never stand alone; if
they were the only cause of complaint, their very isolation
would be their death-warrant. If our boast be well
founded, that we have brought our Constitution near to
perfection, it is very evident that the working classes
have not the benefit of the change. You say that
England had long ago, by wise reforms, anticipated the
changes brought about by bloodshed in France,—that
that we are far in advance of any country in Europe,
our institutions more liberal, our government more
sensitive to the popular wants, the voice of the people
more audible than in any other corner of the world. We
are not inclined to contest this, inasmuch as the question
itself demands a close investigation, and one so elaborate,
that we are unequal to it. Still it is forgotten that laws
have not taken cognizance of many offences against the
welfare of the mass, yet that these very offences may
have eaten deep into the hearts of the sufferers. A nation
may be governed by an oligarchy, though the form of
government be republican, for so it was in the days of
the Italian Republics; Florence under the Medici, Venice

and others are instances of it, and revolutions may break out under a system of institutions whose very motto is freedom. For these very institutions may retain a place in the statute book, when they have long been practically ignored; the changing circumstances of the age may make them of non-effect, and several classes unwittingly combine to keep them in the background. No great political change took place between the Revolution of 1688 and the Reform Bill; still you would not say that the exercise of the political franchise was equally effective during the reigns of the different sovereigns who held the sceptre in that interval, or that the popular voice was heard with the same distinctness in the reigns of William of Orange and George III.

Our argument rather is, that Rookeries are among the seeds of Revolutions; that, taken in connection with other evils, they poison the minds of the working classes against the powers that be, and thus lead to convulsions; and seldom, we repeat it, are such evils found alone; the spirit of justice, which regarded the claims of labour in other respects, would scarcely doom the working man to crowded dwellings and a forfeiture of the commonest blessings God has given us: nor are recent events wanting in the same conclusions.

From the days of the Gracchi till now, the working classes have been turbulent in proportion to their wants; in some cases they have originated commotions,—or if it be not so, it seldom happens that leaders, demagogues, are wanting. Certain disappointed candidates for forensic or legislative honours,—authors, men whose imagination is stronger than their judgment,—men troubled with an unhappy, more than Irish, fluency of speech,—persons, whose ill-success in the occupation which they originally took up has disgusted them, and who suppose they have a destiny to fulfil,—needy men, envious men, vain, ambitious men,—men weary of toil, with an unhealthy distaste for business, or routine, are never wanting. Not seldom the leaders are men fired with a nobler enthusiasm, whom success enrols in the list of patriots,—men scandalised by the real injuries which the working class endures,—men eager for the renovation of their species,—optimists, if you will, yet optimists from sympathy.

Thus, when civil commotions stir the State, these tools are ready at hand. A burst of discontent is confirmed into a radical revolution; the movement loses its first vagueness, has a character, a name, an end; aims at a special reform, the removal of a special grievance, and the words " liberty, equality, and fraternity," have their utterance in national wages, and national workshops.

We are but just emerging from an European revolution,—it may be questioned whether we have emerged,—the agents of change may be recruiting their forces, preparing for some future and better conceived campaign. The revolutions took us by surprise, there were few harbingers of their coming—all seemed profound peace —there had been no fierce battling for popular rights—

no smothered discontent agitating large masses of the people. The cry of anarchy was not a novel thing; men hoping much from it, as from some new and untried medicine, so that demagogues peopled the new era they anticipated with figures which their imagination conjured up. The Continental commotions did not follow upon the heels of transatlantic emancipation; nor did Louis Philippe pay the penalty of feeding disturbances in the colonies of a friendly state. Of a sudden, a cry for reform was heard—a cry artfully evoked by a party—which drew with it, as such cries ever do, a certain amount of sympathy. An attempt was made to stifle that cry, and behold a revolution—a revolution extemporized—a revolution accomplished, not so much in accordance with, but in spite of, the wishes of those who had agitated for reform,—a revolution which took its agents by surprise, which achieved more than they devised, attempted, or desired,—a revolution, just as when children in their sport kindle the tiny flame which, increasing in spite of themselves, involves a household in ruin,—a revolution carried out in spite of, yet not by the defeat, of the army, which had no definite object, which satisfied no one, which all would recall, which has yielded no fruits, which has checked, rather than aided the cause of French and European reform, which has entailed at least as despotic though a stronger government upon the people. Yet, no sooner was this revolution accomplished, than the claims of the mass, hitherto too much lost sight of, were recognised. Had we not witnessed the previous commotion, we should have supposed that a vast social change had taken place. Among the names of those to whom the government was entrusted figured conspicuously that of Albert, *ouvrier* (workman); Albert, workman! What did he there? what business had he there at such a time? It was felt that, if the revolution succeeded, it must succeed by redress; that, despite the political titles in which the change was veiled, at the bottom it was a social one. Workmen had aided in overturning the government, whether that can be called a victory which won no trophies from conquered troops, —whether that can be called a victory where rival combatants did not sustain, as they best might, their respective parts in the arena of the battle field, may be well doubted; but the mass had triumphed when the Reform party were indecisive, the Government supine. St. Antoine had sent her hordes, those hordes had shed blood, and been themselves attacked, not on a grand scale, not that they disputed their positions inch by inch, yet the blood shed was theirs, or that of their opponents; they were the force on which insurrection relied, and by which it prevailed, and they must have their reward. Behold, then, the type of their class, the representative of their claims—Albert, *ouvrier!* The title took men by surprise: a new political banner was unfolded, on which were written the demands of the working classes; Rookeries, the claims of labour, the abolition of privileges, were the real elements of liberty, equality, fraternity. If you doubt this, ask what were among the first institutions?—national workshops, national employers, national wages. We are not concerned in the failure of these chimerical attempts, they were at least the straws thrown up into the air, they showed which way the wind blew.

Lamartine, speaking of an influential class among the labouring population of Paris, says,—" There exists a " mass of workmen, artists, and artisans, belonging to " those employments in which the hand and the mind " are most closely connected, — printers, engravers, " mechanicians, cabinet-makers, locksmiths, carpenters, " and others, forming together a mass of about fifty " thousand. They have among themselves, in their " respective trades, their societies, unions, organisations " for mutual assistance,—orators, delegates, who obtain " a hold upon their confidence, and who discuss their " interests with the contractors*. It was among these

* The historical student should read this book, because written by one who, as much to his own surprise as that of Europe, found himself the director of a revolution. Not that the book is remarkable for profound views ; that it attempts an inquiry into the real causes of the revolution ; its narratives are worked up too much with a view to dramatic effect. Incidents are pregnant only with Lamartine, a crisis takes place at every section of the work ; there is a *Deus intersit*, that *Deus* is Lamartine. The people murmur ; who quells them ?—Lamartine. A thousand sabres glitter in the air ; who sheaths them ?—Lamartine. They want a leader —behold Lamartine ! The fate of France depends upon an orator—listen

" men that the different Socialist schools, which had
" sprung up since 1830, at Paris, Lyons, Rouen, and in
" Germany, recruited the greatest number of their
" followers. The problem, up to this period without
" radical solution, of the inequality of human situations,
" extreme misery by the side of extreme wealth, scandal-
" ised them, as it has scandalised, without effect, all
" the philosophers and religious men of all ages; they
" flattered themselves at having found a solution, some
" by imitation, with Fourier, of the monastic system,—
" others by the brutal Indian system of castes with St.
" Simon; others by the religious united possession of
" land with Pierre Leroux; others by the suppression of
" the sign of riches in specie with Proudhon; the great
" proportion revolting at the impossibility, violence, and
" chimerical projects of these schools, had imagined they
" had found a practical adjustment in the system, at first
" sight less unreasonable, and in appearance less subver-
" sive, of Louis Blanc."

Here then we have the organisation of labour as the
remedy proposed for bad lodgings, scanty food, intermittent wages, and the claims of toil. We are not concerned

to Lamartine! The cry is for a Statesman; Nature is bountiful, and
creates—Lamartine! A certain verse writer of this day, terms a new
poem which he is engaged in, " A series of Mental Tableaux;" Lamartine's work is a series of dramatic tableaux, a second " Henriade," as
though the several wants of the age cried out, and a good spirit gave
them Lamartine! Yet certain facts are elicited, from which the student
may form valuable conclusions.

with the provisions or the fruits of this notable scheme, but rather with the causes which led for a while to its adoption. We are not disciples of this eccentric reformer, nor do we think it necessary to go to Utopia to find a salve for the wounds of our countrymen. Practical men were either beguiled, over-ruled, or frightened into this scheme. Was it that despair made them victims of strange fancies, so that any hot-brained enthusiast had only to create a monster, and the people worshipped it as a God; or was it that their wrongs had made them mad? Men must have been hard driven by poverty to be thus beguiled; and we find accordingly that Louis Blanc, the author of the system, tells us that he proposed this organisation of labour as the remedy for *social ills;* he speaks of the earnings of the labouring classes, and very much does he dwell *on the lodgings* of the workmen, on the French Rookeries, the hot-beds of insurrection, and well he might. When Louis Philippe surrounded himself with troops, previous to the insurrection, he took especial care to guard St. Antoine, the St. Giles's of Paris; the artillery of Vincennes (the Tower of that metropolis) had orders to present itself, at the first summons, at the Faubourg St. Antoine, as though the Rookery quarter of Paris was the focus of insurrection.

Louis Blanc's book is seldom read now its plans have failed; it is only wonderful that they should ever have had a trial, yet it is valuable as showing the social condition of the labourer at that time; very valuable to us, because it gives us an account of the condition of the dwellings—it describes the Rookeries where the working classes lived. The following is a quotation from Doctor Guépin :—" If you would know how the artisan lodges, " enter one of the streets where he dwells, in crowded " poverty, like the Jews of the middle ages, owing to the " popular prejudices, in the quarters set apart for them. " Enter, with stooping head, into one of those alleys " opening from the street, and situated below its level. " The atmosphere there is cold and damp, as in a cellar, " the feet slip upon the dirty soil, and you dread falling " down amid the filth. On each side of the alley, and " below its level, there is a room, sombre, large, and cold, " whose walls drip with damp, dirty water, and which " receives air from a miserable window, too small to " admit the light, and too badly made to exclude the " wind. Open the door, and enter, if the fœtid air does " not cause you to recoil; but take care, for the uneven " floor is neither paved nor boarded, or, if so, is covered " with such a thickness of dirt, that it is impossible to " distinguish whether it is or not. Here are two or three " beds, repaired with rotten string—they are mouldy and " broken down,—a mattress, a coverlet of ragged patch- " work, rarely washed, because it is the only one, some- " times sheets, and a pillow, behind the interior of the bed. " As for drawers and chests, they have no need of them " in these houses. Often a spinning-wheel and weaver's " frame complete the furniture. On the other stories, " the rooms, though drier and better lighted, are equally

" dirty and wretched.   There it is, often without fire in
" the winter, that, by the light of a candle of resin, men
" work fourteen hours a-day for a salary of fifteen
" to twenty sous.   The children of this class, up to the
" moment that by a painful and brutalising toil they can
" increase by a few farthings the incomes of their families,
" pass their life in the mud of the gutters,—pale, blotched,
" and bruised, their eyes red and sunken, or injured by
" scrofulous ophthalmia, they are painful to behold—one
" would imagine them of another nature than the children
" of the rich.   Between the men of the suburbs and
" those of the wealthier quarters, the difference is not so
" great; but there has been a terrible purification ; the
" strongest fruits have ripened, but many have fallen
" from the tree.   After twenty years of age they are
" vigorous, or dead."   Again, we are told : "The number
" of lodging houses of the lowest grade amounted in 1836
" to 243, and that they altogether contained a population
" of 6000 lodgers, of which one-third were women living
" by prostitution or robbery."

France, then, many will say, is in the same condition
as ourselves.   There is at times the same glut of work,
the same minimum of wages ; the same social discomforts,
bad lodgings, scanty furniture, insufficient food, want of
ventilation.   But then the expenses of the French working man are not so great as ours, or his lodging so
dear.

Thus, again, Louis Blanc tells us,—

" Whatever we could add on this subject, the detail of

" the expenditure of this portion of society will speak
" more effectually.

" *Francs annually.*

" Rent for a family 25
 Washing 12
 Fuel 35
 Repair of furniture 3
 Moving (at least once a year) . . . 2
 Shoes 12
 Clothes (they wear old clothes which
   are given them).
 Surgeon . . . . *gratis.*
 Chemist . . . . *gratis.*"

A revolution breaks out, for which it is difficult to find
a sufficient cause. The king was unpopular, yet not so
much as he had been. French society was rotten at the
heart, but the agitation for reform did not seek to remedy
its defects; it was merely got up to extend the elective
franchise. Full soon did the crying evils of the day
claim to be heard,—reform was forgotten,—bread, wages,
work, the rights of labour, the overthrow of the tyranny
of capital, were the watchwords of the insurgents. The
Rookery districts poured forth their thousands. St.
Antoine rallied the combatants—supplied the flames with
fuel,—St. Antoine the stronghold, the citadel, the centre
of the reaction.

Thence did the men who wished to rise upon the
downfall of a monarchical government borrow their emis-

saries : thence did demagogues call spirits from the vasty
deep, and they did come when these did call. What had
they to lose ? what had they at stake ? Success was
justice ; liberty, plenty ; riches perhaps in prospect. The
reformers for a time had their wish—more than their
wish. Louis Philippe was overthrown ; but did they
retain the power they had snatched from him ? For a
time the flames they had kindled were smothered, not
quelled ; yet for how short a time ! Visionary schemes
could not feed the bankrupt and the starveling. A phi-
losophy which set facts and experience at defiance, was
too refined for hunger and sedition. Again they rose, to
be again soothed into patience ; yet a little while,—and
they came again maddened by previous disappointment,
resolved this time not to be cheated of their rights.
Wilder still their theories. Communism, in their hands—
a much injured name ! But one purse, but one storehouse
for the nation's wants and the nation's expenditure, was
the rallying cry of their hosts. Frantic with a government which had only played with their wrongs, maddened by hope deferred, they burst forth as a torrent for
the destruction of all that opposed ; and, after the issue
had long been doubtful, were put down by the practised
soldiery of France, yet not without much bloodshed,
havoc, and ruin. Yet where did the battle rage the
fiercest,—where do houses, riddled by balls, appal the
stranger ? In the Faubourg St. Antoine, in the neighbourhood of the Pantheon and the Jardin des Plantes,
where Rookeries abound,—the native atmosphere of the

refuse of the people, — the nursery of wretchedness, despair, and crime, where men are sheltered who have else no shelter,—where common iniquities bring men together for the common defence. Each Rookery district —and there are several in a city like Paris—was the scene of a separate combat. How desperately the denizens of those retreats struggled, the number of officers and soldiers slain bears fearful witness. After a conflict of four days, unparalleled for its savage ferocity, the anarchists were vanquished, but at a fearful cost,—three or four thousand killed, and double that number wounded, is the very lowest estimate of the loss. At this time 120,000 workmen were receiving state wages; and nearly 10,000 are supposed to have been killed, wounded, and taken prisoners.

The flame which first broke out in France quickly extended through Europe. Berlin, Vienna, Munich, Naples, Rome, Frankfort, Madrid, were the scenes of fierce outbreaks. In most of these capitals the people obtained some triumphs, before they were ultimately quelled; still, the working classes were for the most part the combatants, though the labour question did not assume so prominent a place in the agitation elsewhere as in France.

England escaped, not without a strong demonstration of physical force on the part of the Government. Yet who were they whom the vast array of the 10th of April were in arms to resist. Were they not the inhabitants of our Rookeries? Did not each poor quarter of the town pour forth its multitudes to swell the great gatherings on Kennington Common ? And, as the cellars in Berlin had been the debating-rooms of the insurgents, so the Rookeries of London were the nuclei of the disaf- fected. And when an army was sent to Ireland, against whom was the array set in order ? Against the tenants of mud huts and Irish cabins,—against the remnants of Skibbereen ; those whom fever had spared, who had not been among the victims whom famine had doomed. As if Rookeries, whether in the courts of St. Giles, or in the plains of Tipperary, were not the types of social disease—the abodes of those who were the victims of the plague.

We gather, then, from the survey we have just made, that disturbances and outbreaks spring from social pri- vations and neglect. The history of Europe furnishes too many parallels. Arbitrary laws have held captive mind and body, till, as the mind expanded, it burst the bonds, and men achieved reforms by violence, which wisdom and foresight should have long ago conceded. The poor were neglected, till they pleaded their own cause with arms in their hands, or laid down their own terms as masters whom strength and success allowed to dictate,—or when forcibly repressed, in their very defeat inspired wholesome terror, lest the returning wave, stronger than that which preceded it, should make a further inroad, and engulf what had been hitherto pre- served. So that men in power have given way to reforms, not because prejudiced in their favour, but rather from a conviction that it was wise to yield what they could hold no longer. So that these very reforms have not been so much the redress of political, as social grievances—and the rights of labour recognised, in proportion as the licence of luxury was abridged.

Strong as we are, secure as we have been, we may yet bear to listen to the teaching of history; its lessons are for us—for us, round whom the middle class reared an impregnable rampart, and who have lived through convulsions which shook to the centre the great powers of Europe. That splendid monument of wisdom and courage, the English Constitution, may defy minor attacks— afford to despise them; other nations are only now winning the privileges we enjoy—are only opening their eyes slowly to the light which has long been our birthright. Yet with all this, if we forbear to renovate where time has ravaged, to remedy abuses which none can palliate, the day of retribution must come,—our children may possess an heritage blasted by our neglect, and the swords their fathers have sharpened pierce them to the heart. We cannot defy history, we cannot be so secure, as that the same causes shall not again produce the same effects. Our boasted middle class envies the privileges of the aristocracy,—our aristocracy feels their loss of influence in the national councils. The advocate of free trade elicits cheers in one county; in another, and that an adjoining one, the champion of agriculture is hailed with applause. Surely, then, there are elements of strife, and though opposite combinations greater than these have been dissolved without injury to the nation, there are grounds of apprehension, should either appeal to popular support.

Let us, then, be up and be doing. Our task it is to describe only one social evil, although that a monster, and the parent of a host of ills. Sufficient for us it is to have denounced that we have seen and known, and which has been a source of almost daily disquiet. Grant, if you will, that such an anomaly may exist, and yet England be the home of a peace as profound as that under which we now repose ; calculate, if you will, how many years the strong walls of England's citadel may withstand a storm,—believe it, and there is much to cherish the idea, that our sons and our sons' sons may escape the desolation which has laid waste foreign cities, if only they progress in the same course of temperate reform as their forefathers ;—tell us that every large city must have its back ground of wretchedness ; and still we cannot believe that our countrymen, kind, liberal, generous, wishing that others should participate in the blessings they enjoy, will sit down quietly with the consciousness that such evils are unchecked. Grant that the evil day be staved off, the sore will yet fester, and English life be poisoned by a wound so deep, so rankling. Grant that among us insurrection is a hopeless thing,— vaunt, if you will, with some pride, the social and political blessings which exalt the working man in England above his compeers in other lands ; yet, recollect the spirit which won those blessings is still alive in the breasts of Englishmen, and they who suffer must suffer in sullen silence and brooding discontent. The feudal institutions, much as they degenerated, were conceived upon the idea and in the spirit of brotherhood—union for mutual interest and defence. The lord might call his vassal to the war, but then he protected him in peace; he wrung hard service from him, but deemed as his own the affront offered to his dependent; in the same hall with himself that dependent fed — he was nourished and sustained by his lord. The property of the baron depended much on the fidelity of his retainers,—it was his interest to protect one so closely united to him. Feudal government at length degenerated into an oppression, yet this its early practice knew not, and it was foreign to the theory which gave it birth. Many bodies corporate there are now, though no corporate title distinguish them. Our large manufactories, our foundries, &c., what are they but commercial leagues, in which masses are associated together, obeying one mind, and working out the designs of one employer—not seldom a thousand hands in a single establishment? You may answer, that the numbers engaged in such schemes are too fluctuating to allow of a comparison with our ancient institutions, even if other circumstances permitted it. Yet, fluctuate as they will, these operatives follow only one trade; if dismissed by one employer, they must get work from another in the same branch of commerce. And there is a numerical standard, below which those employed never fall. Many are constantly em-

ployed for years under the same manufacturer, and are,
to all intents and purposes, his dependents; yet where
is the recognition of brotherhood here? Is there the
slightest connection other than that of work and wages
between them? Does the employer know even by name
the men who have been constantly for years employed
in his factory?—has he the most distant idea how they
are lodged, fed, or tended in sickness? Suppose the
employer a man of *active* benevolence, and you might
expect that a little colony would rise in the neighbourhood either of his factory, or the town in which it was
situated—this colony tenanted by his operatives, super-
intended by himself—the place where he gave his little
senate laws. Many such colonies there were in feudal
times—why not now? Is it that the law has made men
less dependent upon the strong arm of their lord and
patron?—or, is it that individual avarice denies the funds,
individual indolence shrinks from the experiment?

We have termed our Rookeries plague-spots; are they
not indeed such? Where are our convicts nursed—the
men whom our distant colonies reject; for whom there
is our vast array of penitentiaries, prison-ships, hulks,
penal settlements, and the like?

These men ply a daily trade in our large towns, their
occupation regulated by laws peculiar to themselves—
their very thefts determined by the nicest and most rigid
calculation. These men exist in bodies; there are particular sections of crime, particular gathering-places, and
bodies corporate. Do not such outcasts hide their heads

in Rookeries, because the very wretchedness of these districts acts as a charm—is their shield; disgusts men so that they shun them—avoid them, as though they were the nurseries of disease ?

And in close connection with such dregs of society does the honest and the hard-working labourer rest his weary head, his children playing with felons' children, learning their habits, infected by their example; and, as a man sinks in the world, here is the receptacle for him; his heart broken, he retreats to scenes like these, to learn by contrast the height from which he has fallen.

You have, as you are bound to have, your remedial schemes. Schools, cramped and crippled as they are by party feuds, which impart religious and secular know-ledge to the children of the poor.

Yet is not the edge of teaching blunted by the habits these Rookeries oppose to it? You teach precepts not merely conducing to present profit, but rather elevating and ennobling the child's nature. What an atmosphere is that of Rookeries to mature them! Dwellings which barely supply the most elementary wants of our being— the scenes where children shall put to proof what they learn;—where the good, the generous, and the noble within is cramped by the narrowness of all around.

Still, we may not despair; whilst our pen traces these concluding pages, an appeal for the needlewomen of England has been answered, as Englishmen should answer the cry of distress, and large already is the contribution which their advocate has obtained from his

countrymen. Oh! that one with eloquence would plead
the cause we have so feebly set forth! that one earnest
for his poorer brethren—known and honoured in his
generation—would arise, to urge the claims of labour
on those who direct it, and on those who are benefited by
its results!

Circumstances are related, tales told of the sufferings
of these needlewomen, which make the blood run cold,—
the needlewomen who people our Rookeries, whom Drury
Lane, Saffron Hill, Wapping, and Shoreditch shelter, if
the term be not a mockery. Mothers toiling by day and
night to earn 3s. 6d. a-week for the support of their
family, and part of that, too, spent in the materials
needed for the work, and then eking out the rest of their
miserable pittance—how? by *involuntary prostitution*.
And these prostitutes, too, not merely the unmarried,
but *married women,*—their husbands consenting because
poverty was killing their children,—these wretched
victims of Mammon putting on the unwilling blandish-
ment, made tempters in spite of themselves, lest their
offspring should starve. Is not the very name of Christi-
anity, we might ask, forgotten in a land which tolerates
such a curse? Are there shopkeepers banded together
to sell articles, spotted with the poison of that which is
more precious than the life-blood of their fellow creatures, and purchasers economising on the infamy of their
countrywomen? Men daring to take the Bible in
their hands, who dole out, under pretence of pay, the
wretched pittance in return for the days of toil and nights

of agony. Not that all the purchasers know the source whence comes the cheapness so precious in their eyes; that the thoughtless many pause to think; that they deck themselves willingly with the spoils of their country's disgrace; but some there *must be, many* who are aware at whose cost this accursed cheapness is achieved, and into what a pit of despair these thoughtless economists are plunging the mothers of our working classes.

No one who pretends to interest himself in the great question of the day,—may we not write of his country's infamy, perhaps his country's ruin,—should be without the pamphlet, entitled " The Needlewomen of England*." It has been before published in, and is now extracted from, the Letter to *The Morning Chronicle.* Every mother should come forward from every class with her superfluities and her savings, to check the unhallowed work which is polluting her countrywomen. We read in Roman history, that when Carthage was brought to the verge of ruin in the last Punic War, the Carthaginians brought their vessels of silver and gold and gave them to the state, which needed them so much, and the women plaited their hair into bowstrings, lest the war should flag; and in our Great Rebellion, many of the colleges of Oxford melted down their plate to support the royal cause. Is no effort to be made to save the mothers of England from prostitution ?

We may not despair. The strong old English spirit

* Printed by Peter Duff and Co.

still warms many a heart, and the strong old English
energy still nerves many a hand among us.

Europe is heaving with the swell of a revolution—a
Jacquerie, and yet a war of opinions too, as Canning
predicted ; and men have stirred the fire, who felt they
were not fed, clothed, paid, lodged as they ought to be.
We have stood firm as a rock, looking on with careful
scrutiny, looking round with jealous vigilance, to detect
the blemishes of our own fabric ; not from fear so much
as sense of duty, not from impulse but inquiry, we have
shaken off our apathy; and men are coming forward with
new schemes, and aiding, by new grants, the distress to
which their eyes at length are opened. What a time,
then, to plead that Rookeries may no longer be—what a
time to speak to the better emotions of English hearts.
England, our beloved country, the mother of freedom,
the asylum of the persecuted, whose sons have gone forth
from their island home to teach the British tongue, and
hand down the British name to empires now just springing
into life ; who, at the cost of twenty millions, willed that
Slavery should be no more. Look around on what she
has done, and think not that her strength is spent, or her
arm unnerved. If Rookeries be the canker-worms, not
of England but of Europe, may she be the first to sweep
them from the land they disgrace ;—may she take the
lead in the holy work, from whom the voice has oft gone
forth which awoke Europe from her slumber. It shames
us to plead with Christian men in arguments which ex-
pediency commends, or where profit must be the medium
of conviction.

We call them by that better, nobler, holier bond to remember that they are brethren. Yes, brothers they are, whose sickness Rookeries aggravate, whose weariness they mock, whose hearts they sear—brothers clinging, with a fondness which poverty cannot shake, to the country which gave them birth—brothers proud of the name that country has won—brothers still bending before the laws which govern them, still sending forth their sons to combat for England's fame, and to bleed in her defence!

Oh! that these our feeble hands might lay one stone of this vast reform—our eyes be permitted to see some part of the good work done in this our age! We stand high, and we deserve it. We alone support a law for the relief of the poor. Such provisions are questionable, yet rather than that the poor should starve, we maintain them; and though founded in fact, syllogisms of the political economist convince us not.

Verily, we are obstinate, in spite of figures even, to maintain a custom, which our fathers valued and our brethren stand by. Let us do more,—remove the necessity of a State assistance, by teaching the poor man to respect himself, and to be proud of his own independence. Love of decency is still a home plant; cherish it by dwellings large enough for its indulgence. Teach men to care for their minds, by showing them you are not indifferent to their bodies. Bind them to you, because you share with them the blessings you enjoy. Evoke their loyalty to their sovereign, when the ruling powers have recognised their claims as subjects. Appeal to their consciences as Christians, by acknowledging first that they have the feelings of men.

Education will be valued by those who have means to improve themselves; religion will thrive when it makes the rich alive to the wants of the poor. A happier day will dawn; 𝕽ookeries will be remembered not by what they are, but as the dungeons of an ancient castle, whose horrors tradition records, but custom has long superseded; like monoliths and cromlechs, relics of an elder age.

Postscript.

FIRE OF LONDON—ITS RAVAGES—ITS EFFECT UPON
Rookeries.

WE have frequently alluded to the Fire of London, and
the effect it had upon the present condition of the
Metropolis; a long account of this great national calamity would have been out of place in the middle of this
volume, but, perhaps, it may be welcome to some few at
the end of the book.   There is, in fact, a striking difference between the older parts of London, and those of
foreign cities, which is mainly owing to the fire.   In
other countries we are enabled to trace the different
periods of domestic, ecclesiastical, or civil architecture, by
the buildings which survive in different parts of the
Metropolis.   In London, the Hôtel de Ville, or Mansion
House, is little more than one hundred years old.   The
City Halls of the olden times must have been glorious
buildings, if we may judge by Crosby Hall; and the
dwelling-houses quaint structures, if the Holborn end of
Staple's Inn is a fair specimen; but the fire has been
fatal to our curiosity in this respect; so that Bristol,
York, and Chester still preserve more models of a by-
gone age than London itself.   The palace of Bridewell,
the residence of Henry VIII.; the remains of John of
Gaunt's House, Old St. Paul's, which, however Inigo

Jones is supposed in his ignorance of Gothic architecture
to have spoiled; the Old Custom House, on the site of
that rebuilt by Charles II., were the victims of this
dreadful catastrophe.

The fire broke out on the 2nd of September, 1666, in
the middle of the night; a high wind aided its fury. The
following is the account given in the *London Gazette*.

" On the 2nd instant, at one of the clock of the
" morning, there happened to break out a sad and de-
" plorable fire in Pudding Lane, near New Fish Street,
" which falling out at that hour of the night, and in a
" quarter of the town so close built, with wooden pitched
" houses, spread itself so far before day, and with such
" distraction to the inhabitants and neighbours, that care
" was not taken for the timely preventing of the farther
" diffusion of it by pulling down houses, as ought to have
" been ; so that this lamentable fire, in a short time,
" became too big to be mastered by any engines in
" working near it. It fell out most unhappily too, that
" a violent easterly wind fomented it, and kept it burning
" all that day and night following, spreading itself to
" Gracechurch Street and downwards, from Cannon
" Street to the waterside, as far as the Three Cranes in
" the Vintry. The people in all parts about it distracted
" by the vastness of it, and their particular care to carry
" away their goods, many attempts were made to prevent
" the spread of it by pulling down houses and making
" great intervals, but all in vain, the fire seizing upon
" the timbers and rubbish, and so continuing itself even

" through these spaces, and raging in a bright flame all
" Monday and Tuesday, notwithstanding His Majesty's
" own and his Royal Highnesses indefatigable and per-
" sonal pains to apply all possible remedies to prevent it,
" calling upon and helping the people with their guards;
" and great number of nobility and gentry, unweariedly
" assisting therein, for which they were requited with a
" thousand blessings from the poor distressed people.

" By the favour of God the wind slackened a little on
" Tuesday night, and the flames meeting with brick
" buildings at the Temple, by little and little it was
" observed to lose its force on that side, so that on
" Wednesday morning we began to hope well, and his
" Royal Highness never despairing or slackening his
" personal care, wrought so well that day, assisted in
" some parts by the Lords of the Council, before and
" behind it, that a stop was put to it at the Temple
" Church, near Holbourn Bridge, Pie Corner, Alders-
" gate, Cripplegate, near the lower end of Bishopsgate
" Street, and Leadenhall Street, at the Standard in
" Cornhill, at the church in Fenchurch Street, near
" Clothworkers' Hall, in Mincing Lane, at the middle of
" Mark Lane, and at the Tower Dock. On Thursday,
" by the blessing of God, it was wholly beat down and
" extinguished; but so as that evening it unhappily burst
" out again fresh at the Temple, by the falling of some
" sparks (as is supposed) upon a pile of wooden build-
" ings; but his Royal Highness, who watched there that
" whole night in person, by the great labour and diligence

" used, and especially by applying powder to blow up
" the houses about it; before day most happily mastered
" it. Divers strangers—Dutch and French—were, during
" the fire, apprehended upon suspicion that they contri-
" buted mischievously to it, who are all imprisoned, and
" informations prepared to make a severe inquisition
" thereupon by my Lord Chief Justice Keeling, assisted
" by some of the Lords of the Privy Council, and some
" principal members of the city, notwithstanding which
" suspicions, the manner of the burning all along in
" a train, and so blown forwards in all its way by strong
" winds, makes us conclude the whole was an effect of an
" unhappy chance, or to speak better, the heavy hand of
" God upon us for our sins, showing us the tenor of his
" judgment in thus raising the fire, and immediately after,
" his miraculous and never enough to be acknowledged
" mercy in putting a stop to it when we were in the last
" despair, and that all attempts for the quenching it,
" however industriously proposed, seemed insufficient.
" His Majesty then sat hourly in council, and ever since
" hath continued making rounds about the City in all
" parts of it, where the danger and mischief was greatest,
" till this morning that he hath sent his Grace the Duke
" of Albemarle, whom he hath called for to assist him in
" this great occasion, to put his happy and successful
" hand to the finishing this memorable deliverance.

" About the Tower, the seasonable orders given for
" plucking down houses to secure the magazines of
" powder, were more especially successful, that part being

" up the wind, notwithstanding which it came almost to
" the very gates of it, so as by this early provision, the
" several stores of war lodged in the Tower, were entirely
" saved. And we have further, this infinite cause par-
" ticularly to give God thanks that the fire did not
" happen in any of those places where His Majesty's
" naval stores are kept, so as though it pleased God to
" visit us with his own hand, he hath not by disfurnishing
" us with the means of carrying on war, subjected us to
" our enemies.

" It must be observed that this fire happened in a
" part of the town where though the commodities were
" not very rich, yet they were so bulky that they could
" not be removed, so that the inhabitants of that part
" where it first began have sustained very great loss ;
" but by the best inquiry we can make, the other parts
" of the town, where the commodities were of greater
" value, took the alarm so early that they saved most of
" their goods of value, which possibly may have dimi-
" nished their loss, though some think that if the whole
" industry of the inhabitants had been applied to the
" stopping of the fire, and not to the saving of their
" particular goods, the success might have been much
" better, not only to the public, but to many of them in
" their own particulars. Through this sad accident it
" is easy to be imagined how many persons were neces-
" sitated to remove themselves and goods into the open
" fields, where they were forced to continue some time,
" which could not but work compassion in the beholders ;

" but his Majesty's care was most signal on this occasion,
" who, besides his personal pains, was frequent in con-
" sulting all ways for relieving those distressed persons,
" which produced so good an effect, as well by his
" Majesty's proclamation, and the orders issued to the
" neighbour justices of the peace to encourage the
" sending in provisions to the markets, which are
" publickly known, as by other directions, that when his
" Majesty, fearing lest other orders might not yet have
" been sufficient, had commanded the Victualler of his
" Navy to send bread into Moorfields for the relief of the
" poor, which for the more speedy supply he sent in
" bisket, out of the sea stores, it was found that the
" markets had been already so well supplied, that people
" being unaccustomed to that kind of bread declined it,
" and so it was returned in great part to his Majesty's
" stores again without any use made of it."

We are told, in another account, that the fire broke
out in a baker's shop in Pudding Lane, in the lower part
of the city, near Thames Street, amongst rotten wooden
houses.   They who are curious in such matters may not
be aware that Cripplegate Church was uninjured, and that
in the churchyard are still some remains of the old city
wall ; the church is a strange medley of architecture, and
the pews and pulpit in the stiff taste of the last two
centuries—great square boxes, whilst above them are
Gothic windows.

" The damage done by the fire is thus computed.
" Burned and consumed 12,000 houses within the walls

" of the city, and above 1,000 more without the walls,
" but all of them within the freedom and liberty of
" London, that is in all 13,000 ; or, as others say,
" 13,200 houses ; there were also destroyed the Cathe-
" dral Church of St. Paul's, which was then being rebuilt,
" and, as to the stone work, almost finished. Also
" eighty-seven parish churches, and six consecrated
" chapels, most of the principal and public edifices, as
" the great Guildhall, wherein were nine several courts
" belonging to the city : the Royal Exchange, the King's
" Custom House, Justice Hall, where the sessions were
" kept eight or nine times in the year for the trial of
" murderers, felons, and other malefactors, the four
" prisons, four of the principal gates of the city, and fifty
" halls of companies, most of which were most magnifi-
" cent structures and palaces. The whole damage sus-
" tained by this fire is almost incredible.

" The damage done is thus estimated :—   £.

	£.
In houses burnt	3,900,000
In churches and public edifices as follows :—The eighty-seven parish churches at £.8,000 each .	696,000
Six chappels at £.2,000 each . .	12,000
The Royal Exchange at	50,000
The King's Custom House at . .	10,000
The fifty-two halls of companies, at £.15,000 each	780,000
Three of the city gates at £.3,000 each	9,000

	£.
The Jail of Newgate	15,000
Four stone bridges	6,000
The Sessions House	7,000
The Guildhall and courts and offices belonging to it	40,000
Blackwell Hall	3,000
Bridewell	5,000
Poultry Compter	5,000
Wood Street Compter	3,000

" To which add :—

Towards building of St. Paul's Cathedral	2,000,000
The wares, household stuffs, monies, and other moveable goods, &c. .	2,000,000
The hire of porters, carts, waggons, barges, boats for removing wares and household stuff	200,000
In printed books	150,000
In wine, tobacco, sugar, and of which the city was then very full	1,500,000
For public works enjoined by Act of Parliament	41,500
	£.11,432,500"

The following causes were supposed to have contributed to the great destruction of property :—

" The fire began between one and two o'clock, after " midnight when all were in a dead sleep.

" It broke out on Saturday night when many of the
" most eminent merchants and others were retired into
" the country, and none but servants left to look to
" their city houses.

" It was in the long vacation, being that particular
" time of the year when many wealthy citizens and
" tradesmen, were wont to be in the country at fairs, and
" getting in of debts, and making up accompts with
" their chapmen.

" The closeness of the building and narrowness of
" the streets where it began did much facilitate the pro-
" gress of the fire, by hindering of the engines to be
" brought to play upon the houses on fire.

" The matter of which the houses were—timber, and
" those very old.

" The dryness of the preceding season, there having
" been a great drought even to that very day, and all
" the time that the fire continued, which had so dried
" the timber, that it was never more apt to take fire.

" The nature of the wares and commodities stowed
" and vended in those parts were most combustible of
" any sold in the whole city—as oil, pitch, tar, cordage,
" hemp, flax, rosin, wax, butter, cheese, wine, brandy,
" sugar. An easterly wind, which is the driest of all
" others, had blown for several days together before,
" and at that time very strongly.

" The unexpected failing of the water thereabouts,
" at that time,—for the engine at the north end of
" London Bridge, called the Thames Water Tower,

" which supplied all that part of the city with Thames
" water, was out of order, and in a few hours was itself
" burnt down,—so that the water pipes which conveyed
" the water from thence through the streets were soon
" empty.

" Lastly, an unusual negligence at first, and confi-
" dence of easily quenching it, and of its stopping at
" several places afterwards, turned at length into con-
" fusion, consternation, and despair,—people choosing
" rather by flight to save their goods, than by a vigorous
" opposition to save their own houses and the whole
" city.

" To all which reasons, must not be past over the
" general suspicion that most then had of incendiaries
" laying combustible stuff in many places, having
" observed divers distant houses to be on fire together,
" and many were then taken up on suspicion*."

Within four or five years the city was nearly rebuilt,
in a more uniform and substantial manner than before;
but if the designs of Sir Christopher Wren had been
carried out, London would indeed have been a fine city.
He intended to have laid out one large street from
Aldgate to Temple Bar, in the middle of which was to
have been a large square, capable of containing the new
church of St. Paul, with a proper distance for the view
all round it. He further intended to have rebuilt all the
parish churches in such a manner as to be seen at the
end of every vista of houses, and dispersed at such a

* SEYMOUR's *Survey of London and Westminster.*

distance from one another, as neither to be too thick nor too thin. All the houses to be uniform, and supported on a piazza like that of Covent Garden; and by the water-side, from the bridge (London Bridge) to the Temple, he had planned a long and broad wharf or quay, wherein he designed to have ranged all the halls that belong to the several companies of the city, with proper warehouses for merchants between, to vary the edifices, and to make it at once one of the most beautiful and most useful ranges of buildings in the world. But, says his encomiast, the hurry of rebuilding, and the disputes about property, prevented this glorious scheme from taking place. It would seem that the great fire was not without its use,—that houses were built on the old found ations, but in a much better and more substantial manner than before, though not so well as if Sir Christopher's plan had been followed. We are apt to think that the crowding of several families into one house is an innovation of later times; it would rather seem to have been the revival of an obsolete practice. The fire rooted out and destroyed Rookeries, and the stringent laws laid down for the rebuilding of the city prevented such abuses for some years; but we find Queen Elizabeth issuing a proclamation at the time of her progress in 1572, from which the following is an extract :—

" Yet where there are a great multitude of people " brought to inhabit in very small rooms, whereof the " greater part seem very poor,—yea, such as live of beg- " ging or worse means,—and they heaped up together

" and in a sort smothered with many families of children
" and servants in one house or small tenement, it must
" needs follow (if any plague or popular sickness should
" by God's permission enter among the multitude), that
" the same would not only spread itself and invade the
" whole city and confines, as great mortality should
" ensue to the same where Her Majesty's personal pre-
" sence is many times required, besides the great con-
" fluence of people from all parts of the realm, by reason
" of the ordinary Terms for Justice there holden, but
" would also be dispersed through all other parts of the
" realm to the manifest danger of the whole body thereof.
" For the remedy whereof, Her Majesty, by good and
" deliberate advice of her Council, doth straightly com-
" mand all manner of persons of what quality soever they
" be, to desist and forbear from any new building of any
" house or tenement within three miles of the gates of
" the said City of London, to serve for habitation or
" lodging for any person, where no former house hath
" been known to have been in the memory of such as
" are now living; and also to forbear from letting, or
" setting or suffering *any more families than one only*
" *to be placed* or to inhabit from henceforth in any
" house that heretofore has been inhabited." And the
authorities are moreover enjoined to prevent " the
" heaping up of multitudes of families in the same
" house, or the converting of any one house into
" multitudes of tenements for dwelling or victualling
" places." They are charged to prevent " the increase of

" many indwellers, or, as they are commonly called,
" *inmates or undersitters,* contrary to the good ancient
" laws."

Before the Fire, we are told, that when old houses were
repaired that were of good amplitude, they would make
two or three tenements of them, to increase the rent,
and these were turned some into ale-houses and let out
to the poorer sort. Great houses also were turned sometimes into alleys, consisting of divers houses. Care was
taken for the preventing of drinking houses, more commonly cellars. Many *sheds* were also set up to serve
for small houses, which did but harbour poor people ;
there were also made holes under the shops for the
poorer sort of artisans.

Such dwellings were not the fruit of municipal arrangements for the housing of the poor, they are the abuses
of them. When men devise deliberate plans for such
ends, they are in general liberal, it may be said ; that as
the carrying out of such plans does not affect the law-
makers, but rather those whom laws control, that there
is not the usual selfish inducement of profit to guide
them. It would be more true to say, that men shrink
from putting on paper that at which they are brought by
custom to connive. The authorities, before the Fire took
place, wished to confine London within a given space,
so that, like continental cities, its suburbs should be
rural districts, not that it should stretch forth its arms in
the form of Brixton, Camberwell, Greenwich, Hackney,
Hampstead, Hammersmith, Wandsworth, and others ;

yet the natural effect of such provision was to crowd as
many persons as could be packed within a given area.
The Fire came and cleared a vast space—cleared, in fact,
almost the whole surface of what was then the City of
London. The Parishes of St. George's, Bloomsbury,
St. James's, St. Martin's, were like what our suburban
districts now are, places where the nobility lived, their
residences having a background of garden, or rather
park.

Oxford Street being Oxford Road, fields intervening
between Gray's Inn and Hampstead, houses scattered
here and there, Rookeries could scarcely have been as
yet established beyond the precincts of the City, so that
when the fire came, it made a wholesale clearance in
these time honoured colonies. How many perished
Strype and others do not tell, and we only gather from
certain enactments curtailing their excess and checking
their extent, that such purlieus were.

The citizens had no sooner looked their losses in
the face than they began to repair them. Heavy were
the burdens entailed upon the funds of that ancient
corporation during many years—deep the groans of the
worthy Seymour as he pondered on or recapitulated the
expense; but men must live, so that very soon a new
city stood in the place of the old one, not certainly a
very picturesque or convenient monument of good taste,
not a very creditable monument to the liberality of the
nation; but a fairer representative than its predecessor
of the liberality of the Londoners—and, considering

the infamous excesses of the court, and the disgusting character of Charles II., as decent a substitute as could be hoped for in old London. In this good work Rookeries had no place, the poor were provided for, as hewers of wood and drawers of water ever must be ; still there were no special injunctions that eight or ten families should live in a single house, nor did alleys seem to enjoy a blissful immunity from the comforts accessible to dwellers in larger thoroughfares.

Among the directions given for rebuilding the city, are provisions for removing abuses ; the streets to be rebuilt were to be free from certain annoyances which their predecessors could not shake off—they were to be raised in the neighbourhood of the Thames to a certain level, because, previous to the fire, these streets were periodically inundated,—sewers were to be formed, and drainage carried out after the best model and on the most scientific plans then known—that in future the city might be spared the wasting plague, so frequent in former times.

That part of the city which was situated near the Thames not only suffered much from inundation previous to the Great Fire, but the ascent was also difficult. It was therefore ordered, after the fire, that all the ground between Thames Street and the river should be raised and made higher by three feet, at the least, above the surface of the ground. Such old streets and passages within the City of London and its liberty as were narrow and incommodious for carriages and passengers, and prejudical to the trade and health of the inhabitants, were to be enlarged. New streets, wharves, and markets were quickly formed. Brick was henceforth to be used instead of wood.

We can have little idea of what London was before the fire*. Doubtless a strange medley,—palaces and hovels, — glorious specimens of the Tudor style, flanked by timber huts,—Inigo Jones' masterpieces concealed by the penthouses of crumbling shops,—the Conduit in Cheapside, a splendid relic of the past, despoiled indeed in Edward the Sixth's time, and shorn of its glory, yet contrasting oddly with the mean buildings which surrounded it,—Gresham's Exchange, in the quaint style perhaps of that still remaining at Antwerp,—Old St. Paul's, multilated by the bad taste of the age, with the stone pulpit where Hooker preached,—Smithfield, still retaining the memory of bloody Mary and the Martyrs' fires, —the goodly hospitals, piety's tributes in the olden time, —the city halls, speaking of the guilds and brotherhoods, with the privileges which municipalities wrought out with their own good swords,—churches where convents lavished their wealth,—the noble's palace and the trader's mansion,—streets which tell better than the most laboured annals the history of different ages,—gates which had fortified the city's rebellion,—thoroughfares which had rung to the cry of " Clubs " and " Prentices,"—hospitals

---

* Whilst these sheets were going through the press, the Writer was gratified by the appearance of a large print of London, before the Fire, by Bogue and Son, of Fleet Street.

for diseases now forgotten,—courts of justice and cellars
of merchandise,—bridges and conduits, inns and prisons,
—squares which of old had witnessed brave feats of arms,
where tournaments once kept up the spirit of a martial
age,—the scenes where fountains ran with wine on festal
days, and pageants arrayed their tasteful flattery for the
new crowned Sovereign,—all alike have perished. The
wasting fire hath invaded halls the architect might have
sketched as models of his craft; stores of records which
enriched a nation's history have perished. And yet we
may not lament;—the plague, whose periodical ravages
were wont to be numbered by its tens of thousands
victims, has fled the land,—the hovels which beckoned
the advancing flames, and aided them in their course,
have ceased to be; and, if the old city hath raised in
their stead structures which taste condemns, they wait
perhaps for the wand of some better age to bid them
vanish; and, if streets still narrow check the traffic, and
stop hurrying concourse, the citizens have still repaired
not a few of their forefathers' errors.

For many a year were city feasts despoiled by the expenses the fire entailed, and imposts still exist which
owe their origin to this great calamity. Yet we, as sons,
reap the benefit of our fathers' tears; the flames swept
away pests which years of litigation might still have
spared, which selfishness would have clung to and
avarice groaned over. Smithfield, not as now, the last
fortress of relaxing covetousness, would have been the
type of kindred shambles; St. Giles, already yielding

to the pressure of awakened common sense, would have been kept in countenance by wood-built Rookeries, and cholera seizing on unnumbered outposts would have outdone the Plague !

We cannot write now of the monument as Pope did—

> " Where London's column pointing to the skies,
> Like a tall bully lifts its head and lies."

Returning charity has erased the scandal, but it is yet a record of our fathers's loss and our gratitude ; they suffered that we might be spared. Old London is no more, but in its stead a vigorous offspring. The past has long blotted out the traces of the fire ; the present enjoys the blessings it bequeathed.

Notes.

Page 12.—"*The opulent and the great, we are told, hastened from town.*"

The Court during the grievous sickness of 1665 resided at Oxford. Defoe says :—" The Court removed early in the " month of June and went to Oxford, where it pleased God to " preserve them, and the distemper did not, as I heard of, so " much as touch them; the Inns of Court were all shut up, " nor were any of the lawyers in the Temple, or Lincoln's " Inn, or Gray's Inn, to be seen there. Whole rows of houses " in some places were shut up close, the inhabitants all fled, " and only a watchman or two left. The very Court, which " was then gay and luxurious, put on a face of just concern " for the public danger. All the plays and interludes which, " after the manner of the French Court, had been set up and " began to increase among us, were forbid to act ; the gaming " tables, public dancing rooms, and music houses, which " multiplied and began to debauch the manners of the people, " were shut up and suppressed ; and the jack puddings, merry " andrews, puppet shows, rope dancers, and such like doings ; " which had bewitched the poor common people, shut up their " shops, finding indeed no trade."

Among the provisions made to prevent the spreading of the infection are the following, which might be usefully applied, should the Cholera again afflict us :—" That special care be " taken that no stinking fish, or unwholesome or musty corn, " or other corrupt fruits, of what sort soever, be suffered to be " sold about the city, or any part of the same; that the " brewers and tippling houses be looked into for musty and " unwholesome casks; that no hogs, dogs or cats, or tame " pigeons or conies, be suffered to be kept within any part of " the city; or any swine to be, or stray in the streets or lanes, " but that such swine be impounded by the beadle or any " other officer, and the owner punished according to act of " common council; and that the dogs be killed by the dog " killers appointed for that purpose." Men of substance generally left town. A singular anecdote is told of a nobleman who was about to quit London; the hall was strewed with packages, and the master of the house was executing some business in a room adjoining, when he heard his black servant asking why the family were about to leave town, and on being informed that the plague was the cause of their departure, he said, " I have been told that the white man's God lived every- " where; now I find that can't be true; master's God does not " live in London, or he would not be in such a hurry to be " gone :" the nobleman was so struck by this speech, that he countermanded the preparations for his journey, and re- mained in London till the cessation of the plague. In one week, we learn from Defoe, there died twelve thousand people ; and, in a particular night, an eminent physician tells us, four thousand people died !

Page 12.—" *We justly reckon our Coal Beds as a great source of national wealth.*"

" It was formerly thought to contribute much to the preser-
" vation of the healthy and good air of the city, that nothing
" was burnt in it but wood and charcoal, even in trades that
" used great quantities of firing ; but about the latter end of
" the reign of Edward I., brewers, dyers, and other artificers,
" beginning to use sea coal, in or near the city, several pre-
" lates, nobles, commoners, and others, inhabitants of the
" villages of Southwark, Wapping, and East Smithfield, com-
" plained thereof, as a public nuisance, to the King, who
" prohibited burning sea coal by proclamation, which being
" disobeyed by many for their private lucre, upon a second
" complaint he issued out a commission of Oyer and Terminer
" to enquire of all such as burned sea coal against his procla-
" mation within the city or ports adjacent, and to punish
" them for the first offence by large fines ; and for the second
" by demolishing their furnaces, kilns, &c. wherein they
" burnt the said coals.   For this end also provision was for-
" mally made against stinks and annoying smells *arising from*
" *killing beasts in the city, which* was once thought to have
" *occasioned a grievous plague* in the reign of Edward the
" Third, who sent his command to the authorities to suffer
" no butcher to kill his cattle nearer the city than Stratford or
" Knightsbridge "——*Seymour.*

Query.—Could this command be put in force against the
present conservators of Smithfield ?

Page 22.—" *Seven Dials, even then the resort of questionable characters.*"

Strype, writing in 1720, thus speaks of this neighbourhood :
—" And on the west side there was a place with a building,
" called Cock and Pye Fields, which was made use of for a
" Laystall for the soil of the streets ; but of late built into
" several handsome streets, and so neatly contrived that every
" street in a straight line fronts the Dyall placed in the midst,
" which is raised on a high pedestal or pillar.   These streets
" are thus named Earls Street, Queen Street, White Lion
" Street," &c.

Page 67.—" *Whole streets, once residences, are now ware-houses, counting houses, and places solely for business.*"

Let the antiquarian, if he wish to put this to the test, take
a walk down to Mark Lare, and inspect some of the houses in
that street, especially 32 and 33, (and No. 50, the house of
Messrs. Arbouin, wine merchants,) not merely the outside, but
the court into which he will enter through a beautiful doorway,
and then let him walk up the stairs of the house, now converted into sets of chambers : from the windows he will have
a view of the neighbouring court-yards, in some of which are
fountains ; in one especially, a little more to the north, a
fountain of very chaste design.   He will then see that our
ancestors displayed infinitely more taste in adorning their
houses, both within and without, than we their descendants.
There is also a fine old front to a house in Aldersgate Street,

which report says was once tenanted by the Duke of Buckingham, the famous Villiers of Charles the Second's time. The reader may not be aware that, in the beginning of the last century, fountains were much more general than at present: there were two in Lincoln's Inn, one with the effigies of a mermaid; one in King now Soho Square, four river gods spouting water; one in the Privy Gardens near Richmond Terrace; one in the Temple, the remains of which are still visible; one in front of old Somerset House; and several behind the City Halls and the old houses in that quarter. Montague House, since converted into the British Museum, was also celebrated for the *jets d'eau* and fountains of its gardens. The fine old mansion in Lincoln's Inn Fields, now tenanted by the *Society for Promoting Christian Knowledge*, belonged to the Duke of Newcastle, of the reign of George II.

Page 40.—" *The inmates suffer much, too, from want of water, ... though the companies have a plentiful supply at command.*"

In the second report of the Health of Towns Commissioners, we have the following interesting information, which shows how much more careful our ancestors were than ourselves :—

" It is however apparent, on a review of the course of legis-
" lation on this subject, that the most serious attention was
" given to works of drainage from the earliest period of our
" constitutional history. The earliest fundamental provisions
" have been based on the footing that such works, as well as
" measures for the maintenance of the free flow of running

" waters, were of general, public, and national, rather than of
" exclusively local consideration. It is held by the first legal
" authorities to be one of the prerogatives of the Crown to
" issue commissions for the protection of the population by
" the enforcement of proper works of drainage; and this pre-
" rogative appears to have been exercised by the issue of
" special commissions, as well after as before the passing of
" statutory provisions on the subject."

Dr. Buckland has entered the lists on this occasion, but
has been ably met by Messrs. Easton and Amos, whose
answer we subjoin.

To the Editor of the " Daily News."

SIR,

WE have perused with regret the reports of the
remarks made by the Very Rev. the Dean of Westminster at
the Hanover Square Rooms, and at the Institute of British
Architects, upon the wells supplying the Trafalgar Square
fountains and the public offices with water; and our regret
arises from the reflection that these reports should attach his
respectable name to a series of mistakes, which a trifling
degree of inquiry would have prevented.

The Very Rev. Dean, after giving a definition of an artesian
well, and affirming that although many wells in London are
so called, not a single real artesian well exists within three
miles of St. Paul's, goes on to observe, that, so far from the
wells in Trafalgar Square being artesian wells, the water does
not rise within forty feet of the surface; that it is pumped up
by means of a steam-engine; that the requisite supply of
water could have been obtained at a much less cost from the

Chelsea Waterworks; and, finally, that the same water is pumped up over and over again.

Now, we are certainly unable to contradict the statement that the wells are not artesian wells; this may or may not be the case, as we are perfectly indifferent to the etymology of the word "artesian;" but in this instance the Dean is made to fight a shadow, for neither the Commissioners of Woods, nor ourselves, have ever called these wells "artesian" wells, by whatever name the public may have chosen to designate them.

There is consequently no attempt at deception of any kind in the case, as the language of the Very Rev. Dean would seem to imply.

We turn to the comparative cheapness of the mode adopted and that proffered by the Chelsea Company; in this case a plain statement is all that is required.

When the question of the supply of water to these fountains first came before the Government, the Chelsea Waterworks Company (which was at that time receiving a large rental for the supply of the public offices) was applied to for the purpose, and we believe their demand was higher for supplying two one-inch jets, than our charges have been for supplying two two-inch jets (carrying, be it observed, four times as much water), and as many of the public offices as used to pay the company about £.1000 per year.

With regard to the assertion that the water is pumped up, over and over again, we beg to say, that for the last three years we have been pumping from 3 to 400 gallons per minute from the well (the pumps originally fixed having been superseded by pumps capable of raising this quantity), not a drop of which has ever been returned to it; the only foundation existing for such a statement is, that the water supplied to the fountains, after doing duty there, is allowed to run back into a catch well, or reservoir near the works, from whence it is again pumped up to be again used in playing them; a plan which is obviously very much cheaper than any by which the Chelsea or other Company could possibly supply them.   We have now erected a large engine at those works, preparatory to supplying the palaces, public buildings, and barracks, round St. James's Park, the Serpentine, and the Hyde Park cavalry barracks; and it will be found, when this is done, that a saving will be effected in the annual expenditure for water equal to a large per centage on the capital laid out.

A considerable portion of the Dean's address is stated in the report to have consisted of remarks on what is designated the fact, that all the so-called artesian wells require incessant deepening, and that in a case where the water now stands sixty feet deep, it would be 120 feet deep in the year 1875, twenty-five years hence. Now, what are the facts in the Orange Street wells, which supply the fountains in Trafalgar Square? Why, that the water in the spring of every year rises higher than it did in 1844, when we first established the works. We lower it slightly in the summer, and towards autumn, but it has always returned to its original height in the following spring; indeed, in April 1847, it rose two feet higher, and should we have a wet winter with snow, we have no doubt that it will rise several feet higher in April next than it did in 1844.

We have, in fact, in our London Chalk Basin something better even than an artesian well, as described in the report, *viz.*, an always-existing receiver for the rains of heaven, which cannot fail so long as these rains themselves do not fail; a fact which the Dean as well as so many others have wholly over-looked.

We can safely affirm that the practical experience we have had during the last twenty-seven years in sinking wells and supplying towns from the chalk formation, had led us to results very different from the theory devised by the Rev. Dean, as regards the quantity of water obtainable from that stratum.

In 1844 we entered into a contract with Her Majesty's Commissioners of Woods, &c., for erecting the waterworks in Orange Street for a given sum, taking on ourselves all risks of supply, &c. We should be willing to enter into a similar contract to supply every house in London with forty gallons of water per day from similar wells for 10s. per year, and pay 5 per cent. on the capital expended.

In our opinion London will never be properly supplied until each house is furnished with spring water for beverage,—as well as with that less pure supply now afforded, which may be employed for sanitary purposes.

We are, Sir,

Your obedient Servants,

EASTON and AMOS.

Grove, Southwark, Dec. 5, 1849.

The intervention of the Crown was often urgently sought, for the public protection against the injurious encroachments of private interests upon the great public water-courses, for mill power, or for fishing weirs.   The 16th chapter of Magna Charta is a defence of the public rights against the growth of such encroachments.   The fourth statute of 25 Edw. III. c. 4, provides for the putting down of mills, weirs, dams, and other obstructions ; and commissions appear to have been issued from time to time, to see the execution of the laws provided therein.   A commission was issued in the third year of Henry IV., for providing the means of conveying pure water to " the " inhabitants of Kingston-upon-Hull, as well as for draining " that town, and removing impure sea or marsh water."

Page 44.—" *The notorious Saffron Hill.*"

Strype tells us, in his edition of Stowe, brought down to 1720, —" Saffron Hill takes its beginning at Field Lane, and runs " northward to Vine Street.   It is a place of small account " both as to buildings and inhabitants, and pestered with small " and ordinary alleys and courts, taken up by the meaner " sort of people, especially the east side unto the Town Ditch, " which separates this parish from St. James's, Clerkenwell, " and over this ditch most of the alleys have a small boarded " bridge, as Castle Alley, Bell Alley, and Blue Ball Alley. " Other places on this hill are Bull Head Alley, and Dobbins' " Alley, both very small and ordinary.   Strangways Street " hath small houses, but something better than the allies, and " hath a passage by the bridge, over the ditch ; Lewis Yard, " pretty, large, and airy, with gardens in the middle, and " indifferent well inhabited—the entrance to it down steps.

" Peter Street hath pretty good new brick buildings, espe-
" cially the lower part by the ditch. Harp Alley, nasty, and
" inconsiderable. Paved Alley, but mean, hath a passage up
" steps to Hatton Garden, and the entrance into it is but ill.
" Lamb Alley, narrow and ordinary, hath a passage into
" Scroop's Court. *But this part is not properly Saffron Hill,*
" but part of Field Lane, which said lane is already spoken of.
" Hatton Court, small and ordinary, &c. &c. Ely Court, very
" handsome, large, with new brick houses, and a freestone
" pavement, and well inhabited : this court lieth between
" Leather Lane and Hatton Garden ; as likewise Ely House,
" Scroop's Court, formerly Scroop's Inn, and belonged to John
" Lord Scroop, after whose death it was let out to some Ser-
" jeants-at-Law, and then called Serjeant's Inn, Holbourn.
" And, upon their removal, it was converted into tenements,
" with gardens unto them. Since which, being old, and the
" houses very much decayed, it is of late rebuilt with very
" good houses, and the place very much enlarged with the ad-
" ditional buildings, leaving yet a great deal of waste ground
" to be built on, which lieth behind Field Lane, which I
" doubt not, in a short time, will all be built into courts and
" allies."

Page 50.—" *The famous Gordon riots broke out in June*
1780."

Mr. Dickens has illustrated this period with his usual felicity.
Lord George Gordon was a madman. Zealous as he was against
Popery, he died, we believe, a proselyte to Judaism. His
followers, at the time he did so much mischief, were the refuse
of the metropolis, ever ready for anything which promises a

scramble. The Lord Mayor of the day was weak and indecisive. The riot seemed to take all the authorities by surprise,
and to paralyse them. When the Cabinet Council was called,
no one of the assembled ministers would sign the commission
authorising the soldiers to act, alleging their scruples as to the
legality of the act. George III. is reported to have seized a
pen, and signed the warrant himself, as well as to have
declared that he would head the troops which were sent to put
down the rioters. In that very interesting book, " Beckford's
" Travels," he speaks of having just left this scene of riot and
disturbance behind. " But a few days ago, thought I within
" myself, I was in the midst of all the tumult and uproar of
" London. This characteristic stillness was the more pleasing
" when I looked back upon those scenes of outcry and horror
" which filled London but a week or two ago, when danger
" was not confined to night only, and to the environs of the
" capital, but haunted our streets at mid-day. Here (Antwerp)
" I could wander over an entire city without beholding a sky
" red and portentous with the light of houses on fire, or hearing
" the confusion of shouts and groans mingled with the reports
" of artillery." Many old people recollect the scenes which
took place. The dead bodies of the rioters, we were informed,
were piled against the Bank ; and five fires were seen at one
time to blaze at different parts of the town. The greatest loss
sustained was that of the famous Lord Mansfield's Library,
many of the books containing manuscript notes of inestimable
value. There is a most interesting account of the whole affair
in a letter of Sir Samuel Romilly's, published in his memoirs,
and dated from his chambers, 7, Gray's Inn Square. In the
burial books of St. Bride's, Fleet Street, is the entry of two

deaths—two youths—one of them a sweep—who were killed
when the mob attacked the Fleet Prison. Mr. Dickens uses
the novelist's licence when he extends the ravages of the
rioters to Essex. Lord Mansfield's house in Bloomsbury
Square was burnt to the ground,—the Fleet Prison and
Newgate much damaged ; the former, we believe, entirely
consumed.

Page 53.—" *Clerkenwell, in the neighbourhood, is famed
for its Printing Houses.*"

St. John's Gate is the only remaining among the many gates
of the city. Ludgate, Cripplegate, and others, have long since
been pulled down. It derives an interest from the fact that
Cave, the original proprietor of the "Gentleman's Magazine,"
lived there : there it was that he was sought by the great
lexicographer and man of letters, Johnson,—sought by the sage
in his poverty ; and there is a touching story of the literary
leviathan being regaled by his patron at some public-house hard
by, where he was introduced to some penny-a-liner of those days,
whom Cave represented as a very great man. Oliver Cromwell long lived in a house still shown in this parish ; and the
registry of his marriage is still preserved in the books of St.
Giles's, Cripplegate; it is spelt Crummell. In this churchyard
John Milton was buried, and there is a small tablet to his
memory. " Clerkenwell was a noted place in old times. The
" famous priory of St. John of Jerusalem stood here, founded
" by Inden Brissett, Baron, and Mary his wife, about the year
" 1100, near unto *Clerks-Well*, besides West Smithfield.
" Which Brissett, having founded the Priory of Nuns, at

" Clerks-Well, bought of them ten acres of land, giving them
" in exchange ten acres of land in his lordship of Welling-
" Hall, in the county of Kent.   St. John's Church was dedi-
" cated by Heraclius, Patriarch of the Holy Resurrection of
" Christ at Jerusalem, in the year 1185, and was the chief seat
" in England of the Religious Knights of St. John of Jerusalem ;
" whose profession was (besides their daily service of God) to
" defend Christians against Pagans, and to fight for the Church,
" using for their habit a black upper garment with a white
" cross on the fore part thereof.   And their good service was
" so highly esteemed, that, when the Order of the Templars
" was dissolved, their lands and possessions were, by Parlia-
" ment, granted unto these, who, after the loss of Jerusalem,
" recovered the Island of Rhodes ; but after the loss thereof,
" 1523, removed to the Isle of Malta, manfully opposing
" themselves against the Turkish invasions.

  " This priory, church, and house of St. John was preserved
" from spoil or pulling down so long as Henry VIII. reigned,
" and was employed as a store house for the King's toils and
" tents for hunting and for the wars.   But in the third of
" Edward VI. the church, for the most part, to wit, the body
" and side aisles, with the great Bell Tower (a most curious
" piece of workmanship, graven, and gilt, and inameled, to
" the great beautifying of the city, and passing all other that
" I have seen), was undermined and blown up with gun-
" powder, the stone thereof was employed in building of the
" Lord Protector's House in the Strand.   That part of the
" Quire which remained, with some side chapels, was, by
" Cardinal Pole (in the reign of Queen Mary) closed up at the
" west end, and otherwise repaired ; and Sir Thomas Tresham,

" Knight, was then made Lord Prior there, with restitution
" of some lands, but the same was again suppressed in the
" first year of Queen Elizabeth."——*Strype's Edition of
Stowe.*

Page 72.—" *Jacob's Island.*"

The line of the Thames which separates Jacob's Island from
the river is bordered by capacious warehouses. The proprietors of these must often be rich capitalists ; but we regret to
say, and experience bears us out, that the owners of such
premises too often confine their charities and their sympathies
to the districts where their dwellings, not their warehouses, are
situated. Many large mansions within ten miles of London
are tenanted by the principals of such establishments ; there
their benefactions enrich the surrounding neighbourhood, but
surely districts like Jacob's Island deserve far more their care
and attention. They can scarcely purchase an immunity from
superintending the interests of the many labourers in their
employ, or by giving, at stated times, large sums to be disbursed among the charitable institutions in their home parish,
rid themselves of still nearer claims. The trade of wharfinger
is profitable ; men realise large sums by it ; many the hands
employed. Where do they live ?—where must they live ?
surely in the close vicinity to their work.

Page 143.—" *Dorchester Labourers.*"

The amount of crime in Dorsetshire exceeds that of any
portion of England of similar extent. Wages are lower—

cottages more wretched—we might say, fever more wasting
—than in any other agricultural district of Great Britain.
The letters of S. G. O. in *The Times*, have made these things
known. An attempt is being made to pull down cottages, and
thus reduce at once the incumbrances of an ill-paid peasantry
and the agricultural population. In one of the illustrated
newspapers of the day is a series of prints, showing what the
homes of the labourers are. A more formidable weapon to
be used against the Protectionists can scarcely be imagined ;
for with all that a corn-tax gave the landlords, they either
could not, or would not, support the men by whom their lands
were tilled. The change which has since taken place, even
should it be proved to be really injurious to the landowner,
only injures a small class comparatively in Dorsetshire ; the
labourers, in this country at least, cannot be worse off than
they have been, and, we regret to say, that the landlords who
have been attacked for this state of things, have not come out
of court as well as we could wish ; they have substituted abuse
for argument, and they failed to convince.

Page 175.—" *As things now are, we have a large class of
middle-men.*"

We doubt if we have Johnsonian authority for the use of
this word. Perhaps the clients of old Rome, the men who
stood between the patrons and the plebeians, are representa-
tives of this class. They took the trouble of letting and
leasing from the shoulders of their patrons, and indemnified
themselves by oppressing those who really tilled the ground.
In Ireland, the term middle-man seems to imply absenteeism ;
the landlord too often spending in Continental cities the sums

which are wrung from the children of the soil, and the middle-
man, one who manages affairs in his absence. Perhaps, in
some instances, there is something like a lease from landlord
to middle-man; or the latter farms the rents; at any rate,
whilst he spares his principal trouble, he intercepts, not wit-
tingly but in effect, the favours his master, if resident, would
bestow on his tenant. An irresponsible person is set over
them; to him they address complaints, he either will not hear
or cannot redress; and though much of the distress of Ireland
be owing to the *perfervidum ingenium* of the people, this ele-
ment of their misery should not be forgotten. The " Tales of
" the Munster Festivals " give us, perhaps, as great an insight
into the Irish character as any book extant. Mr. Lever's
works, especially the " O'Donoghue, " describe the miseries
of Ireland, and their causes. Whilst Great Britain has made
an extraordinary progress, the state of Ireland does not seem
to be much better than it was in the time of Cromwell; one
difference there certainly is: he sold those whom he took
prisoners as slaves for the West Indies, we allow the surplus
population to emigrate. Middle-manship, though under a
somewhat different shape, is at work in the Rookery system.
The landlords of Rookeries are often men who scarcely know
where their property is situated, and these middle-men are the
links between them and the real tenants. Thus these poor
creatures are shut out of the charities which would acrue to
them were there no intermediate agents between them and
the landlord. There would be a really responsible person to
whom application could be made when abuses were palpable;
and the landlord would feel an interest in his tenant. We
fear that the greater part of the poor dwellings in London are
let out in this way; yet it seems obvious that you cannot

build model lodging-houses without putting a stop, or at least giving a check, to this system, whilst at the same time you lower the average of rents which the working classes now pay.

Page 219.—" *Where want, and scanty food, and confined cabins, foster disease.*"

The writer was sent for one Sunday morning to see a poor woman, attacked by Asiatic cholera. It was decidedly the worst, though not the only fatal case he witnessed in the same street. The woman and her husband, with their family, occupied two miserable rooms—rather closets—which smoked in winter, and were stifling in summer, These apartments were situated at the back of a public-house, a small wooden gallery in front, just beneath a sewer, was arrested in its course, and the odour diffused by it fœtid in the extreme. She lingered scarcely twenty-four hours, and then died. In the house opposite lived an old man who soon sickened, as did his next door neighbour, with the same complaint. He, after a most severe struggle, recovered, only to die of weakness within two months of the seizure; and his neighbour is still on a sick bed, suffering from the ill-health which cholera often bequeaths. In the same street, an old woman died after twenty-four hours' suffering, and several fell ill, though they afterwards recovered. The accuracy with which those acquainted with pauper districts can prophesy where fever or disease will settle, is remarkable. Certain portions of the parish are badly drained; these places are well known, and there almost invariably disease alights, as though beckoned to the spot. When the Irish fever was extending throughout London, the writer called the attention of the Commissioners of Pavements to a spot where the drainage was particularly bad. The complaint was promptly attended to, yet not before two children had died in the house opposite.

Page 238.—"*In* 1789, *the year when the Revolution broke out.*"

The seeds of this great commotion had been planted by Louis XIV. He wished to break the power of the nobles, and to extinguish the remains of the feudal system. He drew the landlords, therefore, away from their châteaus, and centralised them, so to speak, in Paris. For this cause, the Metropolis was adorned with fine buildings. Versailles, the most extensive palatial building in Europe, perhaps in the world, was erected, with its statues, its fountains, its gardens, everything around it in a style of lavish magnificence and grandeur; but such a place entailed immense expense upon the nation, and created or fostered a love of show among the nobles. Expensive, and, towards the close of this reign, disastrous wars added their sum to the general distress. The profligacy which was veiled beneath the forms of the Court under Le Grand Monarque, was undisguised under the Regent Orleans, and Louis XV. seems to have set decency at defiance. When you pass along the splendid galleries of Versailles and wander through its gardens, you cease to wonder at the revolution. Money must have been poured out like water to create such a marvel; and courtiers would ape, at a distance, the splendour of their master. Meanwhile a passion for military glory took the place of interest in the useful arts. On the pediment of this gorgeous palace is sculptured the motto of the nation,

" A toutes les gloires de France." Feed them with these, and
what will they not do ?   Let a peaceful sovereign endeavour
to reduce their burdens, and behold a revolution !   Splendid
as were the châteaus of the nobles, read Arthur Young, and
you will find them ever in juxta-position with lands barely
cultivated, and a starving peasantry.

Page 242.—"*And laws, some of which from their severity*
would seem to have been rather the fictions of the
romancer than the records of history."

Mr. Carlyle, in his quaint style thus describes the supposed,
though of course obsolete law to which we allude.—See his
French Revolution, p. 16, Vol. I.   "For the rest, their privi-
" leges every way are much curtailed.   That law, authorising
" a Seigneur, as he returned from hunting, to kill not more
" than two serfs, and refresh his feet in their warm blood and
" bowels, has fallen into disuetude, and even into incredibility,
" for if Deputy Lapoule can believe it, and call for the abro-
" gation of it, so cannot we."

It seems incredible, and certainly we should like to have
the proofs before us, very much doubting the whole story ;
yet during the reign of Louis the XV., within a hundred
years of the present time, Damien, who attempted the Sovereign's life, was put to death by torture.   Goldsmith alludes,
we may recollect, to "Damien's Bed of Steel."

Page 261.—" *An appeal for the Needle-women of England.*"

Emigration is preached up at present as our great national
safety-valve, and this is to be the resource of distressed needlewomen : it is assumed that the country cannot support its

present population ; and New Zealand, the most fertile colony we possess, and the finest climate we have yet discovered, is to be the basis of the rising generation. On the other hand, the Chartist Committees are telling the people that there is sufficient land, if properly cultivated, to maintain a hundred and fifty millions of people. What shall we say to statements so different ? Has the last assertion even a show of truth in its favour ? Emigration, no doubt, has much in its favour. The colonies want, we are glutted with, labour; the strength of the colonies hereafter must be, not English armies, but a native population, and to retain at least the English name and language among them, we must feed them more with English labourers and artisans. Europe, we are told, is worn out ; if it be so, we are wise, before the house tumbles, to look out for the best situation in which to build a new one ; but suppose we take a less gloomy and truer view of the case. The colonies are likely to be more profitable and not so expensive as workhouses, and there seems no reason why we should not, but rather every encouragement to urge us to apply a portion of the rates to promote emigration. In our workhouses, it is well known, a man soon loses self-respect; independence of action is necessarily checked, and the man soon degenerates, despite the increased care taken to improve the inmates. Workhouses are schools of vice—the old women are often known to corrupt the young ; and it is scarce likely that youths will learn prudence and self-control from those, many of whom are doomed for life to inhabit the workhouse from want of both. With much we could wish otherwise, we may still be very proud of our offspring—the United States. In the struggles of future ages, they will rub off much of the rust which still adheres to them, and the present is full of hope. With respect to the assumption of land societies, it seems scarcely possible, under the most favourable circumstances, that the country should feed even its present amount of population. Agricultural science, like every other science, is progressive ; men cannot anticipate. Some agricultural Newton may arise, and treble the produce of our national granary, but as yet there are no signs of his coming. The population is likely to run faster than the progress of science, for science here wants capital, and there is a tendency to withdraw capital from agriculture, to lay down corn land to grass, to make large farms,— farms, in fact, too large for any but a man of property to undertake, and then this landlord farmer will not superintend minutely every portion of his farm. That he may avoid this, he will like to have pasture instead of arable lands, for they are less troublesome ; so that the country, if it ever became wedded to such a system, would produce less rather than more than it does at present. Still, there is a shadow of truth in the assertion of these land societies. Some thousand acres in England are uncultivated—not the commons in the neighbourhood of towns, which ought ever to be preserved for the people's relaxation—not the pasture meadows where rich and poor have the privilege of turning their cattle out during great part of the year—but large tracts of land, such as in Derbyshire, seem only valuable as grouse preserves. Such as in Scotland are parcelled out in deer forests, and the like. When the population is so superabundant, these things should not be ; it savours too much of feudal times, and in the neighbourhood of these hunting grounds, game laws are rigidly enforced—not trespass laws, which very properly would prevent men from breaking down fences, and making paths where there are none—but laws which fine men, because they kill the hare which runs across their garden, or shoot the stray pheasant which has broken bounds. I do not mean to say that, under a better system, we should fulfil the prophecies, or disarm the rancour of the Chartist school ; yet to the right thinking man, it is some satisfaction that he has removed just cause of offence, and that if called on to defend his privileges, they are not such as he would blush to own.

In the pamphlet to which we have alluded, are some sad details, take the following :—" I stitch," says one woman, " the legs of trousers when there are any, but for these five " weeks I have'n't earned more than 1s. 4d., for the party who " gives them to me has'n't had any work himself to do. He " gives me a penny a-pair, and finds me the thread ; four pair " is as much as I can do in the day, from six in the morning " to six at night. I can't see by candle-light. It would not " pay me to have a candle for such work. The most I ever " earned was 2s. the week, and that my girl helped me to a " good bit. Twenty-four pair is more than one hand can do. " That's more than twelve months ago since I did as much " as that. About one shilling a-week some weeks, and some " weeks 9d., and some weeks 6d., and this week it will " be 3d."

Another states—" It is not a farthing more than 3s. a-week " that I earn, take it all the year round, and out of that " there's thread, candle, and firing to be taken away, and that " comes to 1s. a-week for coal, candle, and wood, and 6d. " for thread, leaving about 1s. 6d. for my clear earnings " after working the whole week through. But that's better " than nothing. My husband has lately been in the hos- " pital."

Page 267.—" *The Palace of Bridewell, the residence of Henry VIII.*

" The kings of this realm," says Strype, " have been there
" lodged, and their courts of law have been kept there of old
" time. And, till the 9th of Henry III., the courts were
" kept in the King's House wheresoever he was lodged, as may
" appear by ancient records. King Henry VIII. builded
" there a stately and beautiful house of new, for receipt of the
" Emperor Charles V., who, in the year 1522, was lodged
" himself at the Black Friers, but his nobles in this new
" builded Bridewell, a gallery being made over the water, and
" through the wall of the city, into the Emperor's lodging at
" the Black Friers. King Henry himself oftentimes lodged
" there also, as, namely, in the year 1525, a parliament being
" then holden in the Black Friers. It was converted to its
" present purpose, as a House of Correction, in the reign of
" Edward VI."

The Annalist speaks of a picture hanging near the pulpit in
the Chapel of Bridewell, with these lines on it :—

> This Edward of fair memory the Sixt,
> In whom with greatness goodness was commixt,
> Gave this Bridewell, a palace in old times,
> For a chastising House of vagrant crimes.

Page 282.—" *Gates, which fortified the City's Rebellion.*"

" Gates in the wall of this city," says the Annalist, " in old
" time were four ; to wit, Aldgate for the East, Aldersgate for
" North, Ludgate for the West, and Bridge gate, over the
" river Thames, for the South ; but of later times, for the ease

" of citizens and passengers, divers other gates and posterns
" have been made.   In the reign of Henry II. (saith
" Fitstephen) there were seven double gates in the wall of this
" city, but he nameth them not.   It may, therefore, be sup-
" posed he meant for the first the gate next the Tower of
" London, (which then served as a postern, and now so com-
" monly called) for passengers out of the East.   From thence
" through Tower Street, Eastcheap, and Candlewick Street, to
" London-stone, the middle point of the highway; then through
" Budge Row, Watling Street, and leaving St. Paul's Church
" on the right hand, to Ludgate on the West ; the next to be
" Aldgate, Bishopgate, Crepelgate, Aldersgate, Ludgate ; and
" the seventh, the Bridgegate over the Thames.   The posterns
" of these gates were frequently fitted up, and used as prisons :
" they were taken down, with the exception of St. John's Gate,
" Clerkenwell, and Temple Bar, about the year 1760, having
" been found very inconvenient, and blocking up the Causeway."

FINIS.